TROTSKY'S MARXISM
AND OTHER ESSAYS

BY DUNCAN HALLAS

Haymarket
Books

Chicago, Illinois

Haymarket Books
PO Box 180165
Chicago, IL 60618 USA
www.haymarketbooks.org

ISBN: 1-931859-03-5

U.S. Library of Congress Control Number: 2003107743

07 06 05 04 03 02   1 2 3 4 5 6

CONTENTS

Introduction to the 2003 edition | 5

TROTSKY'S MARXISM

Introduction to the 1984 edition | 15

1. Permanent Revolution | 21

2. Stalinism | 37

3. Strategy and Tactics | 55

4. Party and Class | 77

5. The Heritage | 93

OTHER ESSAYS

Trotskyism Reassessed | 113

Against the Stream | 127

Fourth International in Decline:
From Trotskyism to Pabloism, 1944–1953 | 153

Trotsky's Heritage: On the 50th Anniversary of
the Founding of the Fourth International | 171

NOTES | 185

INDEX | 200

INTRODUCTION
TO THE
2003 EDITION

D uncan Hallas's *Trotsky's Marxism* is one of the most succinct and clear introductions to the ideas and politics of Leon Trotsky. This short book is a masterful attempt to make the essentials of Trotsky's Marxism—his ideas and practical activity—accessible to a wider audience. Hallas's book is not a biographical work—like the three-volume series written by Isaac Deutscher.[1] Rather, it is intended as a summary of Trotsky's main contributions to the Marxist tradition and as a guide to political action—above all, working-class political action. The thread that runs throughout the book is the revolutionary role of the working class and the idea that the "emancipation of the working class must be the act of the working class itself."

Trotsky's Marxism was first published by Pluto Press in London in 1979—the centenary of Leon Trotsky's birth. When the book was first published, the world's communist parties saw Trotsky as an enemy of the Russian Revolution and described him as a counter-revolutionary who sided with the bourgeoisie against the "Socialist Fatherland." This was the point of view diligently advanced by the USSR and its ideologues once Stalin took power. So systematic was the Stalinist rewriting of history that Trotsky felt compelled to write a book setting the record straight, *The Stalin School of Falsification,* as well as an autobiography (*My Life*).[2] The official view suffered a serious blow in 1956 when Nikita Khruschev delivered his famous "Secret Speech" at the 20th Congress, admitting some of Stalin's crimes. The revival of working-class struggle—most notably in France in 1968—and the rebirth of the revolutionary left also challenged the Stalinist myths. But as late as 1979, the USSR, while beginning to show signs of crisis, was still intact. The Stalinist communist parties were still the dominant force on the left and in the workers' movement internationally. As a result, Trotsky was still vilified as a counter-revolutionary and an enemy of socialism.

The truth, of course, was much different. Trotsky and the movement he organized to fight the degeneration of the Russian Revolution and Stalin's counter-revolution, represented a valiant attempt to defend the principles of socialism and the Bolshevik tradition in the face of tremendous odds.

The collapse of the USSR led politicians, ideologues, and the mainstream media to declare that communism was dead, and that Marxism could be consigned to the dustbin of history. These post-mortems failed to distinguish between regimes that were communist in name, but which had long before ceased to have anything to do with socialism, and the genuine Marxism of Trotsky and his Bolshevik contemporaries. Indeed, Stalinism was the antithesis of Marxism and of the key principles that sustained the Bolsheviks. The collapse of the USSR and the Eastern European states has not vindicated capitalism but the ideas so clearly articulated and defended by Trotsky. This may explain why to this day, unlike other "disgraced" figures, Trotsky has yet to be "rehabilitated" in Russia.[3]

Trotsky was to pay an enormous price for his opposition to Stalin—indeed, it cost him his life. His family and friends, those who supported him or were alleged to support him, often suffered the same fate. Trotsky went from being second only to Lenin in the Bolshevik Revolution of 1917 and the leader of the Red Army to being named public enemy number one by the Stalinist counter-revolution.

The question arises, why did Stalin succeed in defeating Trotsky? Duncan Hallas addresses part of this question in his introduction to Trotsky's first major critique of the bureaucratization of the Bolshevik Party in power, *Lessons of October,* written in 1923.

> Isaac Deutscher wrote of the political situation in the year 1921: "Whom then did the Bolshevik Party represent? It represented only itself, that is, its past association with the working class, its present aspiration to act as the guardian of the proletarian class interest, and its intention to re-assemble in the course of economic reconstruction a new working class which should be able in due time to take the country's destiny into its hands. In the

meantime the Bolshevik Party maintained itself in power by usurpation."

Deutscher writes "its past association with the working class" for two reasons. First because the working class, as it is sociologically defined, had shrivelled from around three million to around one million in the years of civil war, foreign intervention and devastation from 1918 to 1921. Secondly because the class-conscious minority of this working class, itself a minority within a working population which was mostly peasants, had either been killed during the civil war, been drawn into administration, or had become demoralized. The peasant masses, having got possession of the land, were now indifferent to the Soviet government, or hostile.

The party in power, therefore, had become "substitutionist." Such a state of affairs can perhaps be "carried" for a short time without the party itself being transformed—but not for years on end. By 1924, indeed by 1923 if not earlier, this transformation had taken place. Party and state apparatuses were becoming one. Of course this was still far from the Stalinist tyranny of the future, but the party had effectively become an apparatus party by the early 1920s. The mass recruitment, the "Lenin Levy" decided upon by the thirteenth party conference, inevitably *weakened* the influence of those party members who still had some Marxist training and internationalist ideas. These included, of course, the supporters of Kamenev and Zinoviev, who soon found themselves in opposition to Stalin, the apparatchik-in-chief, and as impotent as Trotsky. Both were later to face trial and execution.[4]

Apparently, Stalin himself confirmed the basic outline of this analysis. Why did Stalin win? Or more accurately, what was the social basis of Stalin's support? Stalin provided an answer to this question, according to Slavoj Zizek's recently published *Revolution at the Gates*. Zizek writes:

> In the diaries of Georgi Dimitroff, recently published in German, we get a unique glimpse into how Stalin was fully aware of what brought him to power, giving an unexpected twist to his well-known slogan "People (cadres) are our greatest." When, at a dinner in November 1937, Dimitroff praises the "great luck" of the international workers—that they had such a genius as their leader, Stalin—Stalin answers: "I do not agree with him. He even expressed himself in a non-Marxist way.... Decisive are the middle cadres" (November 7, 1937). He puts it even more clearly a paragraph earlier: "Why did we win over Trotsky and others? It is well known that, after Lenin, Trotsky was the most popular in our land.... But we had the support of the middle cadres and they explained our grasp of the situation to the

masses.... Trotsky did not pay any attention to the middle cadres."[5]

In short, Trotsky's strength dependend upon the organizational and political strength of the working class (which was on the wane in the 1920s), whereas Stalin drew his strength from the growing bureaucratic party apparatus.

Trotsky distinguished himself on the Russian revolutionary left while still a young man. He developed views that were not only highly original but ideas that broke with a number of accepted notions among western Marxists. Unlike both the Bolshevik and Menshevik Parties, he argued that the coming revolution in Russia would not be limited to bourgeois power.

Trotsky advanced his theory of "permanent revolution" initially as an analysis specific to Russian conditions. But even before Trotsky drew out the more general application of the theory of permanent revolution, he became the target of attacks by the "triumvirate"—the alliance of Zinoviev, Kamenev, and Stalin—that dominated the bureaucracy in the period of Lenin's illness and death.

Although Trotsky developed an alliance later in the 1920s with Kamenev and Zinoviev, who had become opponents of Stalin, by then Stalin's power had grown too strong. In 1927, Trotsky was expelled from the Bolshevik Party and in 1928 sent into exile. It is in this period of isolation that Trotsky believed he made his most important contribution to the Marxist movement. It is no exaggeration to say that it was Trotsky's efforts in this period that kept alive the tradition of Marx and Lenin through the period of defeats suffered by the world working-class movement in the 1930s.

This is not at all to minimize or play down Trotsky's role in the Russian Revolution itself. But, as Trotsky himself put it, the Russian Revolution would have taken place without him. The survival of the revolutionary Marxist tradition, however, required his efforts.

> I think that the work in which I am engaged now, despite its extremely insufficient and fragmentary nature, is the most important work of my life—more important than 1917, more important than the period of the Civil War or any other....
>
> I cannot speak of the "indispensability" of my work, even about the period from 1917–1921. But now my work is "indispensable" in the full sense of the word. There is no arrogance in

this claim at all. The collapse of the two Internationals has posed a problem which none of the leaders of these Internationals is at all equipped to solve. The vicissitudes of my personal fate have confronted me with this problem and armed me with important experience in dealing with it. There is now no one except me to carry out the mission of arming a new generation with the revolutionary method over the heads of the leaders of the Second and Third International.[6]

Trotskyism was immediately forced to the margins of the working-class movement—and this isolation was compounded by the economic and social conditions after the Second World War. The emphasis on upholding the banner of "Marxism" produced some unwanted distortions—propagandism, sectarianism, and an emphasis on the word rather than the deed.

Nevertheless, revolutionary Marxism survived. As Duncan sums it up:

> What then had been achieved? A good deal, in spite of everything. The *living* continuity of the tradition of Marx and Lenin had been maintained, although by very slender forces, and it had been *enriched* by application to new problems. Trotsky's heritage, embodied in his writings, is a major and very important part of our political armory. Now these writings would not, for the most part, have been produced at all but for Trotsky's extreme tenacity in seeking to create a revolutionary cadre in the struggle to change the course of events.[7]

The distortions of the Trotskyist movement—compounded by Trotsky's insistence that Russia continued to be in some sense a workers' state even after workers had ceased to control it—led after his death to the Trotskyist movement drifting away from its core emphasis on workers' self-emancipation. The articles included in this book after *Trotsky's Marxism* trace these developments. These articles may at first appear to have only historical significance. But the thread running throughout all of the essays included in this volume is the centrality of the working class in the struggle for a new society. It is this thread that Trotsky preserved and that Hallas emphasized in his critical assessment of Trotsky and the Trotskyist movement.

As Hallas himself wrote in a 1988 introduction to his articles "Against the Stream" and "Fourth International in Decline" (included in this volume):

> If I had to write an account of the development of the Fourth International from scratch today, I would change some of the em-

phases and add some new material. Yet the general thesis would remain substantially unaltered.

More fundamentally, does it matter now? It does. We, our tendency, came out of the Trotskyist tradition, the only living tradition to have survived the Stalinist and bourgeois reaction in the 1930s and 1940s. Trotskyism had fought not only to preserve but also to develop and apply the revolutionary ideas of Marx and Lenin which centered around the conception of socialism and the self emancipation of the working class.

And yet we broke with it? No we did not. We broke with its degeneration in order to preserve its essential core.[8]

Duncan Hallas was a lifelong revolutionary. He died last year, in 2002, at the age of 77. He was an exceptional and talented man, an orator and polemicist—and yet was proudly ordinary. His writing, speaking, and his manner were direct, concise, and clear. He was also, as one of his lifelong comrades, Nigel Harris, put it, one of the most erudite revolutionaries in the movement.

Duncan Hallas was one of the most admired speakers for the socialist movement. As a teenager in the mid-1970s, I still remember traveling from Central London to East London countless times to hear Duncan's series of meetings at (if memory serves me right) the Centerprise Bookshop. Duncan was in top form. It wasn't only Duncan's speaking that was memorable, but the way he interacted with all those who attended. He would be attentive and try to answer question after question, calmly and patiently—even if he would mutter something under his breath after speaking to someone who was particularly antagonistic. The content and manner of his argumentation were deliberate, systematic, and convincing. But it was also the cadence and tempo of Duncan's speaking that captured the attention of the audience.

It is no exaggeration to say that Duncan played a key role in training a generation of revolutionaries to build in the heart of world imperialism. More than 25 years have passed since Duncan made his first trip to the United States. He made several trips to the U.S. in the 1970s and 1980s to help build a small and young revolutionary organization, the International Socialist Organization. His 1983 tour of the U.S. is one of the most memorable events any of us were involved in organizing. The majority of talks that Duncan gave were titled "The Meaning of Marxism"—after the pamphlet that he authored[9]—and also because

1983 was the centenary of Karl Marx's death. One of the meetings was recorded and transcribed, and appeared in the centerfold of the newspaper *Socialist Worker*.

> Capitalism is a very special sort of class society. Marx was enthusiastic about the progress it had made possible. The capitalist class, he wrote, "during its rule of scarcely 100 years has created more massive and more colossal productive forces than have all preceding generations together."
>
> Since that was written, the productive forces have been multiplied many times over. There is no longer any necessary reason for poverty or social classes on a world scale. The qualification about "on the world scale" is important, though.
>
> Capitalism created a world market, an international division of labor and a world economy. That omelette cannot be unscrambled without a catastrophic fall in output, a fall so great that it would destroy the material basis for socialism—highly developed productive forces. That is why Marx and Engels said, "Workers of the world unite"—and that is why real socialists must be internationalists.
>
> Possibilities and potentials are one thing. The means to realize them are another. Marx believed that capitalism itself had created the force that could overthrow it and establish a classless society—the modern wage-earning working class.
>
> Socialism, for Marx, as for the International Socialist Organization, is the self-emancipation of the working class, and it is nothing else. There is no socialism without collective, democratic rule by the people who do the work and create the wealth. The claim that countries like Russia and Poland are socialist is simply fraudulent.
>
> Note, too, "self-emancipation." Nobody can replace actual working-class struggle in the fight for socialism. The attempt to do so always leads to reactionary results.
>
> But isn't the working class divided, under the influence of ruling-class ideas—racist, sexist, nationalist ideas? All that is true, and it can be changed in struggle. It is a long, hard and complicated struggle. It is also the only cause worth fighting for.
>
> I have given the barest outline of some of Marx's ideas. The incredible richness of his thought nowadays supports a whole industry—a growth industry until very recently—of commentaries on commentaries on Marx and so on, ad infinitum.
>
> The people who make a living out of this, and not a bad living either, are not Marxists—although most of them think they are. Why not? Because as Marx wrote as a young man, "The philosophers have only interpreted the world in various ways. The point, however, is to change it." To be a Marxist, you have to be a fighter in the cause of the working class, nationally and internationally, as Marx himself was.

One hundred years ago this month, Frederick Engels—Marx's lifelong friend and coworker—spoke these words at the old man's funeral. They cannot be bettered: "For Marx was before all else a revolutionist. His real mission in life was to contribute, in one way or another, to the overthrow of capitalist society…. Fighting was his element. And he fought with a passion, a tenacity and a success such as few could rival."[10]

Engels' words could as easily be applied to Duncan Hallas's own life and commitment to building the revolutionary working-class movement for self-emancipation.

Ahmed Shawki
June 2003
Chicago, Illinois

TROTSKY'S MARXISM

Acknowledgements

This little work owes its existence to the encouragement, advice and practical help of Tony Cliff.

Insofar as its treatment of Trotsky's thought is in any way unusual, it is very heavily dependent on Cliff's own appreciation and critique from 1947 onwards. Of course, Cliff is not responsible for every emphasis I have made.

Three other specific acknowledgements must be made. To Nigel Harris, whose writings and conversation have considerably modified my own first assessment of Trotsky; to John Molyneux, whose *Marxism and the Party* has influenced me more than may appear from a superficial view of our respective writings on the subject; and to Chanie Rosenberg who converted my handscript into type in the odd intervals of a very active political life and without whose efforts it would never have seen the light of day.

Duncan Hallas
July 1979

Duncan Hallas's other publications include *The Labour Party: Myth and Reality* (1981), *Days of Hope: The General Strike of 1926* (1981, with Chris Harman) and *The Comintern* (1984).

INTRODUCTION
TO THE
1984 EDITION

LEON TROTSKY was born in 1879 and grew to manhood and to consciousness in a world that has passed away, the world of the social-democratic Marxism of the Second International.

In any generation there are many possible mental worlds, rooted in the widely differing circumstances, social organization, and ideologies that coexist at any one time. That of social democracy was the most advanced, the closest approximation to a scientific, materialist world outlook that then existed.

For Lev Davidovitch Bronstein (the name of Trotsky was borrowed from a jailer), son of a Ukrainian Jewish peasant family, to attain that outlook was remarkable enough. The older Bronstein was a well-to-do peasant, a kulak—otherwise Trotsky would have received very little formal education—and he was a Jew in a country where anti-Semitism was officially encouraged and actual pogroms not rare. At any rate, the young Trotsky became, after an initial period of romantic revolutionism, a Marxist. And very soon, under the condition of tsarist autocracy, a professional revolutionary and a political prisoner. First arrested at the age of 19, he was sentenced to four years' deportation to Siberia after spending 18 months in jail. He escaped in 1902, and, from then until his death, revolution was his profession.

This small book is concerned with ideas rather than events. Least of all is it an attempt at a biography. Isaac Deutscher's three volumes, whatever view is taken of the author's political conclusions, will remain the authoritative biographical study for a very long time.

Yet, any attempt to present a summary of Trotsky's ideas runs into an immediate difficulty. Much more than most of the great Marxist thinkers (Lenin is an outstanding exception), Trotsky was concerned throughout his life with the immediate problems facing revolutionaries in the workers' movement. Nearly everything he said or wrote relates to some immediate issue, to some current struggle. The contrast with what has come to be called "Western Marxism" could hardly be more marked. A sympathetic chronicler of this latter trend has written, "The first and most fundamental of its characteristics has been the structural divorce of this Marxism from political practice."[1] That is the last thing that could ever be said of Trotsky's Marxism. Therefore, it is necessary to present, in however sketchy and inadequate a fashion, some elements of the background against which Trotsky formed his ideas.

Russia was backward, Europe advanced. That was the basic idea of all Russian Marxists (and not of Marxists alone, of course). Europe was advanced because its industrialization was well developed *and* because social democracy, in the form of sizeable workers' parties professing allegiance to the Marxist program, was growing fast. For Russians (and to some extent generally), the parties of the German-speaking countries were the most important. The social-democratic parties of the German and Austrian empires were expanding workers' parties that had adopted fully Marxist programs (the German Erfurt program of 1891, and the Austrian Heinfeld program of 1888). Their influence on Russian Marxists was immense. The fact that Poland, whose working class was already stirring, was partitioned between the empires of the tsar and the two Kaisers strengthened the connection. Rosa Luxemburg, it will be recalled, was born in Russian-occupied Poland, but became prominent in the German movement. There was nothing out of the way in this. Social democrats then regarded "national" boundaries as secondary.

In terms of ideas, this growing movement (illegal in Germany between 1878 and 1890, but polling one and a half million votes on a restricted suffrage in the latter year) was sustained by the synthesis of early Marxism and late 19th century developments that had been achieved by Frederick Engels. His *Anti-Dühring* (1878), an attempt at an overall, scientifically grounded worldview, was the basis for the popularizations (or vulgarizations) of Karl Kautsky, the "pope of Marxism," and of the more profound expositions of the Russian G.V. Plekhanov.

In this exciting intellectual/practical world—for Engels and his disciples and imitators had established a link between theory and practice in the workers' party—the young Trotsky grew intellectually and soon became something more than a disciple of his elders. His respect for Engels was immense. Yet he was, within a few years of his first assimilation of the Marxist world outlook, to challenge the then Marxist orthodoxy on the question of the backward countries. But first he was to meet the émigré leaders of Russian Marxism and to play a prominent role in the 1903 congress of the Russian Social Democratic Labor Party—the real founding conference.

Trotsky escaped from Verkholensk in Siberia, hidden under a load of hay, in the summer of 1902. By October, he had arrived at the directing center of Russian social democracy, then situated near Kings Cross station in London. Lenin, Krupskaya, Martov, and Vera Zasulich all lived in the area, and from here *Iskra,* the organ of the advocates of a centralized, disciplined party, was produced and dispatched to the underground in Russia. Trotsky was soon involved in the disputes within the *Iskra* team—Lenin wished to add him to the editorial board; Plekhanov resolutely opposed the idea—and so came to know at close quarters the future leaders of Menshevism, Plekhanov and Martov, as well as Lenin.

The split in the *Iskra* group was already gestating. It came into the open at the congress in the summer of 1903. The *Iskra*-ists stood together in resisting the demands of the Jewish socialist organization, the Bund, for autonomy so far as work among Jewish people was concerned, and in resisting the reformist tendency of the economists. Then came the split in the *Iskra* group itself into the Bolshevik majority and the Menshevik minority. It was not clear-cut at first—the issues themselves were not yet clear. Plekhanov sided with Lenin initially; Trotsky supported the Menshevik leader Martov.

Two years later, Trotsky was back in Russia. The revolution of 1905 was underway. In the course of it, Trotsky rose to his full height. Still only 26 years old, he became the most prominent single revolutionary leader and an internationally known figure. He emerged from the background of small-group and émigré politics transformed into a magnificent orator and mass leader. As president of the Petrograd Soviet, he was able to exert a considerable degree of tactical leadership and demonstrated that sure touch and iron nerve that were to characterize him in the greater upheavals of 1917.

The 1905 Revolution was crushed. The tsarist army was shaken but not broken. Out of the experience—the "dress rehearsal," Lenin called it—the divergent tendencies in social democracy moved further apart. Trotsky, still nominally a Menshevik, developed his own unique synthesis, the theory of permanent revolution.

The next decade was spent in the small émigré circles again, and in futile attempts to unite what were by now incompatible tendencies. Then came the war, antiwar activity, and, in February 1917, the overthrow of the tsar. Trotsky joined the Bolshevik party, by now a real mass workers' party, in July, and such was his force of personality, talent, and reputation that within a few weeks he stood second only to Lenin in the eyes of the mass of its supporters. He was entrusted with the actual organization of the October uprising and, at the age of 38, became one of the two or three most important figures in party and state. A little later, he would also become one of the most significant leaders of the *world* communist movement, the Communist International. He was the main creator and director of the Red Army, and was influential in every field of policy.

From these heights, Trotsky was destined to be cast down. The fall was not simply a personal tragedy. Trotsky rose as the revolution rose and fell as the revolution declined. His personal history is fused with the history of the Russian Revolution and international socialism. From 1923, he led the opposition to the growing reaction in Russia—to Stalinism. Expelled from the party in 1927, and from the USSR in 1929, his last 11 years were spent in a heroic struggle against impossible odds to keep alive the authentic communist tradition and embody it in a revolutionary organization. Vilified and isolated, he was finally murdered on Stalin's orders in 1940. He left behind a fragile international organization and a body of writings that is one of the richest sources of applied Marxism in existence.

This book concentrates on four themes. They do not exhaust Trotsky's contribution to Marxist thought, not by any means, for he was an exceptionally prolific writer with unusually wide interests. Nevertheless, his life's work was centrally concerned with these four questions, and the bulk of his voluminous writings relate to them in one way or another.

They are, first, the theory of "permanent revolution," its rele-

vance to the Russian Revolutions of the 20th century and to subsequent developments in the colonial and semicolonial countries—what is today often called the Third World. Second, the
outcome of the Russian October Revolution and the whole question of Stalinism. Trotsky made the first sustained attempt at a
historical materialist analysis of Stalinism, and his analysis, whatever criticism may have to be made of it, has been the starting
point for all subsequent serious analysis from a Marxist point of
view. Third, the strategy and tactics of mass revolutionary parties
in a wide variety of situations, a field in which Trotsky's contribution was not inferior to that of Marx and Lenin. Fourth, the
problem of the relationship between party and class, and the historical development that reduced the revolutionary movement to
a fringe status with respect to the mass workers' organizations.

Isaac Deutscher described Trotsky, in his last years, as "the
residuary legatee of classical Marxism." He was that, and more
besides. It is this that gives Trotsky's thought its enormous con-
temporary relevance.

CHAPTER I

PERMANENT REVOLUTION

URING THE last third of the 18th century, the industrial revolution, the most profound change in the whole history of the human race since the development of agriculture in the remote past, gained an irresistible momentum in one small corner of the world, in Britain. But the British capitalists soon had imitators in those other countries where a bourgeoisie had gained power or come near to gaining power.

By the beginning of the 20th century, industrial capitalism completely dominated the world. The colonial empires of Britain, France, Germany, Russia, the U.S., Belgium, the Netherlands, Italy, and Japan covered by far the greater part of the world's land surface. Those essentially precapitalist societies that still preserved a nominal independence (China, Iran, the Turkish Empire, Ethiopia, etc.) were, in fact, dominated by one or another of the great imperialist powers or informally partitioned between them—the term "spheres of influence" expresses it exactly. Such token "independence" as remained was due solely to the rivalries of competing imperialisms (Britain versus Russia in Iran; Britain versus France in Thailand; Britain versus Germany—with Russia as an also-ran—in Turkey; Britain, the U.S., Germany, Russia, France, Japan, and various minor contenders, all against each other, in China).

Yet the countries conquered or dominated by the industrial capitalist powers were *not,* generally speaking, transformed into replicas of the various "mother countries." On the contrary, they remained essentially preindustrial societies. Their social and economic development was profoundly influenced—profoundly distorted—by conquest or dominance, but they were not, typically, transformed into the new type of society.

Marx's famous description of the ruin of the Indian textile industry (which had been based on high-quality products made by independent artisans) by cheap Lancashire machine-made cotton piece goods still stands as a good rough outline of the initial impact of Western capitalism on what is now often called the "Third World": impoverishment and social retrogression.

This process of "combined and uneven development," to use Trotsky's expression, led to a situation (still with us in all essentials) in which the greater part of the world's population had not only not advanced socially and economically, but had been thrown backwards. What then, was (and, indeed, is) the way forward for the mass of the people in these countries?

Trotsky, as a young man of 26, made a profoundly original contribution to the solution of this problem. It was a solution rooted both in the realities of the uneven development of capitalism on a world scale and in the Marxist analysis of the true significance of industrial development—the creation, at one and the same time, of the material basis for an advanced classless society and of an exploited class, the proletariat, that is capable of raising itself to the level of a ruling class and, through its rule, of abolishing classes, the class struggle, and all forms of alienation and oppression.

Trotsky, naturally, developed his ideas in relation to Russia in the first instance. It is therefore necessary to look at the ideological background to the disputes among Russian revolutionaries in the late 19th and early 20th centuries in order to understand the full import of his contribution. But not only Russian revolutionaries. There was, after all, a real international movement at that time.

> Once Europe is reorganized, and North America, that will furnish such colossal power and such an example that the semi-civilized countries will follow in their wake of their own accord. Economic needs alone will be responsible for this. But as to what social and political phases these countries will then have to pass through before they likewise arrive at socialist organization, we today can only advance rather idle hypotheses, I think. One thing alone is certain; the victorious proletariat can force no blessings of any kind on any foreign nation without undermining its own victory by so doing.[1]

So Engels wrote to Kautsky in 1882. He was not thinking of Russia. The countries mentioned in this letter are India, Algeria,

Egypt, and the "Dutch, Portuguese, and Spanish possessions." Nevertheless, his general approach is representative of the thinking of what was to become the Second International (from 1889 onward). The course of political development would follow the course of economic development. The revolutionary socialist movement that would destroy capitalism and lead ultimately to the dissolution of the proletariat and all classes (after a period of proletarian dictatorship) into the classless society of the future would develop where capitalism and its inseparable concomitant, the proletariat, had first developed.

Russian Marxists, by whom the pioneer Emancipation of Labor group was founded the year after Engels' letter was written, had to place Russia in this historical scheme. Plekhanov, the leading light of the group, had no doubts. The Russian Empire, he argued in the 1880s and 1890s, was an essentially precapitalist society and therefore was destined to go through the process of capitalist development before the question of socialism could be addressed. He firmly rejected the idea, with which Marx himself had once toyed, that Russia might, depending on developments in Europe, avoid the capitalist stage of development altogether and achieve a transition to socialism on the basis of a peasant movement overthrowing the autocracy and seeking to preserve the elements of traditional communal ownership of land (the Mir) that still existed in the 1880s.

Plekhanov's views, developed in polemics with the "peasant road to socialism" school (the Narodniks), became the starting point for all subsequent Russian Marxism. That capitalism was in fact developing in Russia, that the Mir was doomed, that a special "Russian road to socialism" was a reactionary illusion—these ideas were basic for the next generation of Russian Marxists, for Lenin, a few years later for Trotsky, and for all their associates. The first three volumes of Lenin's *Collected Works* consist very largely of criticism of the Narodniks and demonstrations of the inevitability—and progressive character—of capitalism in Russia. The *Iskra* group, founded in 1900 to create a unified national organization out of the scattered social-democratic groups and circles, based itself firmly on the view that the industrial working class was the basis for that organization.

Three questions arose: First, what was the *relationship* between the political roles of the working class (still a small minority), the bourgeoisie, and the peasantry (the great majority); hence, what was the *class character* of the coming revolution in Russia; finally, what was the relationship between the revolution and the working-class movements of the advanced countries of the West?

The different answers given to these questions were one of the two main issues (the other being the nature of the revolutionary party) that defined what would become fundamentally divergent tendencies. To understand Trotsky's theory of permanent revolution, it is necessary to look briefly at these answers, as they appeared in developed form after the 1905 Revolution.

Menshevism

The Menshevik view can be summarized in this way: The state of the development of the productive forces (that is, Russia's general economic backwardness combined with a small but significant and growing modern industry) defines what is possible—a *bourgeois* revolution, like that of 1789–94 in France. Therefore, the bourgeoisie must come to power, establish a bourgeois-democratic republic that will sweep away the remnants of precapitalist social relations, and open the road to a rapid growth of the productive forces (and so of the proletariat) on a *capitalist* basis. The struggle for the socialist revolution will thus, eventually, come onto the agenda.

The political role of the working class is, therefore, to push the bourgeoisie forward against tsarism. It must preserve its political independence—meaning, centrally, that social democrats cannot enter into a revolutionary government alongside nonproletarian forces.

As to the peasantry, it cannot play an *independent* political role. It can play a secondary revolutionary role in support of the essentially urban bourgeois revolution and, after that revolution, will undergo more or less rapid economic differentiation into a layer of capitalist farmers (which will be conservative), a layer of small holders, and a layer of landless agricultural proletarians.

There is no organic connection between the Russian bourgeois revolution and the European workers' movement, although the Russian Revolution (if it occurs before the socialist revolution in the West) will invigorate the Western social democracies.

Actually, Menshevism was a rather variegated tendency. Different Mensheviks put different emphases on the several parts of this scheme (which, as presented, is essentially Plekhanov's), but all accepted its general contours.

The 1905 Revolution showed its fundamental flaws. The bourgeoisie would not play the part allocated to it. Of course, Plekhanov, a profound student of the great French Revolution, never expected the Russian bourgeoisie to lead a ruthless struggle against tsarism without enormous pressure from below. Just as the Jacobin dictatorship of 1793–94, the decisive culmination of the French Revolution, had come to power under the violent pressure of the *sans-culottes,* the plebeian masses of Paris, so in Russia the working class could be the real driving force, *compelling* the bourgeoisie's political representatives (or a section of them) to take power. But 1905 and its aftermath demonstrated that there was no "Robespierrist" tendency in the Russian bourgeoisie. Faced with revolutionary upsurge, it rallied to the tsar.

Already in 1898, the manifesto drawn up for the abortive First Congress of Russian Social Democrats had declared:

> The farther east one goes in Europe, the more the bourgeoisie becomes in the political respect weaker, more cowardly, and meaner, and the larger are the cultural and political tasks which fall to the share of the proletariat.[2]

It was not a matter of geography but of history. The development of industrial capitalism and of the modern proletariat had made the bourgeoisie everywhere, even in countries where industrialization was embryonic, a conservative class. Indeed, the failure of the revolution in Germany in 1848–49 had demonstrated this much earlier.

Bolshevism

The Bolsheviks' view started from the same premises as the Mensheviks'. The coming revolution would be, and could only be, a *bourgeois* revolution in terms of its class nature. It went on to reject outright any reliance on pressuring the bourgeoisie and to propose an alternative. "The transformation of the economic and political situation in Russia along bourgeois-democratic lines is inevitable and inescapable," wrote Lenin in his famous pamphlet *Two Tactics of Social Democracy in the Democratic Revolution* (July 1905).

> No power on earth can prevent such a transformation, but the combined action of the existing forces which are effecting it may result in either of two things, may bring about either of two

forms of that transformation. Either (1) matters will end in "the revolution's decisive victory over tsarism," or (2) the forces will be inadequate for a decisive victory, and matters will end in a deal between tsarism and the most "inconsistent" and most "self-seeking" elements of the bourgeoisie.

We must be perfectly certain in our minds as to what real social forces are opposed to tsarism...and are capable of gaining a "decisive victory" over it. The big bourgeoisie...cannot be such a force. We see that they do not even want a decisive victory. We know that owing to their class position they are incapable of waging a decisive struggle against tsarism; they are too heavily fettered by private property, by capital and land to enter into a decisive struggle. They stand in too great a need of tsarism, with its bureaucratic, police, and military forces for use against the proletariat and peasantry, to want it to be destroyed. No, the only force capable of gaining "a decisive victory over tsarism" is the *people*, i.e., the proletariat and the peasantry.... "The revolution's decisive victory over tsarism" means the establishment of the *revolutionary-democratic dictatorship of the proletariat and the peasantry....*

It can only be a dictatorship, for realization of the changes urgently and absolutely indispensable to the proletariat and the peasantry will evoke desperate resistance from the landlords, the big bourgeoisie, and tsarism.... But of course it will be a democratic, not a socialist dictatorship.... At best, it may bring about a radical redistribution of landed property in favor of the peasantry, establish consistent and full democracy, including the formation of a republic, eradicate all the oppressive features of Asiatic bondage, not only in rural but also in factory life, lay the foundation for a thorough improvement in the conditions of the workers and for a rise in their standard of living, and—last but not least—carry the revolutionary conflagration into Europe. Such a victory will not yet by any means transform our bourgeois revolution into a socialist revolution.[3]

The Menshevik line was not simply a mistake, Lenin argued, it was the expression of an unwillingness to carry through the revolution. Menshevik determination to cling to the bourgeois liberals must lead to paralysis. The peasantry, on the other hand, had a genuine interest in the destruction of tsarism and the remnants of feudalism on the land. Therefore, the "democratic dictatorship"—a provisional revolutionary government, with representatives of the peasantry included alongside social democrats—was the appropriate "Jacobin" regime that would crush the reaction and establish "a democratic republic (with complete equality and self-determination for all nations), confiscation of the landed estates, and an eight-hour working day."[4]

Trotsky's solution

Trotsky rejected the reliance on a "revolutionary bourgeoisie" as firmly as Lenin. He ridiculed the Menshevik scheme as

> an extra-historical category created by journalistic analogy and deduction...because, in France, the Revolution was carried through to the end by democratic revolutionaries—the Jacobins—therefore the Russian Revolution can transfer power only into the hands of a revolutionary bourgeois democracy. Having thus erected an unshakeable algebraic formula of revolution, the Mensheviks then try to insert into it arithmetical values which do not in fact exist.[5]

In every other respect Trotsky's theory of permanent revolution, which owed a good deal to the Russo-German Marxist Parvus, differed from the Bolshevik position. First, and crucially, it ruled out the possibility that the peasantry could play an *independent* political role:

> The peasantry cannot play a leading revolutionary role. History cannot entrust the muzhik with the task of liberating a bourgeois nation from its bonds. Because of its dispersion, political backwardness, and especially of its deep inner contradictions which cannot be resolved within the framework of a capitalist system, the peasantry can only deal the old order some powerful blows from the rear, by spontaneous risings in the countryside, on the one hand, and by creating discontent within the army on the other.[6]

This was identical with the Menshevik line and followed Marx's own assessment of the French peasantry as a class.

Because "the town leads in modern society," only an urban class can play a *leading* role, and because the bourgeoisie is not revolutionary (and the urban petty bourgeoisie in any case is incapable of playing the part of *sans-culottes*),

> the conclusion remains that only the proletariat in its class struggle, placing the peasant masses under its revolutionary leadership, can "carry the revolution to the end."[7]

This *must* lead to a *workers'* government; Lenin's "democratic dictatorship" is simply an illusion:

> *The political domination of the proletariat is incompatible with its economic enslavement. No matter under what political flag the proletariat has come to power, it is obliged to take the path of socialist policy. It would be the greatest utopianism to think that the proletariat, having been raised to political domination*

by the internal mechanism of a bourgeois revolution, can, even if it so desires, limit its mission to the creation of republican-democratic conditions for the social domination of the bourgeoisie.[8]

But this leads to an immediate contradiction. The common starting point of all Russian Marxists was precisely that Russia lacked both the material and human basis for socialism—a highly developed industry and a modern proletariat making up a large fraction of the population and having acquired organization and consciousness as a class "for itself," as Marx had put it. Lenin had denounced forcefully, in *Two Tactics,*

> the absurd and semi-anarchist idea of giving immediate effect to the maximum program and the conquest of power for a socialist revolution. The degree of economic development (an objective condition), and the development of class consciousness and organization of the broad masses of the proletariat (a subjective condition inseparably bound up with the objective condition) make the immediate and complete emancipation of the working class impossible. Only the most ignorant people can close their eyes to the bourgeois nature of the democratic revolution which is now taking place [in 1905].[9]

From a Marxist standpoint, Lenin's argument is incontestable so long as matters stand on the ground of Russia alone. It is perhaps necessary, in view of subsequent developments, to stress this elementary point. Socialism, for Marx and for all those who regarded themselves as his followers at that time, is the self-emancipation of the working class. It therefore presupposes both large-scale modern industry and a class-conscious proletariat capable of self-emancipation. Trotsky was nevertheless convinced that only the working class was capable of playing the leading role in the Russian Revolution and, if it did so, could not fail to take power into its own hands. What then?

> The revolutionary authorities will be confronted with the objective problems of socialism, but the solution of these problems will, at a certain stage, be prevented by the country's economic backwardness. *There is no way out from this contradiction within the framework of a national revolution.* The workers' government will from the start be faced with the task of uniting its forces with those of the socialist proletariat of Western Europe. Only in this way will its temporary revolutionary hegemony become the prologue to a socialist dictatorship. Thus, permanent revolution will become, for the Russian proletariat, a matter of class self-preservation.[10]

Engels' original hypothesis is turned upside down. The *un-even* development of capitalism leads to a *combined* development in which backward Russia becomes, temporarily, the vanguard of an international socialist revolution.

The theory of permanent revolution remained central to Trotsky's Marxism to the end of his life. In only one important respect did his post-1917 ideas on the question differ from those outlined here. The pre-1917 version depended heavily on spontaneous working-class action. As we shall see, Trotsky was in this period a strong opponent of "Bolshevik centralism" and rejected in practice the conception of the leading role of the party. In 1917, he reversed his position on this issue. His subsequent applications of the theory of permanent revolution were structured around the role of the revolutionary workers' party.

The outcome

All theory, at least all theory that has any pretensions to be scientific, finds its ultimate test in practice. "The proof of the pudding," as the Lancashire saying goes, "is in the eating." But the *decisive* practical test may be delayed long after the deaths of the theorist and his or her supporters and opponents.

Unlike the physical sciences—where it is always possible *in principle* to set up experimental tests (even though the technical means to carry them through may not be immediately available)—Marxism, as the science of social development (and, indeed, its bourgeois rivals, the pseudo-sciences of economics, sociology, and so on), cannot be tested according to some arbitrary time scale but only in the course of historical development and, even then, only provisionally. The reason is simple enough, although the consequences are immensely complicated. "Men make their own history," Marx said, "although they do not do so under conditions of their own choosing." The "voluntary" acts of millions and tens of millions of people, who are, of course, themselves historically conditioned, pressing against constraints imposed by the whole course of previous historical development (of which the millions are, typically, unaware), produces effects more complex than the most far-sighted theorist can foresee. The degree of *on s'engage, et puis...on voit* (get stuck in, and then we'll see), which was Napoleon's aphoristic description of his military science, must always be considerable for revolutionaries engaged in a conscious attempt to shape the course of events.

The Russian revolutionaries of the early 20th century were more fortunate than most. For them, the decisive test came very quickly. In 1917, the Mensheviks, the opponents *in principle* of participation in a nonproletarian government, joined a government of opponents of socialism in order to prosecute an imperialist war and hold back the tide of revolution. It verified *in practice* Lenin's 1905 prediction that they were the "Gironde" of the Russian Revolution. That same year, the Bolsheviks, the advocates of the democratic dictatorship and a coalition provisional revolutionary government, after an initial period of "critical support" for what Lenin, on his return to Russia, called "a government of capitalists," turned decisively toward the seizure of power by the *working class* under the impact of Lenin's *April Theses* and the pressure of the revolutionary workers in their ranks.

This year, 1917, saw Trotsky brilliantly vindicated when Lenin, in effect although not in words, adopted the permanent revolution perspective and abandoned the democratic dictatorship without ceremony. It also saw Trotsky in practice isolated and impotent to affect the course of events in the great revolutionary crisis of 1917 until, in July, he led his smallish and largely intellectual following into the mass Bolshevik party. It therefore saw Lenin's long, hard struggle (which Trotsky had denounced for more than a decade as "sectarian") for a *workers'* party, free from the ideological influence of petty-bourgeois "Marxists" (so far as such independence can be achieved by organizational means), no less brilliantly vindicated.[11]

Trotsky had been proved right on the central strategic issue of the Russian Revolution, but, as Tony Cliff justly remarks, he was "a brilliant general without an army to speak of."[12] Trotsky never subsequently forgot that fact. He was later to write that his breach with Lenin on the question of the need for a disciplined workers' party in 1903–04 was "the greatest mistake of my life."

The October Revolution put the Russian working class in power. It did so in the context of a rising tide of revolutionary revolt against the old regimes in Central and, to a lesser degree, Western Europe. Trotsky's perspective, and Lenin's after April 1917, depended crucially on the success of the *proletarian* revolution in at least "one or two" (as Lenin, always cautious, put it) advanced countries. As events unfolded, however, the power of the established social-democratic parties (which proved in practice, from August 1914 on, to have become conservative and nationalistic) and the vacillations and evasions of the leaders of the mass "centrist" breakaways from them between 1916 and 1921, aborted the revolutionary movements in Germany, Austria, Hungary, Italy, and elsewhere before the proletarian revolution could be achieved or, where temporarily achieved, consolidated.

Trotsky's analysis of the consequences of these facts will be examined later. But first it will be useful to look at the second Chinese Revolution (of 1925–27) and its outcome in terms of Trotsky's theory.

The Chinese Revolution, 1925–27

The Chinese Communist Party (CCP) was founded in July 1921, against a background of rising anti-imperialist feelings and working-class militancy in the coastal cities where the newly created but sizeable industrial working class was struggling to organize itself. Tiny and composed at first entirely of intellectuals, the CCP was able in a few years to become the effective leadership of the newly born labor movement.

China was then a semi-colony, partitioned informally between British, French, United States, and Japanese imperialisms. German and Russian imperialism had been eliminated by war and revolution before 1919. Each imperialist power maintained its own "sphere of influence" and supported "its own" regional baron, warlord, or national government. Thus, the British, then the dominant imperialist power, gave arms, money, and "advisers" to Wu P'ei-fu, the dominant warlord in Central China, who controlled the districts along the Yangtse River. The Japanese rendered the same services to Chang Tso-lin, warlord of Manchuria. Lesser military gangsters, each one shiftingly attached to one or another imperialist power, controlled most of the rest of the country.

The exception, a very partial exception, was Canton and its hinterland. Here, Sun Yat-sen, the father of Chinese nationalism, had established some sort of a base on a program of national independence, modernization, and social reforms with a vague "leftist" veneer. Sun's party, the Kuomintang (KMT), a fairly formless and ineffective body before 1922, depended on the toleration of the local "progressive" warlord.

However, after preliminary moves from 1922 onward, the KMT leaders made an agreement with the government of the USSR, which in 1924 sent political and military advisers to Canton and began to supply arms. The KMT became a centralized party with a relatively efficient army. Moreover, from late 1922, the members of the CCP were sent into the KMT "as individuals." Three of them even sat on the KMT Executive. This policy, which had met with some resistance in the CCP, was imposed by the Executive of the Communist International. The CCP was, in effect, tied to the KMT.

Then, in the early summer of 1925, a mass strike movement—partly economic in origin, but rapidly politicized in the repression attempted by foreign troops and police—broke out in Shanghai and spread to the major cities of Central and South China, including Canton and Hong Kong. With many ups and downs, an enormous mass movement of revolt existed in the cities until early 1927. At various times, a situation of dual power existed, with CCP-led strike committees constituting "Government Number Two." In those same years, peasant revolts broke out in a number of important provinces. The warlord regimes were shaken to their foundations. The KMT sought to ride the storm with the help of the CCP and then to exploit it to conquer national power without social change. Early in 1926, the KMT was admitted to the Communist International as a sympathizing party!

Trotsky, although still a member of the political bureau of the Russian party, was effectively excluded from direct influence on policy by 1925. According to Isaac Deutscher, he called for the withdrawal of the CCP from the KMT in April 1926.[13] His first substantial written criticism dates from September.

> The revolutionary struggle in China has, since 1925, entered a new phase, which is characterized above all by the active intervention of broad layers of the proletariat. At the same time, the commercial bourgeoisie and the elements of the intelligentsia linked with it are breaking off to the right, assuming a hostile attitude towards strikes, communists, and the USSR. It is quite clear that in the light of these fundamental facts the question of revising relations between the Communist Party and the Kuomintang must necessarily be raised....
>
> The leftward movement of the masses of Chinese workers is as certain a fact as the rightward movement of the Chinese bourgeoisie. Insofar as the Kuomintang has been based on the

political and organizational union of the workers and the bourgeoisie, it must now be torn apart by the centrifugal tendencies
of the class struggle....

The participation of the CCP in the Kuomintang was perfectly
correct in the period in which the CCP was a propaganda society
which was only preparing itself for future *independent* political activity but which, at the same time, sought to take part in the ongoing national liberation struggle.... But the fact of the Chinese
proletariat's mighty awakening, its desire for struggle and for independent class organization, is absolutely undeniable.... Its [the
CCP's] immediate political task must now be to fight for direct independent leadership of the awakened working class—not of
course to remove the working class from the national-revolution-
ary struggle, but to assure it the role of not only the most resolute
fighter, but also of political leader with hegemony in the struggle
of the Chinese masses....

To think that the petty bourgeoisie can be won over by clever
maneuvers or good advice within the Kuomintang is hopeless
utopianism. The Communist Party will be more able to exert direct and indirect influence upon the petty bourgeoisie of town
and country the stronger the party is in itself, that is, the more
the party has won over the Chinese working class. But that is
possible only on the basis of an independent class party and
class policy.[14]

This was totally unacceptable to Stalin and his associates.
Their policy was to cling to the KMT and to force the CCP to
subordinate itself, no matter what. In this way, they hoped a reli-
able ally of the USSR could be kept going in South China and,
perhaps, later could take power nationally.

This policy was justified theoretically by reviving the "democratic dictatorship" thesis. The Chinese Revolution was a bourgeois revolution, and therefore, the argument went, a democratic
dictatorship of the proletariat and peasantry should be the aim.
In order to preserve the worker-peasant bloc, the movement
must confine itself to "democratic" demands. The socialist revolution was not on the agenda. The difficulty presented by the
fact that the KMT was manifestly *not* a peasant party was met
by the argument that actually it was a multiclass party, a "bloc
of four classes" (bourgeoisie, urban petty bourgeoisie, workers,
and peasants).

What does this mean anyway—bloc of four classes? Have you
ever encountered this expression in Marxist literature before? If
the bourgeoisie leads the oppressed masses of the people under
the bourgeois banner and takes hold of state power through its

leadership, then this is no bloc but the political exploitation of the oppressed masses by the bourgeoisie.[15]

The real point is that the bourgeoisie would capitulate to the imperialists. Therefore, the KMT would inevitably play a counter-revolutionary role.

> The Chinese bourgeoisie is sufficiently realistic and acquainted intimately enough with the nature of world imperialism to understand that a really serious struggle against the latter requires such an upheaval of the revolutionary masses as would primarily become a menace to the bourgeoisie itself.... And if we taught the workers of Russia from the very beginning not to believe in the readiness of liberalism and the ability of petty-bourgeois democracy to crush tsarism and to destroy feudalism, we should no less energetically imbue the Chinese workers from the outset with the same spirit of distrust. The new and absolutely false theory promulgated by Stalin-Bukharin about the "immanent" revolutionary spirit of the colonial bourgeoisie is, in substance, a translation of Menshevism into the language of Chinese politics.[16]

The outcome is well known. Chiang Kai-shek, military chief of the KMT, mounted his first coup against the left in Canton in March 1926. The CCP, under Russian pressure, submitted. When Chiang's army launched the "Northern Expedition," a wave of working-class and peasant revolt destroyed the warlord forces, but the CCP, faithful to the "bloc," did its best to prevent "excesses." Before Chiang entered Shanghai in March 1927, the warlord forces were defeated by two general strikes and an insurrection led by the CCP. Chiang ordered the workers to be disarmed. The CCP refused to resist. Then, in April, they were massacred, and the labor movement was beheaded.

There followed a split in the KMT. The civilian leaders, fearing (correctly) that Chiang was out to become military dictator, set up their government in Wuhan (Hankow). The CCP was now required by the Comintern to support this "left" KMT regime, and supplied its ministers of labor and agriculture. Its leader, Wang Ching-wei, used them to serve his turn and then, after a few months, carried out his own coup. Subsequently, he even headed the puppet government of Japanese-occupied China. The CCP was driven underground and rapidly lost its mass base in the towns. At each crucial confrontation, it had used its hard-earned influence to persuade the workers not to resist the KMT.

Then, because a critical stage had been reached in the inner-party struggle in Russia, the Stalin-Bukharin ruling group in the Communist Party of the Soviet Union (CPSU) made a 180-degree turn. From repeated capitulations to the KMT, the CCP was forced into an outright putsch. Stalin and Bukharin needed a victory in China in order to fend off the criticisms of the opposition (which they planned to expel) at the 15th Congress of the CPSU in December 1927. A new Comintern emissary, Heinz Neumann, was sent to Canton, where he attempted to stage a coup d'état in early December.

The CCP still had a serious underground force in the city. Five thousand communists, mostly local workers, took part in the uprising. But there had been no political preparation, no agitation, no involvement of the mass of the working class. The communists were isolated. This "Canton Commune" was crushed in approximately the same time it had taken to crush Blanqui's insurrection in Paris in 1839—two days—and for the same reasons. It was a putsch, undertaken without regard to the level of the class struggle and the consciousness of the working class. The outcome was a massacre even greater than that of Shanghai. The CCP ceased to exist in Canton.

The theory of permanent revolution had been strikingly confirmed again—in a negative sense. Imperialist domination of China got a further lease of life.

Suppose, however, the CCP had followed the same course the Bolsheviks had followed after April 1917. Was a proletarian dictatorship really possible in a country as backward as China in the 1920s? Trotsky was open-minded:

> The question of the "non-capitalistic" path of development of China was posed in a conditional form by Lenin, for whom, as for us, it was and is ABC wisdom that the Chinese Revolution, left to its own forces, that is, *without the direct support of the victorious proletariat of the USSR and the working class of all countries,* could end only with the broadest possibilities for capitalist development of the country, with more favorable conditions for the labor movement.... But first of all, the inevitability of the capitalist path has by no means been proved; and secondly—the argument is incomparably more timely for us—the bourgeois tasks can be solved in various ways.[17]

It will be necessary to return to that last point. In the second half of the 20th century, a series of revolutions occurred, from

Angola through to Cuba and Vietnam to Zanzibar (now part of Tanzania), that were certainly not proletarian revolutions and were certainly not bourgeois revolutions in the classic sense. Trotsky did not foresee such a development, nor did anyone else in his time. The theory of permanent revolution, decisively confirmed in the first half of the 20th century, must obviously be reconsidered in the light of these later developments. The question will be taken up in Chapter 5 below.

CHAPTER 2

STALINISM

T HE DREAM of and the hope for a classless and truly free society are very old. In Europe, they are well documented from the 14th century onward in the fragments that survive of the ideas of many rebels and heretics. "When Adam delved and Eve span, who was then the gentleman?" went the rhyme popular during the great English peasant revolt of 1381. And, of course, similar sentiments can be identified (however overladen with ruling-class ideology) in early Christianity and early Islam and, in varying degrees, in societies very much older than these.

Marx introduced a fundamentally new idea that can be summarized as follows: The aspirations of the most advanced thinkers and activists of past (preindustrial) generations, however admirable and inspiring for the future, were utopian in their own time in the simple sense that they were unrealizable. Class society, exploitation, and oppression are inevitable so long as the development of the productive forces and the productivity of labor (related but not identical concepts) are at a comparatively low level. With the growth of industrial capitalism, such things are no longer *inevitable,* provided capitalism is overthrown. A classless society, based on (relative) plenty, is now possible. Moreover, the instrument for achieving such a society—the industrial proletariat—has been brought into existence by the development of capitalism itself.

These ideas were, of course, the common coin of pre-1914 Marxism. All revolutionaries in the Marxist tradition took them for granted. But the society that came out of the Russian October Revolution was not a free and classless society. Even at an

early stage, it deviated a long way from Marx's view of a workers' state (as explained in *The Civil War in France*) or Lenin's development of Marx (as expounded in *State and Revolution*).
Later, it grew into a monstrous despotism.

It would be difficult to exaggerate the importance of these
facts. The existence first of one state and then a whole series of
states claiming to be "socialist" that are repulsive caricatures of
socialism must be reckoned as a major factor in the survival of
"Western capitalism."

Right-wing propagandists argue that Stalinism, or something
like it, is the inevitable result of expropriating the capitalist class.
Social-democratic propagandists, on the other hand, argue that
Stalinism is the inevitable consequence of "Bolshevik centralism," and that Stalin was "Lenin's natural heir."

Trotsky made the first *sustained* attempt at a historical materialist analysis of Stalinism—of the actual outcome of the Russian Revolution. Whatever criticisms can be made of it—and
some will be made here—it has been the starting point for all
subsequent serious analysis from a Marxist point of view.

What was the social reality of the Russia of 1921, when
Lenin was still chair of the Council of People's Commissars and
Trotsky still the People's Commissar for War? Speaking in support of the New Economic Policy (NEP) in the USSR in late
1921, Lenin argued:

> If capitalism gains by it, industrial production will grow, and the
> proletariat will grow too. The capitalists will gain from our pol-
> icy and will create an industrial proletariat, which in our coun-
> try, owing to the war and to the desperate poverty and ruin, has
> become declassed, i.e., dislodged from its class groove, and has
> ceased to exist as a proletariat. The proletariat is the class which
> is engaged in the production of material values in large-scale
> capitalist industry. Since large-scale capitalist industry has been
> destroyed, since the factories are at a standstill, the proletariat
> has disappeared. It has sometimes figured in statistics, but it has
> not been held together economically.[1]

The proletariat "has ceased to exist as a proletariat"! What then
becomes of the proletarian dictatorship, the proletariat as ruling
class?

War and civil war wrecked Russian industry—already very
weak by Western standards. From the October Revolution until
March 1918, when the "monstrous robber treaty" of Brest

Litovsk was signed with Germany, revolutionary Russia remained at war with Germany and Austria-Hungary. The following month, the first of the "allied" armies of intervention—the Japanese—landed at Vladivostok and began to push on into Siberia. They were not to withdraw finally until November 1922. In those years, detachments of 14 foreign armies (including those of the United States, Britain, and France) invaded the territory of the revolutionary republic. "White" generals were armed, supplied, and supported. At the height of the intervention, in the summer of 1919, the Soviet republic was reduced to a rump state in central European Russia, around Moscow, with a few outlying bastions precariously held. Even in the following summer, when the "white" armies had been decisively beaten, one-quarter of the entire available grain supply of the Soviet republic had to be sent to the western army group fighting the Polish invaders.

This at a time when the cities were depopulated and starving. More than half of the total population of Petrograd (Leningrad) and nearly half that of Moscow had fled to the countryside. Such industry as could be kept going was devoted almost entirely to war—and this was made possible only by "cannibalization," the steady sacrifice of the productive base as a whole in order to keep a fraction of it working. These were the circumstances in which the Russian proletariat, a small minority to start with, disintegrated.

The facts are known well enough and are set out in some detail in, for example, the second volume of E.H. Carr's *The Bolshevik Revolution*.[2] By 1921, total industrial output stood at roughly *one-eighth* of the 1913 figure, itself a wretchedly low figure by German, British, or U.S. standards. The revolution survived by means of enormous exertion, directed by a revolutionary dictatorship that far surpassed the Jacobin dictatorship of 1793 in its mobilizing capacity. But it survived at the cost of a ruined economy, and it remained isolated. By 1921, the European revolutionary movement was clearly at an ebb.

What concerns us here are the social consequences of these facts. The so-called war communism of 1918–21 had been, in reality, a siege economy of the most brutal and brutalizing kind. In essence, it consisted of forced requisitioning of grain from the peasantry, the cannibalization of industry, universal conscription, and massive coercion to win the war for survival.

Before the revolution, a substantial part of the peasants' grain production had been diverted to the cities (directly or via exports) in the form of rents, interest payments, taxes, compensation payments, and so on, to the old ruling classes. Tsarist Russia had been a major grain exporter. Now, with the destruction of the old order, that link was cut. The peasants produced for consumption—or for exchange. But the ruin of industry meant that there was nothing, or nearly nothing, to exchange— hence, forced requisitioning.

The revolution had survived in an overwhelmingly peasant country because of the support—usually passive, but sometimes active—of the peasant masses who had gained from it. With the end of the civil war, they had no more to gain, and the revolts in 1921, in Kronstadt and Tambov, showed that the peasantry and sections of the remnants of the working class were turning against the regime.

The NEP of 1921 onward recognized this fact above all and introduced a fixed tax (levied in grain, since money had become worthless under war communism) in place of the arbitrary requisitioning of that era. Second, it allowed the revival of private trade and private small-scale production (retaining the "commanding heights" for the state). Third, it opened the gates (pretty unsuccessfully) for foreign capital to exploit "concessions." Fourth, and this was vitally important, the NEP introduced the strict enforcement of the principle of profitability in most of the nationalized industries, along with a strict financial orthodoxy, based on a gold standard, to produce a stable currency and to impose the discipline of the market on public and private enterprises alike.

These measures, introduced between 1921 and 1928, did indeed produce an economic revival. It went slowly at first, and then more quickly, until by 1926–27, the levels of *industrial* output of 1913 were reached and, in a few cases, exceeded. In the case of *disposable* foodstuffs (mainly grain), the growth was much slower. Output grew, but the peasantry, no longer exploited as in 1913, consumed much more of its output than before the revolution, so the cities continued to exist on short rations.

Achieved by capitalist or quasi-capitalist measures, this economic recovery had corresponding social consequences.

And now the cities we ruled over assumed a foreign aspect; we felt ourselves sinking into the mire—paralyzed, corrupted.... Money lubricated the entire machine just as under capitalism. A million and a half unemployed received relief—inadequate relief—in the big towns.... Classes were reborn under our very eyes; at the bottom of the scale the unemployed received 24 rubles a month, at the top, the engineer (i.e., the technical specialist) receiving 800, and between the two, the party functionary with 222, but obtaining a good many things free of charge. There was a growing chasm between the prosperity of the few and the misery of the many.[3]

As a result of the NEP, the working class did undergo a numerical revival from the low point of 1921, but it did not revive politically—or not on a scale sufficient to shake the power of the bureaucrat, the "Nepman," and the kulak. The whip of mass unemployment—much more severe proportionately in the Russia of the twenties than in the Britain of the thirties—was a major factor.

A distorted workers' state

The disintegration of the working class had reached an advanced stage when, toward the end of 1920, the so-called trade union debate broke out in the Russian Communist Party (RCP). The issue at stake was, on the surface, whether or not workers needed trade union organization to defend themselves against "their own" state. At a deeper level, the conflict was about much more fundamental questions.

Did the workers' state of 1918 still exist? Soviet democracy had, in practice, been destroyed in the civil war. The Communist Party had "emancipated" itself from the need for majority working-class support. The soviets had become rubber stamps for party decisions. Moreover, the process of "militarization" and "commandism" within the Communist Party had grown apace, and for the same reasons.

Against these developments, the Workers' Opposition in the party revolted. They called for "autonomy" for the unions, denouncing party control and appealing to a tradition of "workers' control of production" (a party demand in an earlier period). If adopted, these measures would have meant the end of the regime—for the bulk of what remained of the working class was by now decidedly indifferent, if not anti-Bolshevik. So, too, increasingly, was the mass of the peasantry, which was the great majority of the population. "Democracy" under these conditions could only mean counterrevolution—and a right-wing dictatorship.

The party had been driven to substitute itself for a vanishing working class and, within the party, the leading bodies had increasingly asserted their authority over a growing but ill-assorted membership. (The RCP had, in round figures, 115,000 members in early 1918; 313,000 by early 1919; 650,000 by the summer of 1921—a shrinking minority of them workers at the bench.)

The party had become the trustee for a working class that, temporarily it was hoped, had become incapable of managing its affairs. But the party itself was not immune from the immensely powerful social forces generated by industrial decline, low (and falling) productivity of labor, cultural backwardness, and barbarism. Indeed, for the party to act as "trustee," it was necessary to deprive the mass of its membership of any effective say in the direction of events—for they too had come to reflect the backwardness of Russia and the decline of the working class.

Trotsky's solution to this dilemma was, at first, to persist resolutely along the substitutionist course.

> It is necessary to create amongst us the awareness of the revolutionary historical birthright of the party. The party is obliged to maintain its dictatorship, regardless of temporary wavering in the spontaneous moods of the masses, regardless of the temporary vacillations even in the working class. This awareness is for us the indispensable unifying element.[4]

This attitude led him to argue that the unions ought to be absorbed into the state machine (as later happened under Stalin, in fact though not in form). There was no need or justification for even relative union autonomy; it merely served as a focus for discontent rather than a means of exerting party control.

Lenin's arguments against this position in December 1920 and January 1921 are important for the later development of Trotsky's analysis of the USSR. They were, belatedly, to become its foundation.

> Comrade Trotsky speaks of a "workers' state." May I say that this is an abstraction. It is natural for us to write about a workers' state in 1917; but it is now a patent error to say, "Since this is a workers' state without any bourgeoisie, against whom then is the working class to be protected and for what purpose?" The

whole point is that this is not quite a workers' state. That is where comrade Trotsky makes one of his main mistakes.[5]

A month later, he wrote:

> What I should have said is: "A workers' state is an abstraction. What we actually have is a workers' state with this peculiarity, firstly, that it is not the working class but the peasant population that predominates in the country, and, secondly, that it is a workers' state with bureaucratic distortions."[6]

A bureaucratically distorted workers' state in a predominantly peasant country. In the next stage, the NEP, Trotsky was to adopt this view and to deepen its content. It is not relevant here to describe in detail the fate of the Left Opposition (1923) and the United Opposition (1926–27), in both of which Trotsky played the leading role.[7] Suffice it to present some of their major views.

The Left and United Oppositions had pressed for the democratization of the party, the curbing of its apparatus, and a planned program of industrialization, financed by squeezing the kulak and the Nepman, to combat unemployment, revive the working class economically and politically, and so recreate the basis of soviet democracy. "The material position of the proletariat within the country must be strengthened both absolutely and relatively (growth in the number of employed workers, reduction in the number of unemployed, improvement in the material level of the working class)," declared the platform of the Opposition.

> The chronic lagging of industry, and also of transport, electrification, and building, behind the demands and needs of the population, of public economy, and the social system as a whole, holds as in a vice the entire economic turnover of the country.[8]

The inner contradiction of this position was that, on the one hand, to democratize the party would allow both peasant and proletarian discontent to find an organized expression; on the other hand, to increase state pressure on the new rich (especially the richer peasants) would reproduce some of the extreme tensions of war communism that had driven the party first to suppress all legal extra-party opposition and then to eliminate inner-party opposition and establish the dictatorship of the apparatus.

In the event, the matter was not put to the test. It was not simply the economy that was held "as in a vice." The Opposi-

tion was in like case. Its program challenged the material interests of all three classes that principally benefited from the NEP:
bureaucrats, Nepmen, and kulaks. The Opposition could not
prevail without that revival of working-class activity that was its
sole possible basis of support, but that, in turn, was made enormously difficult by the social and economic conditions of the
NEP, so long as the revolution remained isolated.

Stalin, chief and spokesman of the conservatized layer of
party and state officials who actually ruled the country, vigorously resisted *both* the demand for planned industrialization and
the demand for democratization (as did his allies on the far right
of the party, notably Bukharin and his supporters). This was the
social content of "Socialism in One Country," advocated by the
ruling group from 1925. It was a declaration for the status quo
against "upheavals" of any kind, against revolutionary expecta-
tions and an active policy abroad.

As late as April 1924, Stalin himself had summarized what
was then still the accepted view:

> For the overthrow of the bourgeoisie, the efforts of one country
> are enough—to this the victory of our own revolution testifies.
> For the final victory of socialism, for the organization of social-
> ist production, the efforts of one country, especially a peasant
> country like ours, are not enough—for this we must have the ef-
> forts of the proletarians of several advanced countries.[9]

It was a paraphrase of Lenin and no more than a statement of
the social and economic realities. But this orthodox view, once
the common property of Russian Marxists of all tendencies, had
the disadvantage of emphasizing the provisional character of the
regime and its dependence, for a socialist development, on revolutions in the West. This was now profoundly unacceptable to
the ruling layers. "Socialism in One Country" was their declaration of independence from the workers' movement.

After the final defeat of the Opposition and his exile from
Russia, Trotsky summed up the experience in an article written
in February 1929:

> After the conquest of power, an independent bureaucracy differ-
> entiated itself out from the working-class milieu and this differ-
> entiation...[which] was at first only functional, then later became
> social. Naturally, the processes within the bureaucracy developed
> in relation to profound processes underway in the country. On
> the basis of the New Economic Policy a broad layer of petty

bourgeoisie in the towns reappeared or newly came into being. The liberal professions revived. In the countryside, the rich peasant, the kulak, raised his head. Broad sections of officialdom, precisely because they had risen above the masses, drew close to the bourgeois strata, and established family ties with them. Increasingly, initiative or criticism on the part of the masses was viewed as interference.... The majority of this officialdom which has risen up over the masses is profoundly conservative.... This conservative layer, which constitutes Stalin's most powerful support in his struggle against the Opposition, is inclined to go much further to the right, in the direction of the new propertied elements, than Stalin himself or the main nucleus of his faction.[10]

The political conclusion drawn from this analysis was the danger of a "Soviet Thermidor." On the 9th of Thermidor (July 27, 1794), the Jacobin dictatorship was overthrown by the Convention and replaced by a rightist regime (the Directory, from 1795), which presided over a political and social reaction in France and paved the way for Bonaparte's dictatorship (from 1799). Thermidor marked the end of the great French Revolution.

A Russian Thermidor now threatened.

Elements of a Thermidorean process, to be sure one that is completely distinctive, may also be found in the land of the Soviets. They have become strikingly evident in recent years. Those who are in power today either played a secondary role in the decisive events of the first period of the revolution or were outright opponents of the revolution and only joined it after it was victorious. They now serve for the most part as camouflage for those layers and groupings which, while hostile to socialism, are too weak for a counterrevolutionary overturn and therefore seek a peaceful Thermidorean switching back onto the track leading to bourgeois society; they seek to "roll downhill with the brakes on," as one of their ideologists has put it.[11]

This, however, had not yet happened. Nor was it inevitable. The workers' state was still intact, although eroded. The outcome, Trotsky believed,

will be decided by the course of the struggle itself as the living forces of society fight it out. There will be ebbs and flows, whose duration will depend to a great extent on the situation in Europe and throughout the world.[12]

To summarize, there were three basic forces at work in the USSR: the forces of the right—the neocapitalist elements, kulaks, Nepmen, etc., for whom a big section of the apparatus "in power today" serve "for the most part as a camouflage"; the working class, represented politically by the now-suppressed Opposition; and the "centrist bureaucracy," Stalin's faction at the top of the machine, which is not itself Thermidorean, but which rests on the Thermidoreans and zigzags from left to right in its attempts to hold power. It had zigged rightwards from 1923 to 1928; then came the left zag.

"The course of 1928–31," Trotsky wrote in the latter year,

> if we again leave aside the inevitable waverings and backslid-ings—represents an attempt of the bureaucracy to adapt itself to the proletariat, but without abandoning the principled basis of its policy or, what is most important, its omnipotence. The zigzags of Stalinism show that the bureaucracy is not a class, not an independent historical factor, but an instrument, an executive organ of the classes. The left zigzag is proof that no matter how far the preceding right course has gone, it nevertheless developed on the basis of the dictatorship of the proletariat.[13]

Therefore, the working class still, in some sense, held power—or at least had the possibility of recovering power without a funda-mental upheaval.

> The recognition of the present Soviet state as a workers' state not only signifies that the bourgeoisie can conquer power only by means of an armed uprising but also that the proletariat of the USSR has not forfeited the possibility of subordinating the bureaucracy to it, of reviving the party again, and of regenerat-ing the regime of the dictatorship—without a new revolution, with the methods and on the road of *reform*.[14]

By the time this was written, it was, factually, without any foundation. The "three forces" analysis was hopelessly out-dated. In the 1920s it had been a realistic (if provisional) attempt at a Marxist analysis of the course of development in the USSR. The neocapitalist classes, and their influence on the right wing of the ruling party, were real enough in 1924–27. The vacillating role of Stalin's ruling faction was, *at that time,* as described. But there had been a *fundamental* change in 1928–29.

By 1928, the NEP was entering its final crisis. Nepmen and kulaks had a vital interest in maintaining it and expanding yet further the concession to petty capitalism, urban and rural. The leading members of the bureaucracy, and their vast clientele in the lower ranks of the bureaucratic hierarchy, had no such vital interest. They had a *vital* interest only in resisting democratization in party and state. They had allied themselves with the forces of petty capitalism (and the Bukharinist right wing of the party) against the Opposition, against the danger of working-class revival. But when, with the Opposition crushed, the bureaucracy was faced with a kulak offensive, the "grain strike" of 1927–28, it demonstrated that its essential basis was state property and the state machine, neither of which had any *organic* connection with the NEP. It vigorously defended its interests against its allies of yesterday.

The kulaks controlled practically all the marketable grain, the surplus over and above peasant consumption. (The most generally accepted estimate is that one-fifth of peasant farmers produced four-fifths of the grain sold on the market.) Their attempt to force up prices by withholding their stocks from the market forced the bureaucracy to resort to requisitioning. Once started on this course, which undermined the fundamental basis of the NEP, they were driven to take over the Opposition's industrialization program, which they did in a most extravagantly exaggerated form, and to undertake the forced collectivization of agriculture, the "liquidation of the kulaks as a class." The first "five-year plan" was launched.

Trotsky interpreted this as a (temporary) lurch to the left by the Stalinist bureaucracy, as an attempt *"to adapt itself to the proletariat."* He was profoundly mistaken. These were the very years in which the proletariat in the USSR was atomized and subjected, for the first time, to a truly totalitarian despotism. Real wages fell sharply. Although money wages rose considerably, prices rose much faster. In general, meaningful statistics ceased to be published after 1929 (itself a significant fact), but one calculation, published in the USSR long after the event (1966), showed real wages as 88.6 in 1932 (1928 = 100). "The correct real wage index, if only we knew it, would...be well below 88.6," comments Alex Nove, the source of this information.[15]

The five-year plan ushered in a period of directing the economy according to an overall plan, of rapid industrial growth, the forcible collectivization of agriculture, the destruction of the remaining political and trade union rights of the working class, the rapid growth of social inequality, extreme social tension, and forced labor on a mass scale. It also heralded Stalin's personal dictatorship and his regime of police terror and, a little later, the murder by shooting or by slow death in the labor camps of the vast majority of the original cadres of the Communist Party and, indeed, of the majority of Stalin's own faction of the 1920s, together with an uncertain but *very* large number of other citizens of the USSR and of many foreign communists. In short, it ushered in the high tide of Stalinism.

That Trotsky could initially see all this as a turn to the *left* (although he was not aware of the full facts until some years later) indicates that he had relapsed into substitutionism so far as looking at the USSR was concerned. It was a mistake that he was never able to correct fully. The argument that the bureaucracy was not an independent historical factor but an instrument, an executive organ of other classes, had been decisively refuted when that same bureaucracy simultaneously crushed the kulaks and atomized the workers.

In the early 1930s, it was still possible to argue about the facts. The newly born totalitarian regime imposed a blackout of real news and substituted its own monolithic propaganda machine. Trotsky was less deceived by this than almost anyone else. It was his theoretical concept and framework that led him to advocate the prospect of "reform" in the USSR at this time. A famous, and profoundly misleading, analogy of the USSR with a bureaucratized trade union originated in this period. It was, at least, logically coherent so long as the reform strategy persisted.

The workers' state, Thermidor, and Bonapartism

In October 1933, Trotsky abruptly changed his position, arguing now that the regime could not be reformed. It had to be overthrown. The path of "reform" was no longer feasible. Only revolution could destroy the bureaucracy:

> After the experiences of the last few years it would be childish to suppose that the Stalinist bureaucracy can be removed by means of a party or soviet congress. In reality, the last congress of the Bolshevik Party took place at the beginning of 1923, the Twelfth Party Congress. All subsequent congresses were bureaucratic parades. Today, even such congresses have been discarded. No normal "constitutional" ways remain to remove the ruling clique. The bureaucracy can be compelled to yield power into the hands of the proletarian vanguard only by force.[16]

The "bureaucratized trade union" had to be *smashed,* not reformed. It is true that this article contains the statement: "Today the rupture of the bureaucratic equilibrium in the USSR would almost surely serve in favor of the counterrevolutionary forces," but this equivocal position soon gave way to a revolutionary one.

With characteristic honesty, Trotsky went on to criticize and revise his own earlier "reformist" perspective, writing in 1935:

> The question of "Thermidor" is closely bound up with the history of the Left Opposition in the USSR.... In any case the positions on this issue in 1926 were approximately as follows: The group of "Democratic Centralism" (V.M. Smirnov, Sapronov, and others who were hounded to death in exile by Stalin) declared, "Thermidor is an accomplished fact." The adherents of the platform of the Left Opposition...categorically denied this assertion.... Who has proved to be correct?...
>
> The late V.M. Smirnov—one of the finest representatives of the Old Bolshevik school—held that the lag in industrialization, the growth of the kulak and of the Nepman (the new bourgeois), the liaison between the bureaucracy and the latter, and, finally, the degeneration of the party, had progressed so far as to render impossible a return to the socialist road without a new revolution. The proletariat had already lost power.... The fundamental conquests of the October Revolution had been liquidated.[17]

Trotsky's conclusion was:

> The Thermidor of the Great Russian Revolution is not before us but already far behind. The Thermidoreans can celebrate, approximately, the tenth anniversary of their victory. [That is, it had occurred around 1925.][18]

So, had the democratic centralists been right in 1926? Yes and no, Trotsky now said. Right about the Thermidor, wrong about its significance. "The present political regime in the USSR is a regime of 'Soviet' (or anti-Soviet) Bonapartism, closer in type to the empire rather than the Consulate." *But,* he continued, "in its social foundations and economic tendencies the USSR remains a workers' state."[19]

In terms of formal analogies, all this was plausible enough. As Trotsky pointed out, both the Thermidoreans and Bonaparte represented a *reaction* on the basis of the bourgeois revolution, not a return to the *ancien régime*. The fact remains that Trotsky, no less than Smirnov, had previously considered the "Soviet Thermidor" in a fundamentally different light. "The proletariat had already lost power" was the essence of Smirnov's thesis, and that Trotsky strongly denied at the time. For him, the party, however bureaucratized, still represented the working class. The working class, unlike the bourgeoisie, could only hold power through its organizations.

"Comrades," he had declared in 1924,

> none of us wishes to be or can be right against the party. In the
> last instance the party is always right, because it is the only his-
> toric instrument which the working class possesses for the solu-
> tion of its fundamental tasks.... One can be right only with the
> party and through the party because history has not created any
> other way for the realization of one's rightness.... The English
> have the saying "My country right or wrong." With much
> greater justification we can say: My party, right or wrong—
> wrong on certain specific issues or at certain moments.[20]

But the party—the Russian party—had become the instrument
first of Thermidor and now Bonapartism; that was Trotsky's position at the end of 1933. Since the party had ceased to be an instrument of the working class—its regime had to be overthrown
"by force"—and since, admittedly, the Russian workers had no
other instrument (and were in fact atomized and terrorized),
what could be left of the workers' state?

Nothing. That was the only possible conclusion if the terms
were to retain the meaning everyone had taken for granted until
then. A new revolution, "a victorious revolutionary uprising,"
was necessary for the working class to regain power in the
USSR. The working class had lost power and there was no
peaceful, constitutional way for it to capture power again.
Therefore, the workers' state no longer existed. A counterrevolution had taken place.

Trotsky firmly rejected these conclusions. He was therefore
forced to make a fundamental shift in his definition of a workers'
state.

> The *social* domination of a class (its dictatorship) may find ex-
> tremely diverse *political* forms. This is attested by the entire his-
> tory of the bourgeoisie from the Middle Ages to the present day.
> The experience of the Soviet Union is already adequate for the
> extension of this sociological law—*with all the necessary
> changes*—to the dictatorship of the proletariat as well.... Thus
> the present-day domination of Stalin in no way resembles the
> Soviet rule during the initial years of the revolution.... But this
> usurpation was made possible only because *the social content of
> the dictatorship of the bureaucracy is determined by those pro-
> ductive relations that were created by the proletarian revolution.*
> In this sense we may say with complete justification that the dic-
> tatorship of the proletariat found its distorted but indubitable
> expression in the dictatorship of the bureaucracy.[21]

Trotsky held this position, in essence, for the last half decade of his life. His book *The Revolution Betrayed* (1937) elaborates it with a wealth of detail and vivid illustration. The *fundamental* nature of the break with his own earlier views can hardly be overstated. It was one thing to argue (as Lenin had done) that a workers' state could be bureaucratically distorted, deformed, degenerated, or whatever. Now what was being asserted was that the dictatorship of the proletariat had no *necessary* connection with any actual workers' power at all. The dictatorship of the proletariat now came to mean, first and foremost, state ownership of industry and economic planning (although planning hardly existed under the NEP); it could remain extant even if the working class was atomized and subjected to a totalitarian despotism.

It must be said in Trotsky's favor that he was dealing with an entirely new phenomenon. He, like all the Oppositionists in the 1920s, had seen the danger of a collapse of the regime due to pressure from the growing forces of petty capitalism. That was what Thermidor had meant to all of them. The actual outcome was quite unexpected. State property not only survived, but expanded rapidly. The bureaucracy did *in fact* play an independent role, a fact Trotsky would never fully admit. The resulting regime was, at that time, unique.

No restoration of the bourgeoisie had taken place. Moreover, at a time of profound industrial depression in the West, rapid economic growth occurred in the USSR, a point Trotsky repeatedly emphasized in support of his contention that the regime was not capitalist.

Prognosis

In his 1938 *Transitional Program*, Trotsky wrote:

The Soviet Union emerged from the October Revolution as a workers' state. State ownership of the means of production, a necessary prerequisite to socialist development, opened up the possibility of rapid growth of the productive forces. But the apparatus of the workers' state underwent a complete degeneration at the same time: it was transformed from a weapon of the working class into a weapon of bureaucratic violence against the working class, and more and more a weapon for the sabotage of the country's economy. The bureaucratization of a backward and isolated workers' state and the transformation of the bureaucracy into an all-powerful privileged caste constitute the most convincing refutation—not only theoretically but this time practically—of the theory of socialism in one country.

The USSR thus embodied terrific contradictions. But it still remained a *degenerated workers' state*. Such is the social diagnosis. The political prognosis has an alternative character: either the bureaucracy, becoming ever more the organ of the world bourgeoisie within the workers' state, will overthrow the new forms of property and plunge the country back to capitalism; or the working class will crush the bureaucracy and open the way to socialism.[22]

Why should this be so? Trotsky was convinced that the bureaucracy was highly unstable and politically heterogeneous. All sorts of tendencies "from genuine Bolshevism to complete fascism" existed within it, he claimed in 1938. These tendencies were related to social forces, including

conscious capitalist tendencies...mainly the prosperous part of the collective farms...[which] provides itself with a wide base for petty-bourgeois tendencies of accumulating personal wealth at the expense of general poverty, and are consciously encouraged by the bureaucracy.[23]

Within the bureaucracy,

fascist, counterrevolutionary elements, growing uninterruptedly, express with ever-greater consistency, the interests of world imperialism. These candidates for the role of compradores consider, not without reason, that the new ruling layer can ensure their positions of privilege only through rejection of nationalization, collectivization, and monopoly of foreign trade in the name of the assimilation of "Western civilization," i.e., capitalism.... Atop this system of mounting antagonism, trespassing ever more on the social equilibrium, the Thermidorean oligarchy, today reduced mainly to Stalin's Bonapartist clique, hangs on by terroristic methods.... The extermination of the generation of Old Bolsheviks and of the revolutionary representatives of the middle and young generations has acted to disrupt the political equilibrium still more in favor of the right, bourgeois, wing of the bureaucracy, and of its allies throughout the land. From them, i.e., from the right, we can expect ever more determined attempts in the next period to revise the socialist character of the USSR and bring it closer to the pattern of "Western civilization" in its fascist form.[25]

It is interesting that Trotsky at this time should draw attention to the similarities between fascism and Stalinism, when the Popular Front was still at its height. "Stalinism and fascism, in spite of a deep difference in social foundation, are symmetrical phenomena. In many of their features they show a deadly similarity," he wrote in *The Revolution Betrayed*.[24] And again, "As in the fascist countries, from which Stalin's *political* apparatus does not differ save in more unbridled savagery."[26] What they have in common—the destruction of each and every independent workers' organization and the atomization of the working class—is very striking. But, on the assumption that there was a "deep difference in social foundation," had a *fascist* workers' state come into being?

Most important, however, is the question of the "restorationist" tendencies of the bureaucracy. There is no substantial argument in Trotsky's writings at this period, other than that on the right of inheritance:

> Privileges are only half their worth if they cannot be transmitted to one's children. But the right of testament is inseparable from the right of property. It is not enough to be the director of a trust; it is necessary to be a stockholder.[27]

Thus demonstrating the pressure on the bureaucracy to abandon its own control of the USSR in favor of becoming junior partners (compradores) of the various imperialist powers.

In Trotsky's view, the Soviet Union was still "a contradictory society halfway between capitalism and socialism.... In the last analysis, the question [forward to socialism or back to capitalism] will be decided by a struggle of living social forces, both in the national and the world arena."

That struggle had already developed in such a way as to strain Trotsky's analysis to the very limits in the last years before his death.

CHAPTER 3

STRATEGY AND TACTICS

T HE IDEAL of an international workers' movement is as old as, if not indeed older than, the *Communist Manifesto* itself, with its call, "Workers of the world unite." In 1864 (the First International), and again in 1889 (the Second International), attempts were made to give it an organizational expression.

The Second International collapsed in 1914, when its big parties in the warring states broke with internationalism and supported the governments of the German and Austrian Kaisers, the English king, and the French bourgeois Third Republic. It was not that they had been taken by surprise. Pre-war congresses had drawn attention repeatedly to the menace of imperialism and militarism, the growing threat of war, and the need for the workers' parties to stand firm against their own governments—indeed to "utilize the crisis engendered by war to hasten the downfall of capitalist class rule," as the Stuttgart Congress of the International had put it in 1907.

The subsequent capitulations of 1914, a stunning defeat for the socialist movement, led Lenin to declare, "The Second International is dead.... Long live the Third International!" Five years later, in 1919, the Third International was actually founded. Trotsky played a major role in its early years.

Later, with the rise of Stalinism in the USSR, the International was prostituted in the service of the Stalinist state in Russia. Trotsky, more than anyone else, fought against this degeneration. Many of his most valuable writings on the strategy and tactics of revolutionary workers' parties relate to the Third International, the Comintern, both in the period of its rise and in the period of its subsequent decline.

Sweeping aside the half-heartedness, lies, and corruption of the outlived official Socialist parties, we Communists, united in the Third International, consider ourselves the direct continuators of the heroic endeavors and martyrdom of a long line of revolutionary generations from Babeuf to Karl Liebknecht and Rosa Luxemburg.

If the First International presaged the future course of development and indicated its paths; if the Second International gathered and organized millions of workers; then the Third International is the International of open mass action, the International of revolutionary realization, the International of the deed.[1]

Trotsky was 40 years old and at the height of his power when he wrote the *Manifesto of the Communist International,* from which the above lines are taken. As the People's Commissar for War of the embattled Soviet Republic, he was second only to Lenin as the recognized spokesperson of world communism. His outlook at this time was not, of course, especially distinctive. It was the common outlook of the whole Bolshevik leadership, an outlook that did not exclude sharp differences of opinion on this or that issue, but that was essentially homogeneous.

However, Trotsky was to become in time the outstanding advocate of the ideas of the Communist International in its heroic period. Events unforeseen by any of the revolutionary leaders of 1919—or by their opponents—later reduced to a handful the bearers of this authentic communist tradition; Trotsky came to tower over them as a giant among Lilliputians. Time and again, in his writings in the late 1920s and the 1930s, Trotsky would refer to the decisions of the first four congresses of the Comintern as the model of revolutionary policy. What were these decisions and in what circumstances were they adopted?

It was March 4, 1919. Thirty-five delegates meeting in the Kremlin voted, with one abstention, to constitute the Third, or Communist, International. It was not a very weighty or representative gathering. Only the five delegates from the Russian Communist Party (Bukharin, Chicherin, Lenin, Trotsky, and Zinoviev) represented a party that was both a mass organization and a genuinely revolutionary one. Stange, of the Norwegian Labor Party (NAP), came from a mass party, but, as events were to prove, the NAP was far from revolutionary in practice. Eberlein, of the newly formed Communist Party of Germany (KPD), represented a real revolutionary organization, but one that was still only a few thousand strong. Most of the other delegates represented very little.

The majority took it for granted that an "International" without some real mass support in a number of countries was nonsense. Zinoviev, for the Russians, argued that mass support existed in fact. The weakness of many of the delegations was accidental. "We have a victorious proletarian revolution in a great country.... You have in Germany a party marching to power which in a few months will establish a proletarian government. And are we still to delay? No one will understand it."[2]

That the socialist revolution was an immediate prospect in Central Europe, above all in Germany, was not doubted by any of the delegates. In Eberlein's words: "Unless all the signs are deceptive, the German proletariat is facing the last decisive struggle. However difficult it may be, the prospects for communism are favorable."[3] Lenin, the most sober and calculating of revolutionaries, had said in his opening speech that "not only in Russia, but in the most developed capitalist countries of Europe, Germany for example, civil war is a fact...the world revolution is beginning and growing in intensity everywhere."[4]

This was not fantasy. In November 1918, the German Empire, until then the most powerful state in Europe, had collapsed. Six people's commissars—three social democrats and three independent social democrats—replaced the Kaiser's government. Workers' and soldiers' councils had covered the country and wielded effective power. True, the social-democratic leaders, who dominated them, bent all their efforts toward reconstituting the old capitalist state power under a new "republican" guise. That was all the more reason for creating a revolutionary International with a strong centralized leadership to guide and support the struggle for a Soviet Germany. And that struggle, in spite of the bloody suppression of the Spartakus rising in January 1919, appeared to be developing. "From January to May 1919, with offshoots reaching into the height of the summer, a bloody civil war was waged in Germany."[5] A month after the Moscow meeting, the Bavarian Soviet Republic was proclaimed.

The other great Central European power, the Austro-Hungarian Empire, had ceased to exist. The successor states were in varying degrees of revolutionary ferment. In German-speaking Austria, the only effective armed force was the social-democratic controlled Volkswehr (People's Army). In Hungary, the Soviet

Republic was proclaimed on March 21, 1919. All the new or re-constituted states—Czechoslovakia, Yugoslavia, even Poland—were highly unstable.

The role of the socialist leaderships was crucial. The majority now supported counterrevolution in the name of "democracy." Most of them claimed to be, indeed once had been, Marxists and internationalists. In 1914, they had capitulated to "their own" ruling classes. They were now, in this critical time, *the* major prop of capitalism, using socialist phrases and the credit estab-lished by their years of opposition to the old regimes before 1914 to prevent the establishment of workers' power. Their attempt to reconstitute the Second International at a meeting in Berne was advanced as a further, urgent reason for proclaiming the Third.

As early as 1914, Lenin had written: "The Second Interna-tional is dead, overcome by opportunism.... Long live the Third International."[6] Now, 18 months after the October Revolution, the slogan was to be turned into reality. What was its essential political basis? It rested on two fundamental planks: revolution-ary internationalism and the soviet system as the means whereby the workers would rule society. The main resolution of the 1919 Congress declared:

> Democracy assumed different forms and was applied in different degrees in the ancient republics of Greece, the medieval cities, and the advanced capitalist countries. It would be sheer non-sense to think that the most profound revolution in history, the first case in the world of power being transferred from the ex-ploiting minority to the exploited majority, could take place within the time-worn framework of the old, bourgeois parlia-mentary democracy, without drastic changes, without the cre-ation of new forms of democracy, new institutions that embody the new conditions for applying democracy.[7]

Soviets or parliament? After the October Revolution, the Russian Communist Party (RCP) had dispersed the newly elected Constituent Assembly, in which the Social-Revolutionary peasant party had a majority, in favor of soviet power. After the November revolution, the German Social Democratic Party (SPD) had dissolved the workers' and soldiers' councils, in which it had a majority, in favor of the National Assembly, in which it did not.

In both cases, the question of constitutional forms was really a question of class power. The effect of the RCP's action was to create a workers' state. The effect of the SPD's action was to create a bourgeois state, the Weimar Republic.

Marx had written, after the Paris Commune, that in the transition from capitalism to socialism, the form of the state "can only be the revolutionary dictatorship of the proletariat." The social democrats had come, in practice, to reject the essence of the Marxist theory of the state, that all states are class states, that there is no "neutral" state. They had come to reject their own previous position on the inevitability of revolution in favor of "peaceful" parliamentary roads to socialism.

Yet the Weimar Republic was every bit as much a product of the violent overthrow of the previous state as the Russian Soviet Republic had been. Mutinous soldiers and armed workers, not voters, overthrew the German Empire. The same was true of the successor states of Austria-Hungary. But the greater transformation, the destruction of capitalism, was to be achieved by the ordinary mechanisms of bourgeois democracy! In reality, this meant the abandonment of socialism as the aim.

The Third International, in its 1919 "platform," sharply restated the Marxist position. "The victory of the working class lies in shattering the organization of the enemy power and organizing workers' power; it consists in the destruction of the bourgeois state machine and the construction of the workers' state machine."[8] There could be no question of socialism through parliament. Lenin, in 1917, had quoted with approval Engels' statement that universal suffrage is "an index of the maturity of the working class. It cannot and never will be anything more in a modern state."[9] Just after the Moscow conference, he wrote, "No bourgeois republic, however democratic, ever was or could have been anything but a machine for the repression of the working people by capital, an instrument of the dictatorship of the bourgeoisie, the political rule of capital."[10]

The workers' republic, based on workers' councils, was truly democratic.

> The essence of soviet power lies in this, that the permanent and sole foundation of the entire state power, of the entire state apparatus, is the mass organization of those very classes which were oppressed by the capitalists, that is the workers and semi-workers (peasants who do not exploit labor).[11]

This was something of an idealization of Russia, even in 1919, but the "deviations" were accounted for by the backwardness of the country, the still raging civil war, and foreign intervention.

Trotsky then, and until his dying day, supported all these ideas without the slightest reservation. He was at one with Lenin on the questions of bourgeois democracy and reformism in 1919, and he never changed his mind.

The delegates' meeting in Moscow had constituted the new International on the basis of uncompromising internationalism, a decisive and final split with the traitors of 1914, workers' power, workers' councils, the defense of the Soviet Republic, and the perspective of revolution in the near future in Central and Western Europe. The problem now was to create the mass parties that could make all of this a reality.

Centrism and ultraleftism

> Parties and groups only recently affiliated to the Second International are more and more frequently applying for membership in the Third International, though they have not become really communist.... The Communist International is, to a certain extent, becoming fashionable.... In certain circumstances, the Communist International may be faced with the danger of dilution by the influx of wavering and irresolute groups that have not yet broken with their Second International ideology.[12]

So wrote Lenin in July 1920. The assumption of the 1919 Congress of the Comintern, that a truly *mass* revolutionary movement existed in Europe, was shown to be correct in the coming year.

In September 1919, the Bologna Congress of the Italian Socialist Party voted by a large majority, and on the recommendation of its executive, to affiliate to the Communist International. The Norwegian Labor Party, the NAP, confirmed its affiliation, and the Bulgarian, Yugoslav (ex-Serbian), and Romanian parties joined, as well. The first three of these were important organizations. The NAP, which, like its British counterpart, was based on trade union affiliation, completely dominated the Norwegian left, and the Bulgarian Communist Party had the support from the beginning of virtually the whole Bulgarian working class. The Yugoslavian Communist Party returned 54 deputies in the first (and only) free elections held in the new state.

In France, the Socialist Party, SFIO, which had more than doubled its membership—from 90,000 to 200,000—between

1918 and 1920, had swung far to the left and was flirting with Moscow. So were the leaders of the German Independent Social Democrats, the USPD, an organization that was rapidly gaining ground at the expense of the SPD. The Swedish left Social Democrats, the Czechoslovak left wing, and smaller parties in other countries (including the British Independent Labor Party) had essentially the same line. Pressure from their ranks was forcing them to pay lip service to the October Revolution and to negotiate for admission to the Communist International.

"The desire of certain leading 'center' groups to join the Third International," wrote Lenin, "provides indirect confirmation that it has won the sympathy of the vast majority of class-conscious workers throughout the world, and is becoming a more powerful force with each day."[13] But these parties were not revolutionary communist organizations. Their traditions were those of pre-war social democracy—revolutionary in words, passive in practice. And they were led by men who would try any twist or turn in order to keep control and prevent the adoption of genuine revolutionary strategy and tactics.

Without the bulk of the members of these parties, the new International could not hope to exert a decisive influence in Europe in the short term. Without a break with the centrist leaders, it could not hope to exert a *revolutionary* influence. Nor was the situation much different with the mass parties already inside the International. The Italian Socialist Party, for example, had centrists and even some thoroughgoing reformists in its leadership.

The struggle against centrism was complicated by another factor. Strong ultraleftist currents existed inside many of the communist organizations. And outside them were some important syndicalist trade union organizations that had moved close to the Third International but still rejected the need for a communist party. To gain and integrate these big forces was a difficult and complex operation. It required a struggle on several different fronts.

The decisions of the Second Congress were of fundamental importance. In a sense, this was the real founding congress. It took place during the height of the war with Poland, when the Red Army was nearing Warsaw. In Germany, an attempt to establish a military dictatorship, the Kapp putsch, had just been defeated by mass working-class action. In Italy, the factory occupations were about to begin. The mood of revolutionary optimism was stronger than ever. Zinoviev, president of the International, declared: "I am deeply convinced that the Second World Congress of the CI is the precursor of another world congress, the world congress of Soviet Republics."[14]

All that was needed were real mass communist parties to lead the movement to victory. One of Trotsky's major interventions in the congress was concerned with the *nature* of such parties:

> Comrades, it may seem fairly strange that three-quarters of a century after the appearance of the *Communist Manifesto,* discussion should arise at an International Communist Congress over whether a party is necessary or not.... It is self-evident that if we were dealing here with Messrs. Scheidemann, Kautsky, or their English co-thinkers, it would not, of course, be necessary to convince these gentlemen that a party is indispensable for the working class. They have created a party for the working class and handed it over into the service of bourgeois and capitalist society.... Just because I know that the party is indispensable, and am well aware of the value of the party, and just because I see Scheidemann on the one side and, on the other, American or Spanish or French syndicalists who not only wish to fight against the bourgeoisie but who, unlike Scheidemann, really want to tear its head off—for this reason I say that I prefer to discuss with these Spanish, American, and French comrades in order to prove to them that the party is indispensable for the fulfillment of the mission which is placed upon them—the destruction of the bourgeoisie.... Comrades, the French syndicalists are conducting revolutionary work within the unions. When I discuss today, for example, with Comrade Rosmer, we have a common ground. The French syndicalists, in defiance of the traditions of democracy and its deceptions, have said: "We do not want any parties, we stand for proletarian unions and for the revolutionary minority within them which applies direct action...." What does this minority mean to our friends? It is the chosen section of the French working class, a section with a clear program and organization of its own, an organization where they discuss all questions, and not alone discuss but also decide, and where they are bound by a certain discipline.[15]

This, Trotsky argued, was the root of the matter. The revolutionary syndicalists were much closer to constituting a *communist* party than the centrists who took the idea of a party for granted. The syndicalist position was not entirely adequate—something had to be added: "an inventory...which concentrates the entire experience accumulated by the working class. That is how we conceive our party. That is how we conceive our International."[16] It could not be primarily a propaganda organization.

Speaking at the Comintern Executive (ECCI) against the Dutch ultraleft Gorter, who had accused the Comintern of "chasing after the masses," Trotsky declared:

> What does Comrade Gorter propose? What does he want? Propaganda! This is the gist of his entire method. Revolution, says Comrade Gorter, is contingent neither upon privations nor economic conditions but on mass consciousness; while mass consciousness is, in turn, shaped by propaganda. Propaganda is here taken in a purely idealistic manner, very much akin to the concept of the 18th-century school of enlightenment and rationalism.... What you now want to do amounts essentially to replacing the dynamic development of the International by methods of individual recruitment of workers through propaganda. You want some sort of simon-pure International of the elect and select.[17]

The passive, propagandist type of ultraleftism was not the only variety represented in the early Comintern. In 1921, a putschist tendency developed in the leadership of the German party. In March of that year, in the absence of a revolutionary situation nationally (locally, in parts of central Germany, something like a revolutionary situation existed), the party leadership tried to force the pace, to *substitute* the party militants for a true mass movement. The result of this "March Action" was a serious defeat—party membership dropped from about 350,000 to around 150,000.

A "theory of the offensive" was used to justify the KPD tactics. In a speech in the summer of 1921, Trotsky noted:

> There was advanced the so-called theory of the offensive. What is the gist of this theory? Its gist is that we have entered the epoch of the decomposition of capitalist society, in other words, the epoch when the bourgeoisie must be overthrown. How? By the offensive of the working class. In this purely abstract form it is unquestionably correct. But certain individuals have sought to convert this theoretical capital into corresponding currency of smaller denominations and they have declared that this offensive consists of a successive number of smaller offensives.

He went on:

> Comrades, the analogy between the political struggle of the working class and military operations has been much abused. But up to a certain point one can speak here of similarities.... In military respects we, too, had our March days, speaking in Ger-

man and our September days, speaking in Italian [the reference
is to the failure of the Italian Socialist Party to exploit the revolutionary crisis of September 1920]. What happens after a partial defeat? There sets in a certain dislocation of the military
apparatus, there arises a certain need for a breathing spell, a
need for reorientation and a more precise estimation of the reciprocal forces.... Sometimes all this becomes possible only under
the conditions of strategic retreat....

But to understand this properly, to discern in a move, backwards, in a retreat, a component part of a unified strategic
plan—for that a certain experience is necessary. But if one reasons purely abstractly and insists on always moving
forward...on the assumption that everything can be superseded
by an added extension of revolutionary will, what results does
one then get? Let us take for example the September events in
Italy or the March events in Germany. We are told that the situation in these countries can be remedied only by a new offensive.... Under these conditions we would suffer an even greater
and much more dangerous defeat. No comrades, after such a defeat we must retreat.[18]

The united front

In fact, by the summer of 1921, the Comintern leadership
had decided that a strategic retreat in a more general sense was
necessary. Trotsky wrote in *Pravda* in June:

In the most critical year for the bourgeoisie, the year 1919, the
proletariat of Europe could undoubtedly have conquered state
power with minimum sacrifices, had there been at its head a
genuine revolutionary organization, setting forth clear aims and
capably pursuing them, i.e., a strong Communist Party. But
there was none.... During the last three years the workers have
fought a great deal and suffered many sacrifices. But they have
not won power. As a result the working masses have become
more cautious than they were in 1919–20.[19]

The same thought was expressed in the *Theses on the World Situation,* of which Trotsky was the author, adopted at the Third
Comintern Congress in July 1921:

During the year that has passed between the second and third
congresses of the Communist International, a series of working-
class risings and struggles have ended in partial defeat (the advance of the Red Army on Warsaw in August 1920, the
movement of the Italian proletariat in September 1920, the rising of the German workers in March 1921). The first period of
the postwar revolutionary movement, distinguished by the spontaneous character of its assaults, by the marked imprecision of

its aims and methods, and by the extreme panic which it aroused amongst the ruling classes, seems in essentials to be over. The self-confidence of the bourgeoisie as a class, and the outward stability of their state organs, have undeniably been strengthened.... The leaders of the bourgeoisie are even boasting of the power of their state machines and have gone over to an offensive against the workers in all countries, both on the economic and on the political front.[20]

Soon after the congress, the ECCI began to press the parties to shift the emphasis of their work toward the united front. The essence of this approach was very clearly summarized by Trotsky early in 1922:

> The task of the Communist Party is to lead the proletarian revolution...to achieve it, the Communist Party must base itself on the overwhelming majority of the working class.... The party can achieve this only by remaining an absolutely independent organization with a clear program and strict internal discipline. That is why the party was bound to break ideologically with the reformists and centrists.... After assuring itself of the complete independence and ideological homogeneity of its ranks, the Communist Party fights for influence over the majority of the working class.... But it is perfectly self-evident that the class life of the proletariat is not suspended during this period preparatory to the revolution. Clashes with industrialists, with the bourgeoisie, with the state power, on the initiative of one side or the other, run their due course.
>
> In these clashes—insofar as they involve the vital interests of the entire working class, or its majority, or this or that section— the working masses sense the need of unity in action, of unity in resisting the onslaught of capitalism or unity in taking the offensive against it. Any party which mechanically counterposes itself to this need of the working class for unity in action will unfailingly be condemned in the minds of the workers.
>
> Consequently the question of the united front is not at all, either in point of origin or substance, a question of the reciprocal relations between the Communist parliamentary fraction and that of the Socialists, or between the Central Committees of the two parties.... The problem of the united front—*despite the fact that a split is inevitable in this epoch between the various political organizations basing themselves on the working class*— grows out of the urgent need to secure for the working class the possibility of a united front in the struggle against capitalism.
>
> For those who do not understand this task, the party is only a propaganda society and not an organization for mass action....
>
> Unity of front consequently presupposes our readiness, within certain limits and on specific issues, to correlate in practice our

actions with those of reformist organizations, to the extent to which the latter still express today the will of important sections of the embattled proletariat.

But, after all, didn't we split with them? Yes, because we disagree with them on fundamental questions of the working-class movement.

And yet we seek agreement with them? Yes, in all those cases where the masses that follow them are ready to engage in joint struggle together with the masses that follow us and when they, the reformists, are to a lesser or greater degree compelled to become an instrument of this struggle....

A policy aimed to secure the united front does not of course contain automatic guarantees that unity in action will actually be attained in all instances. On the contrary, in many cases and perhaps even the majority of cases, organizational agreements will be only half-attained or perhaps not at all. But it is necessary that the struggling masses should always be given the opportunity of convincing themselves that the non-achievement of unity in action was not due to our formalistic irreconcilability but to the lack of real will to struggle on the part of the reformists.[21]

The Fourth Comintern Congress (1922), which was largely concerned with the united front, was the last Lenin attended and the last that Trotsky regarded as essentially correct in its decisions. A decade later, in a statement of fundamental principles, he summarized his attitude to the experience of the early Comintern:

The International Left Opposition stands on the ground of the first four congresses of the Comintern. This does not mean that it bows before every letter of its decisions, many of which had a purely conjunctural character and have been contradicted by subsequent events. But all the essential principles (in relation to imperialism and the bourgeois state, to democracy and reformism, problems of insurrection, the dictatorship of the proletariat, on relations with the peasantry and the oppressed nations, work in the trade unions, parliamentarianism, the policy of the united front) remain, even today, the highest expression of proletarian strategy in the epoch of the general crisis of capitalism. The Left Opposition rejects the revisionist decisions of the Fifth and Sixth World Congresses [1924 and 1928].[22]

The year 1923 saw the emergence of the triumvirate of Stalin, Zinoviev, and Kamenev on the one hand, and of the Left Opposition on the other. In Europe, it saw two crippling defeats for the Comintern. In June, the Bulgarian Communist Party, a mass party enjoying the support of virtually the entire working class, adopted a position of "neutrality," or rather complete passivity, in the face of the right-wing coup against the Peasant Party government. Then, after the bourgeois-democratic regime had been destroyed, a military dictatorship established, and the mass of the population cowed, it launched (on September 22) a sudden insurrection, without any serious political preparation. It was smashed, and a ferocious White Terror ensued. In Germany, a profound economic, social, and political crisis occurred, precipitated by the French occupation of the Ruhr and astronomic inflation that, literally, made money worthless. "In the autumn of 1923 the German situation was more desperate than at any time since 1919, the misery greater, the prospect apparently more hopeless."[23] A rising was planned for October, after the Communist Party had formed a coalition government with Social Democrats in Saxony, but canceled at the last minute. (In Hamburg, the cancellation was not received in time; an isolated insurrection occurred and was crushed after two days.)

Trotsky believed that a historic opportunity had been missed. From this time on, the policy of the Comintern became increasingly determined, first, by the requirements of Stalin's faction in the inner-party struggle in the USSR and, later, by the foreign policy requirements of Stalin's government. After a brief "left" oscillation in 1924, the Comintern was pushed in a rightist direction until 1928, then into ultraleftism (1928–34), and finally far to the right in the Popular Front period (1935–39). Each of these phases was analyzed and criticized by Trotsky. It is convenient to present his critique using three examples.

The Anglo-Soviet Trade Union Committee

Aside from the Chinese Revolution of 1925–27, which has already been discussed, the policy (under Comintern direction) of the Communist Party of Great Britain (CPGB) up to and during the general strike of 1926 was the most important indictment Trotsky made of the Comintern in its first rightist phase.

The general strike of May 1926 was a decisive turning point in British history—and it was an unmitigated defeat for the working class. It brought to an end a long, though not uninterrupted, period of working-class militancy, led to the prolonged dominance of the unions by their openly class-collaborationist right wing, and led to the massive reinforcement of Labor Party reformism at the expense of the Communist Party.

In 1924–25, the tide in the trade union movement was flowing leftward. The CP-inspired Minority Movement, founded in 1924 around the slogans "Stop the Retreat" and "Back to the Unions," was gaining considerable influence. At the same time, the official movement was coming under the influence of a group of leftist officials. And, from the spring of 1925, the Trades Union Congress (TUC) collaborated with the Soviet Trade Union Federation through the "Anglo-Soviet Joint Trade Union Advisory Committee," a fact that gave the General Councilors a certain "revolutionary" aura and a cover against critics on the left.

The essence of Trotsky's criticism was that the CPGB, on Moscow's urging, was building up trust in these left bureaucrats (the central CP slogan was "All Power to the General Council"!), who were certain to betray the movement at a critical stage (as they did, of course), rather than struggling to build independently among the rank and file, using whatever cover the "lefts" afforded, but in no way relying on them or encouraging militants to rely on them—on the contrary, counting on their treachery, warning against it, and preparing for it. Trotsky wrote later:

> Zinoviev gave us to understand that he counted upon the revolution finding an entrance, not through the narrow gateway of the British Communist Party, but through the broad portals of the trade unions. The struggle to win the masses organized in the trade unions through the Communist Party was replaced by the hope for the swiftest possible utilization of the ready-made apparatus of the trade unions for the purposes of the revolution. Out of this false position sprang the later policy of the Anglo-Russian Committee which dealt a blow to the Soviet Union, as well as to the British working class; a blow surpassed only by the defeat in China.... As the upshot of the greatest revolutionary movement in Britain since the days of Chartism, the British Communist Party has hardly grown while the General Council sits in the saddle even more firmly than before the general strike. Such are the results of this unique "strategical maneuver."[24]

He did not argue that the policy of independent communist work would necessarily have won the strike.

> No revolutionist who weighs his words would contend that a victory *would have been guaranteed* by proceeding along this line. But a victory was *possible* only along this road. A defeat on this road was a defeat on a road that could lead *later* to victory.[25]

However, this road

> appeared too long and uncertain to the bureaucrats of the Communist International. They considered that by means of personal influence on Purcell, Hicks, Cook, and the others...they would gradually and imperceptibly draw...[them] into the Communist International. To guarantee such a success...the dear friends (Purcell, Hicks, and Cook) were not to be vexed or exasperated...a radical measure had to be resorted to...actually subordinating the Communist Party to the Minority Movement.... The masses knew as the leaders of this movement only Purcell, Hicks, and Cook, whom, moreover, Moscow vouched for. These "left" friends, in a serious test, shamefully betrayed the proletariat. The revolutionary workers were thrown into confusion, sank into apathy and naturally extended their disappointment to the Communist Party itself which had only been the passive part of this whole mechanism of betrayal and perfidy. The Minority Movement was reduced to zero; the Communist Party returned to the existence of a negligible sect.[26]

Reliance on "left" officials is still one of the features distinguishing left reformists from revolutionaries. Trotsky's critique is highly relevant today, not least in Britain.

Germany in the Third Period

The Sixth World Congress of the Comintern (summer 1928) began a process of violent reaction against the rightist line of 1924–28. An ultraleftist line of a peculiarly bureaucratic character was imposed on Communist Parties everywhere, regardless of local circumstances. A reflection of the launching of the first five-year plan and the forced collectivization in the USSR, this new line proclaimed a "Third Period," a period of "ascending revolutionary struggles." In practice, this meant that at a time when fascism was a real and growing danger, especially in Germany, the social democrats were regarded as the main enemy. "In this situation of growing imperialist contradictions and sharpening of the class struggle," declared the Tenth Plenum of the ECCI in 1929,

> fascism becomes more and more the dominant method of bourgeois rule. In countries where there are strong social-democratic parties, fascism assumes the particular form of social fascism, which to an ever-increasing extent serves the bourgeoisie as an instrument for paralyzing the activity of the masses in the struggle against the regime of fascist dictatorship.[27]

It followed that the united front policy, as understood until then, had to be jettisoned. There could be no question of trying to force the mass social-democratic parties and the unions they controlled into a united front against the fascists. They were themselves social fascists. Indeed, added the Eleventh Plenum of the ECCI (1931), social democracy "is the most active factor and pacemaker in the development of the capitalist state towards fascism."[28]

This grotesquely false estimate of the nature of both fascism and social democracy led to the assumption that "strong social-democratic parties" and "a regime of fascist dictatorship" could coexist and indeed *did* coexist in Germany well before Hitler came to power. "In Germany, the Von Papen–Schleicher government, with the help of the Reichswehr, the Stahlhelm, and the Nazis, has established a form of fascist dictatorship," proclaimed the Twelfth Plenum of the ECCI in 1932.[29]

Trotsky wrote and argued against this criminal stupidity with increasing urgency and desperation from 1929 until the catastrophe of 1933. The brilliance and cogency of his works on the German crisis have rarely been equaled, and never excelled, by any Marxist.

The central theme of all these writings was the necessity "For a Workers' United Front Against Fascism," to cite the title of one of the most famous of them. But there was much more than this. Trotsky forced himself to follow in detail the tortuous arguments that Stalin's German acolytes advanced in defense of the indefensible. Thus, his writings of this period take up and refute an extraordinary range of pseudo-Marxist argument and, at the same time, expound with exceptional clarity the "highest expression of proletarian strategy." Only a very small part of them can be referred to here.

> The official press of the Comintern is now depicting the results of the German elections [of September 1930] as a prodigious victory of Communism, which places the slogan of a Soviet Germany on the order of the day. The bureaucratic optimists do not want to reflect on the meaning of the relationship of forces which is disclosed by the election statistics. They examine the figure of Communist votes gained independently of the revolutionary tasks created by the situation and the obstacles it sets up.
>
> The Communist Party received around 4,600,000 votes as against 3,300,000 in 1928. From the standpoint of "normal" parliamentary machines, the gain of 1,300,000 votes is considerable,

even if we take into consideration the rise in the total number of voters. But the gain of the party pales completely beside the leap of fascism from 800,000 to 6,400,000 votes. Of no less significance is the fact that the Social Democracy, in spite of substantial losses, retained its basic cadres and still received a considerably greater number of workers' votes than the Communist Party.

Meanwhile, if we should ask ourselves what combination of international and domestic circumstances could be capable of turning the working class towards Communism with greater velocity, we could not find an example of more favorable circumstances for such a turn than the situation in present day Germany...the economic crisis, the disintegration of the rulers, the crisis of parliamentarianism, the terrific self-exposure of the Social Democracy in power. From the viewpoint of these concrete historical circumstances, the specific gravity of the German Communist Party in the social life of the country, in spite of the gain of 1,300,000 votes, remains proportionately small....

In the meantime, the first characteristic of a real revolutionary party is to be able to look reality in the face....

For the social crisis to bring about the proletarian revolution, it is necessary that, besides other conditions, a decisive shift of the petty-bourgeois classes occurs in the direction of the proletariat. This will give the proletariat a chance to put itself at the head of the nation as its leader.

The last election revealed—and this is its principal symptomatic significance—a shift in the opposite direction. Under the impact of the crisis, the petty bourgeoisie swung, not in the direction of the proletarian revolution, but in the direction of the most extreme imperialist reaction, pulling behind it considerable sections of the proletariat.

The gigantic growth of National Socialism is an expression of two factors: a deep social crisis throwing the petty-bourgeois masses off balance, and the lack of a revolutionary party that would today be regarded by the popular masses as the acknowledged revolutionary leader. If the Communist Party is *the party of revolutionary hope*, then fascism, as a mass movement, is *the party of counterrevolutionary despair*. When revolutionary hope embraces the whole proletarian mass, it inevitably pulls behind it on the road of revolution considerable and growing sections of the petty bourgeoisie. Precisely in this sphere, the election revealed the opposite picture: counterrevolutionary despair embraced the petty-bourgeois mass with such force that it drew behind it many sections of the proletariat....

Fascism in Germany has become a real danger, as an acute expression of the helpless position of the bourgeois regime, the conservative role of the Social Democracy in the regime, and the accumulated powerlessness of the Communist Party to abolish it. Whoever denies this is either blind or a braggart.[30]

To mend the situation, Trotsky argued, it was necessary first of all to shake the Communist Party out of its sterile ultraradicalism. The policy of "bureaucratic ultimatism" ("an attempt to rape the working class having failed to convince it") must be replaced by one of active maneuver grounded in the united front policy.

> It is a difficult task to arouse all at once the majority of the German working class for an offensive. As a consequence of the defeats of 1919, 1921, and 1923, and of the adventures of the "Third Period," the German workers, who on top of that are bound by powerful conservative organizations, have developed strong centers of inhibition. But, on the other hand, the organizational solidarity of the German workers, which has almost altogether prevented until now the penetration of fascism into their ranks, opens the very greatest possibilities of *defensive* struggles. One must bear in mind that the policy of the united front is in general much more effective for the defensive than for the offensive. The more conservative or backward strata are more easily drawn into a struggle to fight for what they have than for new conquests.[31]

All manner of sophistries were employed by the Stalinists to obscure the issue and to represent what had once been Comintern policy as "counterrevolutionary Trotskyism." The united front, it was argued, could come "only from below"; that is, agreements with the social democrats were excluded, but individual social democrats could take part in a "Red United Front"—provided they accepted the leadership of the Communist Party!

And increasingly the fatal illusion—summed up as "After Hitler, our turn"—was encouraged, a perspective of passivity and impotence masked by radical rhetoric, as Trotsky repeatedly stressed. Again and again, he returned to the central issue of the united front, exposing sophistries, brushing aside slanders, and thrusting the point home, as in this brilliant example:

> A cattle dealer once drove some bulls to the slaughterhouse. And the butcher came nigh with his sharp knife.
> "Let us close ranks and jack up this executioner on our horns," suggested one of the bulls.
> "If you please, in what way is the butcher any worse than the dealer who drove us hither with his cudgel?" replied the bulls, who had received their political education in Manuilsky's institute.
> "But we shall be able to attend to the dealer as well afterwards!"

"Nothing doing," replied the bulls, firm in their principles, to
the counselor. "You are trying to shield our enemies from the
left; you are a social-butcher yourself."
   And they refused to close ranks.

—from *Aesop's Fables*[32]

The Communist Party held fast to its fatal course. Hitler came
to power. The workers' movement was smashed.

The Popular Front and the Spanish Revolution

Hitler's victory drove the rulers of the USSR to seek "insur-
ance" by means of a military alliance with the then still dominant Western powers of France and Britain. As an auxiliary to
Stalin's diplomacy—for that is what it had now become—the
Comintern was jerked hard to the right. The Seventh (and last)
Congress was convened in 1935 as a public demonstration that
revolution was definitely off the agenda. It called for the "United
People's Front in the struggle for peace and against the instiga-
tions of war. All those interested in the preservation of peace
should be drawn into this united front."[33]

Those interested in the preservation of peace included the victors of 1918, the French and British ruling classes, the objects of
the new line. "Today the situation is not what it was in 1914,"
declared the ECCI in May 1936.

> Now it is not only the working class, the peasantry, and all work-
> ing people who are resolved to maintain peace, but also the op-
> pressed countries and the weak nations whose independence is
> threatened by war.... In the present phase a number of capitalist
> states are also concerned to maintain peace. Hence the possibility
> of creating a broad front of the working class, of all working peo-
> ple, and of entire nations against the danger of imperialist war.[34]

Such a "front" was, of course, necessarily a defense of the imperialist status quo. A reformist rhetoric had to be liberally employed to conceal this fact and was highly successful—for a time.

In the first phase, popular enthusiasm for unity brought
enormous gains to the Communist Parties. The French party
grew from 30,000 in 1934 to 150,000 by the end of 1936, plus
100,000 in the Communist Youth; the Spanish party grew from
under a thousand at the close of the "Third Period" (1934) to
35,000 in February 1936, to 117,000 in July 1937. The recruits
were armored against criticism from the left by the belief that the
Trotskyists were literally fascist agents.

In May 1935, the Franco-Soviet pact was signed. By July, the Communist Party and the SFIO had come to an agreement with the Radical Party, the backbone of French bourgeois democracy, and in April 1936, the "Front Populaire" of these three parties won a general election on a platform of "collective security" and reform. The CP gained 72 seats campaigning on the slogan "For the strong, free, and happy France," and became an essential part of the parliamentary majority of Leon Blum, the SFIO leader and Front Populaire prime minister. Maurice Thorez, the secretary-general of the French Communist Party (PCF) was able to claim: "We boldly deprived our enemies of the things they had stolen from us and trampled underfoot. We took back the Marseillaise and the Tricolor."[35]

When the electoral victory of the left was followed by a massive wave of strikes and sit-ins—6 million workers were involved in June 1936—the erstwhile champions of "ascending revolutionary struggles" exerted themselves to contain the movement within narrow limits and to end it on the basis of the "Matignon Agreement" concessions (notably the 40-hour week and holidays with pay). By the end of the year, the Communist Party, now to the right of its social-democratic allies, was calling for the extension of the "Popular Front" into a "French Front" by the incorporation of some right-wing conservatives who were, on nationalist grounds, strongly anti-German.

The French party pioneered these policies because the French alliance was central to Stalin's foreign policy, but they were rapidly adopted by the whole Comintern. When the Spanish Revolution erupted in July 1936, in response to Franco's attempted seizure of power, the Spanish CP, part of the Spanish Popular Front that had won the February elections and taken power, did its utmost to keep the movement within the framework of "democracy." With the aid of Russian diplomacy, and of course the social democrats, it was successful. "It is absolutely false," declared Jesus Hernandez, editor of the party's daily paper,

> that the present workers' movement has for its object the establishment of the proletarian dictatorship after the war has terminated.... We communists are the first to repudiate this supposition. We are motivated exclusively by a desire to defend the democratic republic.[36]

In pursuit of this line, the Spanish Communist Party and its

bourgeois allies pushed the policies of the republican government more and more to the right. In the course of the long,
drawn-out civil war, it drove out of the government first the
POUM—a party to the left of the CP that Trotsky had bitterly
criticized for entering the Popular Front in the first place, dis-
arming itself politically and providing a "left" cover for the
Communist Party—and then the left-wing leaders of the Spanish
Socialist Party.

"The defense of republican order while defending property"[37] led to a reign of terror in Republican Spain against the
left. And this paved the way, Trotsky demonstrated, for Franco's
victory. "The Spanish proletariat displayed first-rate military
qualities," he wrote in December 1937.

> In its specific gravity in the country's economic life, in its politi-
> cal and cultural level, the Spanish proletariat stood on the first
> day of the revolution not below but above the Russian prole-
> tariat at the beginning of 1917. On the road to its victory, its
> own organizations stood as the chief obstacles. The command-
> ing clique of Stalinists, in accordance with their counterrevolu-
> tionary function, consisted of hirelings, careerists, declassed
> elements, and in general, all types of social refuse. The represen-
> tatives of other labor organizations—incurable reformists, anar-
> chist phrasemongers, helpless centrists of the POUM, grumbled,
> groaned, wavered, maneuvered, but in the end adapted them-
> selves to the Stalinists. As a result of their joint activity, the camp
> of social revolution—workers and peasants—proved to be sub-
> ordinated to the bourgeoisie, or more correctly, to its shadow. It
> was bled white and its character was destroyed.
>
> There was no lack of heroism on the part of the masses or
> courage on the part of individual revolutionists. But the masses
> were left to their own resources while the revolutionists re-
> mained disunited, without a program, without a plan of action.
> The "republican" military commanders were more concerned
> with crushing the social revolution than with scoring military
> victories. The soldiers lost confidence in their commanders, the
> masses in the government; the peasants stepped aside; the work-
> ers became exhausted; defeat followed defeat; demoralization
> grew apace. All this was not difficult to foresee from the begin-
> ning of the civil war. By setting itself the task of rescuing the cap-
> italist regime, the Popular Front doomed itself to military defeat.
> By turning Bolshevism on its head, Stalin succeeded completely
> in fulfilling the role of gravedigger of the revolution.[38]

Scarcely anyone today (apart from a handful of insignificant
ex-Maoist sectlets) defends the Stalinist line of the "Third Pe-

riod." The Popular Front is a different matter entirely. Allowing for all the differences of time and place, what else, in essence, are "Eurocommunism" and the so-called "historic compromise"? Moreover, some of those well to the left, in formal political terms, of the Eurocommunist trend reproduce the *substance* of the very errors Trotsky fought against, under the heading "Anglo-Soviet Trade Union Committee."

The issues, then, are not only of historical but also of immediate practical interest. Trotsky's writings on strategy and tactics in relation to these great questions are a veritable treasure house. It can be said without any exaggeration that no one else since 1923 has produced work that even approaches the profundity and brilliance of these writings. They are, literally, indispensable to revolutionaries today.

CHAPTER 4

PARTY AND CLASS

MARX AFFIRMED that the emancipation of the working class must be the act of the working class itself; but, he also argued, the ruling classes control the "means of mental production," and therefore the "dominant ideas in any epoch are those of the ruling classes."

From this contradiction arises the necessity for the revolutionary socialist party. The nature of the party and, above all, of its relationship to the working class has been central to socialist movements from the beginning. It has never been merely a "technical" question of organization. At each stage, the disputes about the relationship of party and class—and therefore about the nature of the party—have also been disputes about the objectives of the movement. The arguments about *means* have always been partly arguments about *ends,* and necessarily so. Thus, Marx's own conflicts with Proudhon, with Schapper, with Blanqui, with Bakunin, and many others on this issue were inextricably interwoven with differences about the nature of socialism and the means whereby it was to be achieved.

After Marx's death in 1883, and the death of Engels 12 years later, there was a massive growth of socialist parties. In Russia, there soon emerged what was to become a fundamental conflict about the kind of party that had to be built.

Trotsky's first view of the nature of the revolutionary party was essentially that which later came to be regarded as peculiarly "Leninist." Indeed, according to Isaac Deutscher, Trotsky argued this point of view independently of Lenin while in exile in Siberia in 1901.[1] At any rate, he became an early adherent of *Iskra,* and at the 1903 Congress of the Russian Social Democratic Labor

Party (RSDLP), he spoke strongly for a highly centralized organization: "Our rules...represent the organized distrust of the Party towards all its sections, that is, control over all local, district, national, and other organizations."[2]

He recoiled violently from this position after taking the Menshevik side in the split in the *Iskra* tendency at the Congress. Within a year, Trotsky had become the outstanding critic of Bolshevik centralism; Lenin's methods, he wrote in 1904, "lead to this: the party organization is substituted for the party, the Central Committee is substituted for the party organization, and finally a "dictator" is substituted for the Central Committee."[3]

Like Rosa Luxemburg, Trotsky was suspicious of "party conservatism" in general and placed heavy reliance on spontaneous working-class action:

> The European socialist parties—and in the first place the mightiest of them, the German—have developed their conservatism, which grows stronger in proportion to the size of the masses affected, the efficiency of the organization, and the party discipline. *Therefore, it is possible that the social democracy may become an obstacle in the path of any open clash between the workers and the bourgeoisie.*[4]

To overcome this conservatism, Trotsky relied on the spontaneous sweep of revolution, which, he wrote, under the impact of the 1905 Revolution, "kills party routine, destroys party conservatism."[5] Thus, the role of the party is reduced essentially to propaganda. It is not the vanguard of the working class.

There was, of course, considerable justification for his fears. In Russia, even the Bolshevik party showed itself to be conservative in 1905–07, and again in 1917.[6] In the West, where conservatism had an incomparably greater *material* basis in the privileges of the labor bureaucracies, it played a decisive counterrevolutionary role in 1918–19.

The experience of 1905, in which Trotsky played a quite extraordinary part as an individual without serious party connections (he was a nominal Menshevik at the time but essentially a freelancer), no doubt strengthened his belief in the sufficiency of spontaneous mass action.

In the period of the reaction after 1906, and even in the upturn in the Russian labor movement from 1912, he continued to criticize Bolshevik "substitutionism" and to preach a "unity" of all tendencies that was essentially directed *against* the Bolsheviks. Again, this may have contributed to his slowness in recognizing the dangers of *real* substitutionism after 1920.

Trotsky's position of 1904–17 was shown to be clearly untenable by the course of events. Without Lenin, Trotsky later wrote, there would have been no October Revolution. But it was not simply a question of Lenin arriving at the Finland Station in April 1917. It was a matter of the party that Lenin and his collaborators had built over the previous years. The conservatism of many of the leaders of that party (reinforced, it must be said, by the theoretical scheme of the "democratic dictatorship" that Lenin had defended for so long) would very probably have prevented the seizure of power but for Lenin's unique authority and determination. Without the party, with all its defects, the question could not even arise. "Spontaneous" mass action can sometimes bring down an authoritarian regime. It did so in Russia in February 1917, in Germany and in Austria-Hungary in 1918, and has done so on various occasions since, most recently in Iran.

In 1917, Trotsky adopted the view that for the workers to take and hold power, a party of Lenin's type was indispensable. He never subsequently wavered from it and indeed gave it characteristically sharp expression. In 1932, rebutting the argument that "the interests of the class come before the interests of the party," he wrote:

> The class, taken by itself, is only material for exploitation. The proletariat assumes an independent role only at the moment when from a social class *in itself* it becomes a political class *for itself*. This cannot take place otherwise than through the medium of a party. The party is that historical organ by means of which the class becomes class conscious. To say that "the class stands higher than the party" is to assert that the class in the raw stands higher than the class which is on the road to class consciousness. Not only is this incorrect: it is reactionary.[7]

This conception presents some very obvious difficulties. In particular, experience had shown that the "historical organ" through which a particular working class achieved consciousness could degenerate. How then can party organization be defended?

The historically conditioned instrument

Trotsky was well aware of this problem. He had witnessed the disintegration of the International in 1914, the directly counterrevolutionary role of social democracy in 1918–19, and, of course, the rise of Stalinism.

The passage quoted above continues:

> The progress of a class towards class consciousness, that is, the building of a revolutionary party which leads the proletariat, is a complex and a contradictory process. The class itself is not homogeneous. Its different sections arrive at class consciousness by different paths and at different times. The bourgeoisie participates actively in this process. Within the working class it creates its own institutions, or utilizes those already existing, in order to oppose certain strata of workers against others. Within the proletariat several parties are active at the same time. Therefore, for the greater part of its political journey, it remains split politically. The problem of the united front—which arises during certain periods most sharply—originates therein. The historical interests of the proletariat find their expression in the Communist Party—when its policies are correct. The task of the Communist Party consists of winning over the majority of the proletariat; and only thus is the socialist revolution made possible. The Communist Party cannot fulfill its mission except by preserving, completely and unconditionally, its political and organizational independence apart from all other parties and organizations within and without the working class. To transgress this basic principle of Marxist policy is to commit the most heinous of crimes against the interests of the proletariat as a class.... But the proletariat moves towards revolutionary consciousness not by passing grades in school but by passing through the class struggle, which abhors interruptions. To fight, the proletariat must have unity in its ranks. This holds true for partial economic conflicts within the walls of a single factory as well as such "national" political battles as the one to repel fascism. Consequently the tactic of the united front is not something accidental and artificial—a cunning maneuver not at all; it originates entirely and wholly, in the objective conditions governing the development of the proletariat.[8]

This remarkably clear, coherent, and realistic analysis was not, of course, a timeless sociological generalization. It was rooted in actual historical development. The parties of the Second International had, in their time, helped to create those

> bulwarks of workers' democracy [the workers' organizations, especially the unions] within the bourgeois state...[which] are absolutely essential for taking the revolutionary road. The work of the Second International consisted in creating just such bulwarks during the epoch when it was still fulfilling its progressive historic labor.[9]

The parties of that International were in time rotted from within by adaptation to the societies in which they operated; this development had, of course, a material and not merely an ideological basis. Faced with the test of August 4, 1914, they capitulated to "their own" bourgeoisie (with certain exceptions: the Bolsheviks, the Bulgarians, the Serbs) or adopted an equivocal "centrist" position (the Italians, the Scandinavians, the Americans, and various minorities elsewhere). Out of that capitulation, the inner-party conflicts and splits that it produced, the rising tide of working-class opposition to the war from 1916 onwards, and the revolutions of 1917 and 1918 arose the Communist International, "the direct continuation of the heroic endeavors and martyrdom of a long line of revolutionary generations from Babeuf to Karl Liebknecht and Rosa Luxemburg."[10]

This was now the "historic organ by means of which the class becomes class conscious." The parties of the Communist International had, especially since 1923, committed a series of blunders (Trotsky was not, of course, blind to their earlier mistakes), and increasingly followed opportunist or sectarian policies under the direction of Stalin and his ruling circle in the USSR. Nevertheless, with all its defects, it was a *reality*, not a hypothesis, a reality that commanded the support or sympathy of millions around the world. Indeed, paradoxically, its very defects indicated in a distorted way that it was a truly mass organization. For Trotsky did not subscribe to the simplistic view that the big parties of the Comintern were *merely* instruments of the Stalinist bureaucracy in Russia. The problem was to correct their course. "All eyes to the Communist Party. We must explain to it. We must convince it."[11]

As a matter of political necessity, the party's internal regime must be democratic. Trotsky wrote in 1931:

> The internal struggle trains the party and makes its own road clear to it. In this struggle all the members of the party gain a deep confidence in the correctness of the policy of the party and in the revolutionary reliability of the leadership. Only such a conviction in the rank-and-file Bolshevik, won through experience and ideological struggle, gives the leadership the chance to lead the whole party into battle at the necessary moment. And only a deep confidence of the party itself in the correctness of its policy inspires the working masses with confidence in the party. Artificial splits forced from the outside; the absence of a free and honest ideological struggle...this is what now paralyzes the Spanish Communist Party.[12]

The argument applied generally.

It was, however, not so simple. Soon after his expulsion from the USSR in 1929, Trotsky outlined what he considered to be the basic questions for supporters of the Left Opposition in Europe (attitudes to the Anglo-Russian Trade Union Committee, the Chinese Revolution, and to "Socialism in One Country").

> Some comrades may be astonished that I omit reference here to the question of the party regime. I do so not out of oversight but deliberately. A party regime has no independent, self-sufficient meaning. In relation to party policy it is a derivative magnitude. The most heterogeneous elements sympathize with the struggle against Stalinist bureaucratism.... For a Marxist, democracy within a party or within a country is not an abstraction. Democracy is always conditioned by the struggle of living forces. By bureaucratism, the opportunist elements...understand revolutionary centralism. Obviously, they cannot be our co-thinkers.[13]

It is possible to go through Trotsky's post-1917 writings, and even his writings after 1929 or 1934, and to produce a series of statements, some exalting the virtues of inner-party democracy and condemning "administrative" measures against critics, others arguing the necessity for purges and expulsions. Nor is it a case of quotations wrenched from their context. For Trotsky, the relationship between centralism and inner-party democracy was not constant. It was a question of the *political content* of each in specific but changing circumstances. Trotsky wrote toward the end of 1932:

> The principle of party democracy is in no way identical with the principle of the open door. The Left Opposition has never demanded of the Stalinists that they transform the party into a mechanical sum of factions, groups, sects, and individuals. We accuse the centrist bureaucracy of carrying on an essentially false policy which at every step brings them into contradiction with the flower of the proletariat and of looking for the way out of these contradictions by the strangling of party democracy.[14]

This may appear equivocal. Indeed, in purely formal terms, it *is* equivocal. The solution to the contradiction is to be found in the dynamics of party development. The party, Trotsky believed, cannot grow, in terms of real mass influence as opposed to mere numbers, except through a reciprocal relationship, a process of interaction, with wider and wider layers of workers. For *this,* inner-party democracy is indispensable. It provides the means of feedback of class experience into the party. Such a development is not always possible. Often, objective circumstances rule out such growth. But the party must always be attuned to the possibility. Otherwise it will not be able to seize the chances that occur from time to time.

Therefore, the regime must *at all times* be as open and flexible as possible, consonant with preserving the revolutionary integrity of the party. The qualification is important. For unfavorable circumstances weaken the ties between the party and the layers of advanced workers, and so increase the problem of "factions, groups, sects" that can become an *obstacle* to the growth of inner-party democracy, understood as Trotsky understood it, essentially a mechanism by which the party relates to wider sections of the working class, learning from them and at the same time earning the right to lead them.

The argument is, perhaps, too abstract. To concretize it, consider this passage from Trotsky's *History of the Russian Revolution*, discussing Lenin's isolation from the majority of the party leadership after the February Revolution:

> Against the old Bolsheviks [in April 1917] Lenin found support in another layer of the party, already tempered, but more fresh and more closely united with the masses. In the February Revolution, as we know, the worker-Bolsheviks played the decisive role. They thought it self-evident that the class which had won the victory should seize power.... Almost everywhere there were left Bolsheviks accused of maximalism, even of anarchism. These worker-revolutionists only lacked the theoretical resources to defend their position. But they were ready to respond to the first clear call. It was on this stratum of workers, decisively risen to their feet during the upward years of 1912–14, that Lenin was now banking.[15]

That model appears again and again in Trotsky's writings. A mass party, unlike a sect, is necessarily buffeted by immensely powerful forces, especially in revolutionary circumstances. These forces inevitably find expression inside the party also. To keep the party on course (in practice, to continually correct its course in a changing situation), the complex relationship between the leadership, the various layers of the cadre, and the workers they influence and are influenced by expresses itself and *must* express itself in political struggle inside the party. If that is artificially smothered by administrative means, the party will lose its way.

An indispensable function of the leadership, itself formed by selection in previous struggles, is to understand when to close ranks to preserve the core of the organization from disintegration by unfavorable outside pressures—to emphasize centralism—and when to open up the organization and to use layers of advanced workers inside *and outside* the party to overcome the party conservatism of sections of the cadre and leadership—to emphasize democracy—in order to change course quickly.

All of this implies a very exalted conception of the role of leadership, and this the post-1917 Trotsky certainly had. He was to affirm in 1938 that the "historical crisis of mankind is reduced to the crisis of revolutionary leadership." It was a conception, however, of the organic growth of a leading cadre in relation to the experiences of the party in the actual class struggle. Of course, the leading cadre had to embody a tradition and the experience of the past (from Babeuf to Karl Liebknecht), a knowledge of the strategy and tactics that had been tested in many countries at different times over many years. This knowledge was necessarily, for the most part, theoretical, and Trotsky least of all was inclined to undervalue it. It was a necessary condition for successful leadership but not a sufficient one. The experience of the party in action and of its changing relationship to various sections of workers was the additional, irreplaceable factor, which could be developed only in practice.

An anomaly

In Trotsky's lifetime, only one Communist Party, the CPSU in the USSR, held state power (other than in the areas controlled by the Chinese Communist Party in the 1930s). Trotsky classed them all as "bureaucratic centrist" organizations, that is to say, workers' organizations that vacillated between revolutionary and reformist politics. After 1935, with the Popular Front line, he concluded that they had become social-patriotic, "yellow agencies of rotting capitalism."[16]

But these terms refer to workers' organizations, to parties that are obliged to compete with other parties for support in their own working-class movements. The CPSU, certainly after 1929, if not earlier, was not a party at all in that sense. It was a bureaucratic apparatus, the instrument of a totalitarian despotism. Trotsky conceded this in part: "The party [that is, the CPSU] as a party does not exist today. The centrist apparatus has strangled it," he wrote in 1930.[17] But he did conclude that

PARTY AND CLASS   85

the CPSU was a *fundamentally* different species from the workers' parties outside the USSR.

Even after he had abandoned hope (in October 1933) of a peaceful reform of the regime in the USSR, the confusion remained. Of course it was associated with the belief that even though reform was impossible, the USSR nonetheless remained a degenerated workers' state.

The matter became important a few years after Trotsky's death, when a series of new Stalinist states came into being without proletarian revolutions and with a series of ruling "communist parties" that manifestly were not workers' parties in terms of Trotsky's conception. The contradiction was already built into Trotsky's own post-1933 position.

The thread is cut

We have seen that Trotsky's mature conception of the relationship between party and class was neither abstract nor arbitrary, but was rooted *both* in the experience of Bolshevism in Russia and in the actual historical development that had led to mass communist parties in a number of important countries.

But what if that development runs into the sands? What if the "historically conditioned instrument" fails the test? Trotsky had contemplated the possibility, only to reject it firmly. In 1931, he wrote:

> Let us take another, more remote example for the clarification of our ideas. Hugo Urbahns, who considers himself a "Left Communist," declares the German party bankrupt, politically done for, and proposes to create a new party. If Urbahns were right, it would mean that the victory of fascism is certain. For, in order to create a new party, years are required (and there has been nothing to prove that the party of Urbahns would in any sense be better than Thaelmann's party: when Urbahns was at the head of the party, there were by no means fewer mistakes). Yes, should the fascists really conquer power, that would mean not only the physical destruction of the Communist Party, but veritable political bankruptcy for it.... The seizure of power by the fascists would therefore most probably signify the necessity of creating a new revolutionary party and in all likelihood also a new International. That would be a frightful historical catastrophe. But to assume today that all this is *unavoidable* can be done only by genuine liquidators, those who under the mantle of hollow phrases are really hastening to capitulate like cravens in the

face of the struggle and *without* a struggle.... We are unshakably convinced that the victory over the fascists is possible—not after their coming to power, not after five, ten or twenty years of their rule, but now, under the given conditions, in the coming months and weeks.[18]

But Hitler did come to power. Notwithstanding the brilliance and cogency of Trotsky's arguments, the German Communist Party, with its quarter of a million members and its 6 million votes (in 1932), held fast to its fatal course. It was smashed, without resistance, along with the "social fascists," the trade unions, and each and every one of the political, cultural, and social organizations created by the German working class in the previous 60 years.

In 1931, Trotsky had described Germany as "the key to the international situation.... On the development in which the solution of the German crisis occurs will depend not only the fate of Germany itself (and that is already a great deal) but the fate of Europe, the destiny of the entire world, for many years to come."[19]

It was an accurate forecast. The defeat of the German working class transformed *world* politics. The failure of the Communist Party even to attempt resistance was a blow as heavy as the capitulation of social democracy had been in 1914. It was the August 4 of the Communist International.

What then is left of the "historic organ by means of which the class becomes class conscious"? From 1933 until his death in August 1940, Trotsky wrestled with what proved to be an insoluble dilemma, at that time and long afterward. In June 1932, he had written:

> The Stalinists by their persecution would like to push us on the road of a second party and a fourth international. They understand that a fatal error of this type on the part of the Opposition would slow up its growth for years, if not nullify all its successes altogether.[20]

Now, less than a year later, he was forced to concede, first, that the German party was finished, then a little later (after the Comintern executive declared in April 1933 that its policy in Germany was "completely correct") that *all* the communist parties were finished as revolutionary organizations, that what was needed were "New Communist Parties and the New International" (the title of an article dated July 1933).

The connecting rod between theory and practice had been

cut. Before 1917, Trotsky had relied on spontaneous working-class action to overcome party conservatism. After 1917, he recognized the revolutionary workers' *party* as the *indispensable* instrument of socialist revolution. The lack of such parties rooted in the working class, and possessing mature, experienced cadres, had produced the tragedy of 1918–19: mass revolutionary movements in Germany, Austria, Hungary, and, elsewhere, mass spontaneous struggles, leading to defeat.

The means of overcoming the defeat—the parties of the Communist International—had themselves degenerated to the point where they had become obstacles to a revolutionary solution of new profound social crises.

It was necessary to start again. But what was left to start with? Essentially, there was nothing but small (often tiny) groups, whose common characteristics included isolation from the actual workers' movements and from direct involvement in workers' struggles. The apparent partial exceptions to this generalization—those who could count their members in hundreds or thousands rather than dozens—the Greek Archio-Marxists, the Dutch Revolutionary Socialist Workers Party (RSAP), and, a little later, the Spanish POUM, all proved to be frail reeds, centrists rather than revolutionaries, obstacles rather than allies.

With such forces Trotsky began to reconstruct. He had no choice, unless retreat into passivity or that disguised passivity later called "Western Marxism" is reckoned a choice. But means and ends are inextricably interwoven. With the links to the real workers' movement cut, "Trotskyism," even in Trotsky's lifetime, began to accommodate to its actual milieu—small, radicalized sections of the intellectual strata of the petty bourgeoisie. As we shall see, Trotsky himself fought a long battle against this accommodation. At the same time, the cruel necessities of the situation drove him to adopt positions that, in spite of his will and understanding, assisted in its growth.

The New International

If the Communist Left throughout the world consisted of only five individuals, they would nevertheless have been obliged to build an international organization *simultaneously* with the building of one or more national organizations. It is wrong to view a national organization as the foundation and the Interna-

tional as a roof. The interrelation here is of an entirely different
type. Marx and Engels started the communist movement with
an international document in 1847 and with the creation of an
international movement. The same thing was repeated in the
creation of the First International. The same path was followed
by the Zimmerwald Left in preparation for the Third International. Today this road is dictated far more imperiously than in
the days of Marx. It is, of course, possible in the epoch of imperialism for a revolutionary proletarian tendency to arise in one
or another country, but it cannot thrive and develop in one isolated country; on the very next day after its formation it must
seek or create international ties, an international platform, because a guarantee of the correctness of the national policy can be
found only along this road. A tendency which remains shut in
nationally over a stretch of years condemns itself irrevocably to
degeneration.[21]

Trotsky wrote this, in a polemic with Bordiga's Italian ultra-
left sect, while he was still committed to a policy of reform of the
existing communist parties. He was arguing for an international
faction orienting on an existing international. The logic of that
position, as opposed to the arguments used to sustain it, seemed
irrefutable.

The *arguments* themselves will not withstand critical examination. Marx and Engels did not start with the "creation of an
international movement." The *Communist Manifesto* was written for an already *existing* Communist League (albeit of very
primitive communist ideas) that was international only in the
sense that it existed in several countries. It was essentially a *German* organization, consisting of German émigré artisans and intellectuals in Paris, Brussels, and elsewhere, as well as groups in
the Rhineland and German Switzerland.

The First International started as an alliance between existing
British trade union organizations under liberal influence and existing French ones under Proudhonist influence, and later drew
in other groupings of very diverse character and nationality. Far
from "repeating" the experience of the Communist League, it
was developed on exactly the *opposite* lines—without an initial
programmatic basis and without a centralized organization. The
same is true, to a much lesser degree, of the Second International, which Trotsky does not mention here.

Nor will the reference to the Zimmerwald Left stand, either.
The Zimmerwald *Left* (as opposed to the Zimmerwald current as
a whole) consisted of the Bolshevik Party, a mass national party,

plus more or less isolated individuals ("one Lithuanian, the Pole Karl Radek, two Swedish delegates, and Julian Borchard, the delegate of a tiny group, the German International Socialists").[22]

Practically speaking, Trotsky had no option. He had no base in any workers' movement now. All contact with his supporters in the USSR had ceased by the spring of 1933.[23] It was a matter of pulling together whatever could be pulled together, wherever it existed, to create a political current. Moreover, the argument that an international platform was needed—or a common analysis of the problems of the working-class movement—was indisputable. Trotsky supplied it. But a confusion between ideas and organization, between a political tendency and international *party*, had been introduced. Within a few years, Trotsky tacitly abandoned his conception of the revolutionary party as the "historical organ by means of which the class becomes class conscious" and launched an "International" without a significant base in *any* workers' movement.

First, however, Trotsky attempted to find new forces. The Trotskyist groups were tiny. The power of the Stalinists had forced them into a political ghetto. This, moreover, had a definite social location in a section of the petty-bourgeois intelligentsia. How to break out, proletarianize Trotskyism, and pull significant numbers of workers into new communist parties?

There were enormous obstacles in the way. A major long-term effect of the defeat in Germany was to create such a massive groundswell for unity among working-class militants that the call for new parties and a new International, in other words, for a new split, fell on the stoniest of ground. Trotsky had pioneered the call for the workers' united front against fascism. But as this call began to gain ground in the socialist parties after 1933 (and, soon, in the communist parties, too), Trotsky's followers could be and were represented as splitters; they were now calling for new parties and a new International. Their isolation was reinforced.

After initial attempts to "regroup" with various centrist and left-reformist groups (for example, the British ILP) had foundered (producing a rich crop of polemics against centrism from Trotsky), Trotsky proposed the drastic step of entry into the social-democratic parties. Strictly speaking, this was argued for specific cases—France at first (hence, the term "French Turn")—but it came to be generalized in practice. The arguments were that the social democrats were moving to the left, so creating a more favorable climate for revolutionary work, and that they were attracting new layers of workers and presented an incomparably more proletarian environment than the isolated propaganda groups that Trotskyism inhabited.

The operation was conceived of as short term; a sharp, hard fight with the reformists and centrists, then a split and the founding of the party. "Entry into a reformist or centrist party in itself does not include a long-term perspective. It is only a stage which under certain conditions can be limited to an episode."[24]

The operation failed in its strategic aim; it failed to change the relationship of forces or to improve the social composition of the Trotskyist grouplets. The fundamental reasons for the failure were the consequences of the defeat in Germany and the turning of the Communist International first to the United Front (1934) and then to the Popular Front (1935), the great impact these changes made, and the consequent swing rightward of the whole workers' movement. In addition, Stalin's anti-Trotsky campaign soon had Trotsky and his followers denounced as fascist agents.

The circumstances that had made it possible for revolutionaries to win *mass* leftward-moving centrist parties like the German USPD and the majority of French Socialists to the Communist International in 1919–21 simply did not exist in 1934–35. Whatever mistakes Trotsky or his followers may have made in the course of the "French Turn" can have had only trivial effects by comparison with the effects of the profoundly unfavorable situation.

Some of the gains claimed from the entry tactic were real. It involved a break with many whom Trotsky called "conservative sectarians," that is, those who could not adjust to active politics, as opposed to small circle propagandism in the intellectual milieu.

Toward the end of 1933, Trotsky wrote:

> A revolutionary organization cannot develop without purging itself, especially under conditions of legal work, when not infrequently chance, alien, and degenerate elements gather under the banner of revolution.... We are making an important revolutionary turn. At such moments inner crisis or splits are absolutely inevitable. To fear them is to substitute petty-bourgeois sentimentalism and personal scheming for revolutionary policy. The League [the French Trotskyist group] is passing through a first crisis under the banner of great and clear revolutionary criteria. Under these conditions a splitting off of a part of the

> League will be a great step forward. It will reject all that is un-
> healthy, crippled, and incapacitated; it will give a lesson to the
> vacillating and irresolute elements; it will harden the better sec-
> tions of the youth; it will improve the inner atmosphere; it will
> open up before the League new, great possibilities.[25]

No doubt all this was correct in principle and, in fact, some new
forces were recruited from the socialist youth organizations to
replace those who were eliminated (or, rather, dropped out in
most cases). Nevertheless, the balance of forces—the pathetic
weakness of the revolutionary left—remained basically unaltered. What then?

Trotsky pressed on with the foundation of the Fourth International. After repeatedly stating that it could not be an *immediate* perspective, as the forces were not yet available—as late as
1935, he had denounced as "a stupid piece of gossip" the idea
that "the Trotskyists want to proclaim the Fourth International
next Thursday"[26]—he proposed, within a year, precisely that:
the proclamation of the New International. On that occasion, he
was unable to persuade his followers. By 1938, he had won
them over.

The forces adhering to the Fourth International in 1938 were
weaker, not stronger, than those that had existed in 1934. (The Socialist Workers Party of the U.S. was the only serious exception.)
The Spanish Revolution had been strangled in the meantime. Trotsky justified his decision by a partial and unacknowledged retreat
into the semi-spontaneity he had advocated before 1917, and also
by analogy with Lenin's position in 1914. "The discrepancy between our forces and the tasks on the morrow is much more clearly
perceived by us than by our critics," wrote Trotsky in late 1938.

> But the harsh and tragic dialectic of our epoch is working in our
> favor. Brought to the extreme pitch of exasperation and indigna-
> tion, the masses will find no other leadership than that offered
> by the Fourth International.[27]

But 1917 had shown positively, and 1918–19 negatively,
and, above all, 1936 in Spain had demonstrated the indispens-
ability of parties rooted in their national working classes
through a long period of struggle for partial demands. Trotsky
had recognized this more clearly than most. Now, since such
parties did not exist, and the need was extraordinarily urgent, he
took refuge in a "Weltgeist" of revolution that would somehow
create them out of spontaneous exasperation and indignation,

provided "a spotless banner" were waved aloft. The spontaneous upsurge would, in the course of the war, or soon after, lift the isolated and inexperienced "leaderships" of the Fourth International sections into leadership of mass parties.

The analogy with Lenin in 1914 was doubly inappropriate. When Lenin wrote in 1914: "The Second International is dead.... Long live the Third International," he was already the most influential leader of a real mass party in a major country. Nevertheless, he did not think of calling for the founding of the Third International until one and a half years after the October Revolution and at a time when, he believed, a mass and ascending revolutionary movement existed in Europe. That Trotsky should ignore all this was a tribute to his revolutionary will. Politically, however, this would derail and disorient his followers when, after his death, a very real upsurge passed them by—as was inevitable given their isolation—and would make it much harder for them to develop a realistic revolutionary orientation.

There was an element of near-messianism in Trotsky's conceptions at this time. In a desperately difficult situation, with fascism in the ascendant, defeat piled on defeat for the workers' movement, and a new world war imminent, the banner of revolution had to be flown, the program of communism reasserted, until the revolution itself transformed the situation.

Perhaps it would have been impossible to hold his followers together without something of this outlook, which, if so, was therefore a *necessary* deviation from his mature view. But its later costs were nonetheless real.

CHAPTER 5

THE HERITAGE

THE ESSENCE of tragedy, Trotsky once wrote, is the contrast between great ends and insignificant means. Whatever is to be said about this as a generalization, it certainly epitomizes Trotsky's own plight in the last years of his life. The man who had actually organized the October insurrection, who had directed the operations of the Red armies, who had dealt with—as friend or foe—the mass workers' parties (revolutionary and reformist) through the Comintern, was now reduced to struggling to hold together a scatter of tiny groups, virtually all of them impotent to affect the course of events, even marginally.

He was forced to intervene again and again in a hundred petty squabbles in a score of little grouplets. Some of the disputes did, of course, involve serious issues of political principle, but even these, as Trotsky himself saw clearly, were largely rooted in the isolation of the groups from the actual working-class movement and the influence of their petty-bourgeois milieu—because that was the milieu into which they had been driven and to which so many of them adapted.

Nevertheless, he fought on to the end. Inevitably, his enforced isolation from effective participation in the workers' movement, in which he had once played so big a part, affected to some extent his understanding of the ever-changing course of the class struggle. Not even his vast experience and superb tactical reflexes could substitute entirely for the lack of feedback from the militants engaged in the day-to-day struggle that is possible only in a real communist party. As the period of isolation lengthened, this became more apparent. Compare his *Transitional Program* of

1938 with its prototype, the *Program of Action* for France (1934). In freshness, relevance, specificity, and concreteness in relation to an actual struggle, the latter is clearly superior.

This was certainly not a question of any failing of intellectual power. Some of Trotsky's last unfinished writings, notably *Trade Unions in the Epoch of Imperialist Decay,* are path-breaking contributions to Marxist thought. It is a matter of lack of intimate contact with significant numbers of militants engaged in actual class struggle.

Yet when Trotsky was murdered in August 1940 by Stalin's agent Jacson-Mercader, he did leave behind him a *movement.* Whatever the frailties and failings of that movement, and they were manifold, it was a tremendous achievement. The growth of Stalinism, and then the triumph of fascism in most of Europe, nearly obliterated the authentic communist tradition in the workers' movement. Fascism destroyed it directly. It smashed the workers' organizations wherever it came to power. Stalinism did the same thing by different means, inside the USSR. Outside the USSR, it corrupted and then effectively strangled the revolutionary tradition as a *mass* movement.

It is difficult today to appreciate the full force of the torrent of slander and vilification to which Trotsky and his followers were subjected in the 1930s. The entire propaganda resources of the USSR and of the Comintern parties were devoted to denouncing "Trotskyites" (both genuine and spurious) as agents of Hitler, the Japanese Emperor, and every kind of reaction. The slaughter of the old Bolsheviks in the USSR (some after spectacular "show trials," most by murder without the pretext of a trial) was represented as a triumph for the forces of "socialism and peace," as the Stalinist slogan of the time went. "Every weak, corrupt or ambitious traitor to Socialism within the Soviet Union has been hired to do the foul work of capitalism and fascism," declared the report of the Central Committee to the 15th Congress of Communist Party of Great Britain in 1938.

> In the forefront of all the wrecking, sabotage, and assassination is the fascist agent Trotsky. But the defenses of the Soviet people are strong. Under the leadership of our Bolshevik Comrade Yezhov, the spies and wreckers have been exposed before the world and brought to judgement.[1]

Yezhov, who rose to power on the judicial murder of his predecessor, Yagoda, was the police chief who presided over the slaughter of communists and many, many others in the USSR in 1937–38, at the height of the Stalinist terror.

The official line, pronounced by Stalin himself, was that "Trotskyism is the spearhead of the counterrevolutionary bourgeoisie, waging the struggle against communism."[2] This massive campaign of lies, assisted by the numerous "liberal" and social-democratic fellow travelers who were attracted to the communist parties after 1935, was kept up for more than 20 years. It served to inoculate CP militants against Marxist criticism of Stalinism.

Of at least equal importance for small revolutionary organizations of the time was the general demoralization engendered by the collapse of the Popular Fronts and the approach of the Second World War. Trotsky expressed it vividly in a discussion in the spring of 1939.

> We are not progressing politically. Yes, it is a fact, which is an expression of a general decay of the workers' movement in the last fifteen years. It is the more general cause. When the revolutionary movement in general is declining, when one defeat follows another, when fascism is spreading over the world, when the official "Marxism" is the most powerful organization of the deception of the workers, and so on, it is an inevitable situation that the revolutionary elements must work against the general historic current, even if our ideas, our explanations, are as exact and wise as one can demand.
>
> But the masses are not educated by prognostic theoretical conception, but by general experiences of their lives. It is the most general explanation—the whole situation is against us.[3]

The little Fourth Internationalist movement that survived these glacial conditions under Trotsky's inspiration and guidance was politically scarred by the experience to a greater degree than was immediately apparent. It was subsequently to undergo further mutations. Nevertheless, it was the *only* genuinely communist current of any significance to survive the ice age.

World outlook, 1938–40

At the core of Trotsky's view of the world in his last years was the conviction that the capitalist system was near its last gasp.

> The economic prerequisite for the proletarian revolution has already in general achieved the highest point of fruition that can be reached under capitalism. Mankind's productive forces stag-

nate. Already, new inventions and improvements fail to raise the
level of material wealth,

he wrote in his 1938 program.

> Conjunctural crises under the conditions of the social crisis of
> the whole capitalist system inflict ever heavier deprivations and
> sufferings upon the masses. Growing unemployment, in its turn,
> deepens the financial crisis of the state and undermines the un-
> stable monetary systems. Democratic regimes, as well as fascist,
> stagger from one crisis to another.[4]

As it stands, that could pass as a description of the state of
most of the world economy at the time. As has been said, Trotsky was profoundly impressed by the contrast between this stagnation and the rapid industrial growth of the USSR (there were
other important exceptions, too, that Trotsky did not consider:
industrial output in Japan *doubled* between 1927 and 1936, and
went on growing, and in Hitler's Germany, unemployment virtually disappeared in the drive for rearmament).

But Trotsky was engaged in more than description. He believed that the situation for capitalism was irretrievable. "The
disintegration of capitalism has reached extreme limits, likewise
the disintegration of the old ruling class. The further existence of
this system is impossible," he wrote in 1939.[5] That being so, the
reformist workers' parties could not make any gains for their
supporters, "when every serious demand of the proletariat and
even every serious demand of the petty bourgeoisie inevitably
reaches beyond the limits of capitalist property relations and of
the bourgeois state,"[6] as the 1938 program put it.

That did not mean that the mass parties of reformism would
automatically disappear—historical inertia and the lack of an *obvious* alternative would preserve them for a little while. But they
no longer had any relatively secure basis. They had been destabi-
lized. The shock of war and the postwar crisis would wreck them.
These parties, Trotsky believed, included the Communist Parties.

> The definite passing over of the Comintern to the side of the
> bourgeois order, its cynically counterrevolutionary role through-
> out the world, particularly in Spain, France, the United States
> and other "democratic countries," created exceptional supple-
> mentary difficulties for the world proletariat. Under the banner
> of the October Revolution, the conciliatory policies practiced by
> the "People's Front" dooms the working class to impotence.[7]

He had held, since 1935, that "[n]othing now distinguishes the

Communists from the Social Democrats except the traditional phraseology, which is not difficult to unlearn."[8]

The reality was to prove more complex, a fact that eventually precipitated a fundamental crisis in the Fourth Internationalist movement. Trotsky was pointing to a real trend, but the time scale for its development was very much greater than he thought. After the Hitler-Stalin Pact (August 1939), the Comintern parties stayed loyal to Moscow, and in the "cold war" from late 1948 onward, they did not capitulate to "their own" bourgeoisies, either. Their policies were not revolutionary, but neither were they simply reformist in the ordinary sense. They retained, for nearly 20 years, a "leftist" orientation to the bourgeois state (consolidated by their systematic exclusion from office in France, Italy, and elsewhere after 1947), which made the creation of a revolutionary alternative extremely difficult, even if other factors had been more favorable.

In one great case, China, and some lesser ones (among them Albania, Yugoslavia, and North Vietnam), Stalinist parties actually destroyed weak bourgeois states and replaced them by regimes on the Russian pattern. In particular, the Chinese Revolution of 1948–49 put the classic Trotskyist analysis of the Stalinist parties into question, at any rate for the backward countries. For if it was regarded as a proletarian revolution, the basis of the Fourth International's existence—the essentially counterrevolutionary nature of Stalinism—was destroyed. If, on the other hand, it was, in some sense, a bourgeois revolution—a "New Democracy," as Mao Tse-tung claimed at the time—the theory of permanent revolution was undermined. This aspect of the matter will be considered later. What is relevant here is that the occurrence of the revolution, whatever view was taken of its nature, refurbished the revolutionary image of Stalinism for a long time.

The most important mistake Trotsky made at this time was to assume that capitalism had no way out economically, even if the proletarian revolution was averted. That this was his belief is indisputable. "If, however, it is conceded," he wrote toward the end of 1939,

> that the present war will provoke not revolution but a decline of the proletariat, then there remains another alternative: the further decay of monopoly capitalism, its further fusion with the state, and the replacement of democracy wherever it still remained by a totalitarian regime. The inability of the proletariat to take into its

hands the leadership of society could actually lead under these conditions to the growth of a new exploiting class from the Bonapartist fascist bureaucracy. This would be, according to all indications, a regime of decline, signaling the eclipse of civilization.[9]

Trotsky might, if pressed, have conceded that some temporary economic revival was possible on a cyclical basis. He had been quick to note the limited revival of European capitalism in 1920–21 (and to draw political conclusions from it) and had pointed out a certain revival from the depths of 1929–31 in the early 1930s. But he completely excluded the possibility of a prolonged upward economic movement such as had given birth to reformism as a mass force in the decades before the First World War.

His was a common view on the left at that time. Yet the evidence was already available that large-scale arms production could produce *overall* economic growth—growth that was not at all limited to the arms sector of the economy. Of course, the evidence related to the direct preparations for the Second World War. But, suppose preparing for war could be made permanent or semi-permanent?

In fact, after the Second World War, capitalism experienced a massive revival. Far from economic contraction and decline dominating, there was an even greater economic expansion than during the "classic" imperialist phase before 1914. As Michael Kidron pointed out in 1968, "the system as a whole has never grown as fast for so long as since the War—twice as fast between 1950 and 1964 as between 1913 and 1950 and nearly half as fast again as during the generation before then."[10]

Reformism got an entirely new lease on life in the developed capitalist countries on the basis of a *rising* standard of living for the mass of the working class. That the massive economic revival, the long boom of the 1950s and 1960s, was due mainly to greatly increased state expenditure (in particular, *arms* expenditure) has been disputed, if rather implausibly, by both reformist and Marxist analysts. What cannot be disputed is the *fact* that Trotsky's prognosis was quite wrong. For the political consequences of the boom falsified the prediction that the *immediate* alternatives were *either* proletarian revolution *or* Bonapartist or fascist dictatorship presiding over "the eclipse of civilization." On the contrary, bourgeois democracy and reformist dominance of the workers' movement again became the norm in most of the developed countries.

An indispensable condition for this development was the survival of bourgeois regimes in the great upheavals of 1944–45, when the fascist states were being shattered by the combination of Allied military power and a rising tide of popular revolt. In most European countries, the social-democratic and Communist Parties grew rapidly in this critical phase to play a counterrevolutionary role (in Eastern as well as Western Europe) and the *decisive* counterrevolutionary role in France and Italy.

But Trotsky had taken for granted *both* the revival, in the first stages of revolt, of the established workers' parties (his writings on the Russian Revolution alone suffice to establish that beyond dispute) *and* their counterrevolutionary politics. It was because his perspective was one of economic catastrophe, mass pauperization, and the growth of totalitarian statist regimes as the *only* alternative to proletarian revolution *in the short term,* that he believed that this revival of reformism would be very short-lived—a sort of Kerensky interval. That is why he wrote with such confidence, late in 1938, "During the next ten years the program of the Fourth International will become the guide of millions, and these revolutionary millions will know how to storm earth and heaven."[11]

The mood of messianic expectation induced by such statements made sober and realistic assessments of actual shifts in working-class consciousness, alterations in the balance of class forces, and tactical changes to gain the maximum advantage from them (the essence of Lenin's political practice) extremely difficult for Trotsky's followers.

Mention must be made here of Trotsky's emphasis on the importance of those "transitional demands" that gave his 1938 program its popular name. "It is necessary," he wrote,

> to help the masses in the process of daily struggle to find the bridge between present demands and the socialist program of the revolution. This bridge should include a system of *transitional demands,* stemming from today's conditions and today's consciousness of wide layers of the working class and unalterably leading to one final conclusion: the conquest of power by the proletariat.[12]

Whether it is possible to find slogans or "demands" that meet these exacting specifications depends, very obviously, on circumstances. If, at a given time, "today's consciousness of wide layers" is decidedly non-revolutionary, then it will not be transformed by slogans. Changes in actual conditions are needed. The problem at each stage is to find and advance those slogans that not only strike a chord in at least some sections of the working class (ideally, of course, the whole of it), but that are also capable of leading to working-class *actions*. Often they will not be transitional in terms of Trotsky's very restricted definition.

Of course, Trotsky cannot be held responsible for the tendency of most of his followers to fetishize the notion of transitional demands and even the specific demands of the 1938 program—most obviously the "sliding scale of wages." The emphasis he gave to this matter was, however, excessive, and encouraged the belief that "demands" have some value independently of revolutionary organization in the working class.

The USSR, Stalinism, war, and the outcome

The Second World War began with the German attack on Poland, which was quickly followed by the partition of the territories of the Polish state between Hitler and Stalin. For nearly two years (from the summer of 1939 to the summer of 1941), Hitler and Stalin were allies, and in that period, Stalin's regime was able to annex the Baltic states Bessarabia and Bukovina, as well as the Western Ukraine and Western Belorussia.

From 1935 until then, Stalin's foreign policy had been directed toward achieving a military alliance with France and Britain against Hitler. The Popular Front policy of the Comintern was its counterpart. With the Hitler-Stalin Pact, the Communist Parties swung round to an "antiwar" position, the actual content of which was anything but revolutionary, until Hitler's attack on the USSR (after which, they became superpatriotic in the "Allied" countries).

The Hitler-Stalin Pact and the partition of Poland produced a revulsion against the USSR in left circles outside the Communist Parties (and a fair number of desertions from them, too), which had its impact on Trotskyist groups also. In the biggest of them, the American Socialist Workers Party, an opposition began to question Trotsky's slogan "unconditional defense of the USSR against imperialism," which followed from his definition of the USSR as a "degenerated workers' state," and, soon, that definition itself.

In the course of the dispute that followed, Trotsky gave his analysis of Stalinism in the USSR its final development, and considered—in order to reject—alternative positions. "Let us begin by posing the question of the nature of the Soviet state not on

the abstract sociological plane but on the plane of concrete political tasks," he wrote in September 1939.

> Let us concede for the moment that the bureaucracy is a new
> "class" and that the present regime in the USSR is a special sys-
> tem of class exploitation. What new political conclusions follow
> for us from these definitions? The Fourth International long ago
> recognized the necessity of overthrowing the bureaucracy by
> means of a revolutionary uprising of the toilers. Nothing else is
> proposed or can be proposed by those who proclaim the bureau-
> cracy to be an exploiting "class." The goal to be attained by the
> overthrow of the bureaucracy is the reestablishment of the rule
> of the Soviets, expelling from them the present bureaucracy.
> Nothing different can be proposed or is proposed by the leftist
> critics. It is the task of the regenerated soviets to collaborate
> with the world revolution and the building of a socialist society.
> The overthrow of the bureaucracy therefore presupposes the
> preservation of state property and of the planned economy....
> [I]nasmuch as the question of overthrowing the parasitic oli-
> garchy still remains linked with that of preserving the national-
> ized (state) property, we call the future revolution *political*.
> Certain of our critics (Ciliga, Bruno, and others) want, come
> what may, to call the future revolutions *social*. Let us grant this
> definition. What does it alter in essence? To the tasks of the rev-
> olution which we have enumerated it adds nothing whatsoever.[13]

It is, at first sight, a very powerful argument. But what, then,
of the defense of the USSR?

> The defense of the USSR coincides for us with the preparation of
> world revolution. Only those methods are permissible which do
> not conflict with the interests of the revolution. The defense of the
> USSR is related to the world socialist revolution as a tactical task
> is related to a strategic one. A tactic is subordinated to a strategic
> goal and in no case can be in contradiction to the latter.[14]

If, therefore, the requirements of the tactical operation do in fact
come into conflict with the strategic aim (as Trotsky's left-wing
critics believed it must), then the tactic—defense of the USSR—
must be sacrificed. On that basis, it would seem, Trotsky's critics
(those who considered themselves revolutionaries, that is) might
easily agree to differ with his terminology. Why split over mere
words?

In reality, Trotsky believed, much more was at stake. If the
bureaucracy really constituted a *class* and the USSR a new form
of *exploitative* society, Trotsky argued, then it could not be assumed that Stalinist Russia was the highly exceptional product

of unique circumstances, nor could it be assumed that it was soon doomed to disappear, as he was convinced it was.

Nor could matters be left there. Trotsky drew attention to a view that was "in the air," so to speak, at the end of the 1930s: that "bureaucratization" and "statization" were on the increase everywhere and indicated the shape of society to come—the "totalitarian statism" that he himself expected to develop unless the proletarian revolution followed the war. Orwell's *1984* (published in 1944) expressed the mood. Thus the question became confused with "the world historical perspective for the next decades if not centuries: Have we entered the epoch of social revolution and socialist society, or on the contrary the epoch of the declining society of totalitarian bureaucracy?"[15]

The alternatives were falsely put. The predictions of *The Bureaucratization of the World* (the title of a book by Bruno Rizzi, which Trotsky cited) were impressionistic, not the product of analysis. Nor did it follow that if the USSR were indeed an exploitative society, in the Marxist sense (this is what the apparently scholastic arguments of whether the bureaucracy was a "class" or a "caste"—Trotsky's term—were really about), that it was a *fundamentally new* type of exploitative society. Suppose it was a form of capitalism? If so, all the arguments about "world historical perspective" fall to the ground.

Trotsky was, of course, familiar with the concept of state capitalism. In *The Revolution Betrayed*, he wrote:

> Theoretically, to be sure, it is possible to conceive a situation in which the bourgeoisie as a whole constitutes itself as a stock company which, by means of its state, administers the whole national economy. The economic laws of such a regime would present no mysteries. A single capitalist, as is well known, receives in the form of profit, not that part of the surplus value which is created by the workers of his own enterprise, but a share of the combined surplus value created throughout the country proportionate to the amount of his own capital. Under an integral "state capitalism," this law of the equal rate of profit would be realized, not by devious routes—that is competition among different capitals—but immediately and directly through state bookkeeping. Such a regime never existed, however, and, because of profound contradictions among the proprietors themselves, will never exist—the more so since, in its quality of universal repository of capitalist property, the state would be too tempting an object of social revolution.[16]

Although, Trotsky thought, a system of "integral" (that is, total) state capitalism was theoretically possible, it would not come into existence. But suppose a bourgeoisie had been destroyed by a revolution, and the proletariat—due to its numerical and cultural weakness—failed to take, or having taken, failed to hold, power. What then? A bureaucracy, emerging as a privileged layer (as Trotsky had graphically described in the case of Stalin's bureaucracy in the USSR), becomes the master of the state and the economy. What, actually, would be its *economic* role? Would it not be a "substitute" capitalist class?

It cannot be argued that it is not capitalist because it controls the entire national economy. Trotsky had conceded that, in principle, a statized bourgeoisie could occupy that position. The only *serious* argument that could be advanced, on Trotsky's analysis, is the one he advanced himself: "The bureaucracy owns neither stocks nor bonds." Two points have to be made in this connection. First, the minor point, is that it is simply not true—anyone who can afford it in the USSR [at the time of this writing, in 1979—*ed.*] can buy various kinds of state bonds that bear interest and can be inherited by heirs on the payment of a modest inheritance tax *(much* lower than the corresponding taxes in the West, just as the top rates of income tax are *much* lower in the USSR than in most Western capitalist countries). Second, the major point, from a Marxist point of view, is that the individual capitalist's consumption is, as Marx himself put it, a "robbery perpetrated on accumulation"; that is, it is a drain on resources that could otherwise have gone toward accumulation and is certainly not the major consideration. The *major* consideration is who controls the accumulation process.

Returning to the question in 1939, Trotsky wrote:

> We have rejected, and still reject, this term [state capitalism] which, while it does correctly characterize certain features of the Soviet state, nevertheless ignores its fundamental difference from capitalist states, namely, the absence of a bourgeoisie as a class of property owners, the existence of the state form of ownership of the most important means of production, and finally planned economy made possible by the October Revolution.[17]

Trotsky consistently approached the analysis of Stalinist society from the standpoint of the *form of property,* not the actual social relations of production—although he often used that phrase and, indeed, treated the two as identical. But they are not. In criticizing Proudhon, Marx had explained:

> Thus to define bourgeois property is nothing less than to give an
> exposition of all the social relations of bourgeois production. To
> try to give a definition of property as of an independent relation,
> a category apart—an abstract eternal idea—can be nothing but
> an illusion of metaphysics or jurisprudence.[18]

And so with the USSR. The form of property (state ownership in this case) cannot be considered independently of the social relations of production. The *dominant* relation of
production in the USSR (especially after industrialization) was
the wage labor/capital relationship characteristic of capitalism—
and still is. The worker in the USSR sells a commodity, labor
power, in the same way as a worker does in the United States.
Nor is he or she paid in rations, like a slave, or in a share of the
produce, like a serf, but in money that is spent on commodities,
goods produced for sale.

Wage labor implies capital. There is no bourgeoisie in the
USSR. But there is certainly capital—as Marx defined capital.
Capital, it need hardly be said, does not, for a Marxist, consist
of machinery, raw materials, credits, and so on. Capital is "an
independent social *power,* i.e., as the power of a part of a society
it maintains itself and increases by exchange for *direct living
labor power.* The existence of a class which owns nothing but its
capacity for labor is a necessary prerequisite of capital. It is only
the domination of accumulated, past materialized labor over direct living labor which turns accumulated labor into capital."[19]
Such a state of affairs certainly exists in the USSR.

For Marx, the bourgeoisie's significance was as the "personification of Capital." In the USSR, the bureaucracy fulfils this
function. This last point Trotsky directly denied. For him, the
bureaucracy was merely "a gendarme" in the process of distrib-
ution, determining who gets what and when. But this is inseparable from the direction of the process of capital accumulation.
The implication that the bureaucracy does not direct the accumulation process, that is, does not act as the "personification"
of capital, will not stand a moment's examination. If not the bureaucracy, then who? Certainly not the working class.

The last point illustrates exactly the *essential* distinction between a genuine transitional society (workers' state, dictatorship
of the proletariat), in which wage labor will inevitably persist for
some time, and any form of capitalism. Collective working-class
control over the economy *modifies* (and eventually eliminates)

the wage labor/capital relationship. Take that away, and, in an industrial society, the power of capital is restored. The concept of a workers' state is meaningless without some degree of workers' control over society.

Of course, if the society of the USSR is described as a form of state capitalism, it must be conceded that it is a highly peculiar capitalist society—although, of course, it is *incomparably* closer to capitalist norms than to a workers' state, distorted or otherwise. A discussion of the peculiarities and dynamics of the USSR is not pertinent here. By far the best analysis will be found in Tony Cliff's *State Capitalism in Russia*.[20] What is relevant is Trotsky's failure to examine the actual relations of production in the USSR and its consequences. His final view was that

> [a] totalitarian regime, whether of Stalinist or fascist type, by its very essence can be only a temporary transitional regime. Naked dictatorship in history has generally been the product and symptom of an especially severe social crisis, and not at all of a stable regime. Severe crisis cannot be a permanent condition of society. A totalitarian state is capable of suppressing social contradictions during a certain period, but it is incapable of perpetuating itself. The monstrous purges in the USSR are most convincing testimony of the fact that Soviet society organically tends towards ejection of the bureaucracy.... Symptomatic of this oncoming death agony, by the sweep and monstrous fraudulence of his purge, Stalin testifies to nothing else but the incapacity of the bureaucracy to transform itself into a stable ruling class. Might we not place ourselves in a ludicrous position if we affixed to the Bonapartist oligarchy the nomenclature of a new ruling class just a few years or even a few months prior to its inglorious downfall?[21]

That downfall, it will be recalled, was to be expected either because the bureaucracy, "becoming ever more the organ of the world bourgeoisie...will overthrow the new forms of property," or because of a proletarian revolution (or, of course, foreign conquest). And it was to be expected in the near future—in "a few years or even a few months."

This was the assessment Trotsky bequeathed to his followers, and, like his perspective for Western capitalism, it would disorient them. But the existence of a wing of the bureaucracy wishing to restore capitalism proved to be a myth, at least on any relevant time scale. (Trotsky's belief in it was in flagrant contradiction with his own view of the possibility of totalitarian statism in the developed capitalist countries.)

The USSR emerged from the war stronger than before (relative to other powers) with the bureaucracy firmly in the saddle on the basis of nationalized industry. Moreover, it imposed regimes along the lines of the Russian model in Poland, Czechoslovakia, Hungary, Romania, Bulgaria, East Germany, and North Korea. As has been noted, "indigenous" Stalinist regimes came to power in Albania, Yugoslavia, and, a little later, in China and North Vietnam *without* significant direct intervention by the Russian army. Stalinism, evidently, was not in its "death agony," but was, in the absence of proletarian revolution, an alternative means of capital accumulation to "classical" state monopoly capitalism.

Deflected permanent revolution

The industrial working class played no role whatever in the Chinese Communist Party's conquest of power in 1948–49. Nor did workers play any role *inside* the CCP.

To take the last point first. Whereas, at the end of 1925, workers made up more than 66 percent of the CCP (peasants, 5.0 percent; the rest various urban petty bourgeoisie, among whom intellectuals were prominent), by September 1930, the proportion of workers, by the CCP's own data, was down to 1.6 percent.[22] Thereafter the figure was effectively zero until after Mao Tse-tung's forces had conquered China.

After the defeat of the "Canton Commune" at the end of 1927, the remnants of the CCP retreated deep into the countryside and resorted to guerrilla warfare. The peasant "Kiangsi Soviet Republic" was established, with fluctuating territories in Central China, and, when it was finally overrun by Chiang Kai-shek's forces in 1934, the Red Army undertook the "long march" to Shensi in the far northwest. This heroic operation, carried out against overwhelming odds, took the party-army (it being increasingly difficult to distinguish them) into an area utterly remote from urban life, modern industry, and the Chinese working class. Chu Teh, then the senior military commander, himself admitted, "The regions under the direction of the Communists are the most backward economically in the whole country."[23] And that country was *China,* then one of the most backward countries in the world.

There, for more than 10 years, the CCP forces carried on their struggle for survival against Chiang's armies (although nominally in alliance with Chiang after 1935) and the Japanese invaders. A state machine was constructed in this wholly peasant country on the usual hierarchical and authoritarian lines, consisting of declassed urban intellectuals at the top and peasants at the base. The Japanese army controlled all the areas with significant industrial development from 1937 to 1945, Manchuria (where there was industrial growth), and the coastal cities, where industry (and the proletariat) diminished.

With the Japanese surrender in 1945, Kuomintang (KMT) forces reoccupied most of China with U.S. help, but the utterly corrupt KMT regime was by then in an advanced state of disintegration. After attempts at a national KMT-CCP coalition government had broken down, the CCP conquered its demoralized and fragmenting opponent by purely military means. Massive U.S. military supplies and support to the KMT did not affect the outcome. KMT units, up to divisional and even corps strength, deserted wholesale—often complete with their generals.

Mao's strategy was to encourage these transfers of allegiance and to dampen *any* independent action by either peasants or workers—but especially the latter. The Communist Party was completely divorced from the working class. Before the fall of Peking, Lin Piao, the CCP army commander in the area and later Mao's heir, until his disgrace and death in 1971, issued a proclamation calling on the workers *not* to revolt but to "maintain order and continue in their present occupations. Kuomintang officials and police personnel of the city, county or other level of government institution...are enjoined to remain at their posts."[24] In January 1949, the KMT general in command of the Peking garrison surrendered. "Order" was preserved. One military governor took over from another.

It was the same when the CCP forces approached the Yangtze River and the great cities of Central China, such as Shanghai and Hankow, which had been the storm centers of revolution in 1925–26. A special proclamation issued under the signatures of Mao Tse-tung (head of government) and Chu Teh (army commander in chief) declared that

> workers and employees in all trades will continue to work and that business will continue as usual...officials of the Kuomintang...of various levels...[and] police personnel are to stay at their posts and obey the orders of the People's Liberation Army and the People's government.[25]

A strange revolution with "business as usual"! And so it went on to the end, and the proclamation of the "People's Republic" in October 1949. For these reasons, many of Trotsky's followers, including the leaders of the American Socialist Workers Party, denied that any *real* change had taken place for several years after 1949.

This proved to be wrong. A real overturn had occurred. But of what kind? Central to the theory of permanent revolution was the belief that the bourgeoisie in backward countries was incapable of leading a bourgeois revolution. That was confirmed, yet again. Equally central was the belief that only the working class could lead the mass of the peasantry and urban petty bourgeoisie in the democratic revolution, which would then fuse with the socialist revolution. That proved false. The Chinese working class, in the absence of any *mass* revolutionary workers' movement elsewhere in the world, remained passive. Nor did the peasantry refute Marx's view of their inability to play an *independent* political role. China 1949 was not a peasant movement.

Yet a revolution did occur. China was unified. The imperialist powers were excluded from Chinese soil. The agrarian question, if not "solved," was at any rate resolved so far as is possible, short of socialism, by the liquidation of landlordism. All the *essential* features of the bourgeois (or democratic) revolution, as understood by Trotsky himself, had been achieved, *except* political freedom in which the workers' movement could develop. They had been gained under the leadership of declassed intellectuals, who, in circumstances of general social breakdown, had built a peasant army and conquered by military means a regime rotten to the point of dissolution.

More than 2,000 years earlier, the Han dynasty itself had been founded in similar circumstances, under the leadership of a dynastic founder who, like Mao, came from a rich peasant family. But in the mid–20th century, survival for the new regime depended on industrialization. Chinese Stalinism had its roots in this necessity. It was a development for which Trotsky had failed to allow. In itself, that is neither surprising nor important. But, taken in conjunction with the other unexpected outcomes, it was to have a significant effect on the future of Trotsky's movement.

Only the Chinese case has been considered here—on the grounds of its overwhelming importance—but, earlier, Yugoslavia and Albania, and, later, North Vietnam and Cuba, showed certain similar features. The term "deflected permanent revolution" was introduced by Tony Cliff to describe the phenomenon,[26] so different from the theory of permanent revolution as Trotsky understood it.

Trotskyism after Trotsky

The political dilemmas that faced Trotsky's followers in the years after his death are relevant here for two reasons: first, because Trotsky himself believed in the supreme importance of the Fourth International, and, second, because of the further light they shed on the strengths and weaknesses of his ideas.

Trotsky's uncompromising revolutionary internationalism had steeled his followers to resist an accommodation with the "democratic" imperialism of the Allied camp during the Second World War, in spite of enormous pressure (including the pressure of the overwhelming mass of the working class and most of its best and most militant elements). They had indeed "swum against the stream" and emerged unbowed, in spite of persecution, imprisonment (in the U.S. and Britain, not to mention the Nazi-occupied countries), and executions, which eliminated a significant number of Trotskyist activists in Europe.

They had preserved the tradition against all the odds, recruited new members, and, in some cases at least, had become more working class in composition (this was certainly true of the Americans and the British). They were inspired and fortified by the vision of proletarian revolution in the near future. Thus, the main British group issued as a pamphlet in 1944 its 1942 perspectives document under the title *Preparing for Power!* There were not more than 200 to 300 of them at the time....

This magnificent disregard for immediate and apparently insuperable difficulties, combined with an unshaken faith in the future, was directly inspired by Trotsky's ideas. It was typical of Trotsky's followers everywhere.

Unfortunately, it had another side: a literal belief in the detailed accuracy of Trotsky's 1938–40 world outlook and predictions. Two distinct elements—revolutionary internationalism with faith in the ultimate triumph of socialism, and *specific* assessments of the prospects for capitalism and Stalinism—had become fused. Consequently, attention to the realities of a fast-changing situation became, in the eyes of the more "orthodox" of Trotsky's followers, akin to "revisionism." For several years after 1945, the movement was stuck, in its majority, in the "1938 groove."

When it eventually broke out, a number of different currents emerged, some preserving rather more elements of the authentic communist tradition, others a good many less. Their greatest weakness was their inability, for the most part, to resist fully the gravitational pull of Stalinism and, a little later, in the 1950s and 1960s, Third Worldism. This, in turn, led them away from sustained and single-minded concentration on recreating a revolutionary current in the industrial working class. So their predominantly petty-bourgeois character was reinforced, and a vicious circle was perpetuated.

All that said, it remains true that the heritage of Trotsky's lifelong struggle, the last years of which were carried on under conditions of incredible difficulty, is immensely valuable. To all those Marxists for whom Marxism is a synthesis of theory and *practice,* and not merely more or less learned commentary, it is an indispensable contribution to that synthesis today.

OTHER ESSAYS

TROTSKYISM REASSESSED

I'LL TRY to go through every idea that we are talking about and try to show the roots—where did it come from? Well let's start from when we broke from traditional Trotskyism. Now we broke on one simple thing, on the Russian question. That was the central issue of the time.

Now what did we accept from Trotsky? We accepted from Trotsky first of all that the working class is the agent of the socialist revolution; that the working class is the subject, not the object, but the subject of the socialist revolution; that the criterion to every change in society is what role the working class is playing actively in it....

The second thing we took straight from Trotsky is opposition to all rising bureaucracies. Thirdly we took from Trotsky the theory of the impossibility of socialism in one country, the fact that the pressure of world capitalism distorts development in every workers' state, in this case the Russian workers' state. We also accepted from Trotsky the question of the international nature of the revolution. These things we accepted from him. Now what were the defects, where didn't we agree?

Now what we thought was wrong with Trotsky was this, that if it was true that the working class was the agent of socialist revolution then the form of property is a bloody stupid criterion for deciding whether a state is a workers' state or not.... What the worker as an active agent cares about is the relations

First published in *International Socialism*, first series, issue 99, July 1977. It was reprinted in the *International Socialist Review*, issue 21, January–February 2002.

*in production, in other words what place the worker is in the
process of production; whether the worker comes to a state enterprise like the railways or private enterprise like ICI, he doesn't
come in relation to it as regards the form of property.... Trotsky
was not consistent enough in his own criteria of approach.*

*Second of all, planning is not a criterion for judging the na-
ture of the state because the question is who is being planned
and who is doing the planning.... The central thing is quite simply that we came to the conclusion that workers' control is the
decisive thing in evaluating a workers' state...and therefore a
workers' state is a state where the workers control their destiny.
It cannot be given to them. They have to do it themselves. Once
you abolish the element of workers' control, you abolish the
essence of the workers' state.*

*This was really the first theoretical thing we were faced with
and we are still with it, and when we are faced with new phenomena and new backward countries in the process of industrialization we use the same criteria and the same general
approach, and therefore for us it is not a surprise what happened
to Nkrumah, whatever happens in China....*
—Tony Cliff, from a speech on "Revolutionary Traditions," 1967

T ROTSKYISM HAS come to mean many different things
in the 37 years since Trotsky's death. Widely differing
and often mutually hostile groupings describe themselves
as Trotskyist, and it is not very profitable to attempt to set up a
standard of orthodoxy to judge them by. There are many Trotskyisms. Moreover, those of them that have persisted in an organized form over any considerable period of time have undergone
profound and sometimes repeated changes. For example, the
Mandel tendency is a very different political current today than
it was 10 years ago; and 10 years ago its political content was
markedly different from what it had been 10 years before that.

This article is mainly concerned with Trotskyism as a body of
revolutionary theory and practice as developed by Trotsky in the
decade of his third exile (1929–40). I shall argue, first, that Trotsky fought to preserve the authentic communist tradition, the
tradition of the early Communist International, in the only way
that it could or can be preserved, by developing it and embody-

ing it in a living movement; second, that the extremely unfavorable circumstances of the time not only defeated his efforts so far as immediate large-scale results were concerned, but also led to characteristic distortions and deformations of the tradition itself as it came to be embodied in the various Trotskyist groupings; third, that while Trotsky was aware of this and fought vigorously against certain of the deformations, he himself contributed to fostering some of them.

By "tradition" I mean the doctrine, strategy, and tactics developed by the Comintern in Lenin's time, a development in which Trotsky played a prominent part.

In 1932 Trotsky summarized the matter as follows:

> The International Left Opposition stands on the ground of the first four Congresses of the Comintern. This does not mean that it bows before every letter of its decisions, many of which had a purely conjunctural character and have been contradicted by subsequent events. But all the essential principles (in relation to imperialism and the bourgeois state, to democracy and reformism; problems of insurrection; the dictatorship of the proletariat; on relations with the peasantry and the oppressed nations; soviets; work in the trade unions; parliamentarianism; the policy of the united front) remain even today the highest expression of proletarian strategy in the epoch of the general crisis of capitalism.[1]

There is an important omission here, the nature of the Communist Party—an active, conscious section of the *working class*. Otherwise, it is an accurate condensation of the *indispensable* theoretical basis of a revolutionary Marxist movement.

The post-1923 Comintern deviated rapidly from the line of the first four congresses, first in an opportunist direction (1924–28, with a partial "left" oscillation in 1924), then in an ultra-left direction (1928–34), and finally it completely abandoned the whole basis of communist politics with the lurch into popular frontism from 1935 onward.

Trotsky's superb analysis of these developments, and untiring struggle to reintegrate the authentic tradition with the actual movement, was an enormously important achievement. Our own politics rest upon it. All the more reason, then, to look critically at the weaknesses of the Trotskyist heritage.

The most glaring, of course, is that referred to by Cliff in the speech quoted here. Until late 1933, Trotsky had maintained that the working classes of the USSR had the possibility of "recapturing" the bureaucratized state by peaceful and legal means, "without a new revolution, with the methods and on the road of reform."[2]

However unrealistic in fact, this position enabled Trotsky to reconcile the Marxist conception of the working class as the active agent of the socialist revolution with his description of the USSR under Stalin's dictatorship as a workers' state.

Once this "reformist" perspective was abandoned, as it was in October 1933, there was a built-in contradiction in Trotsky's theoretical system. At the time it did not have any very important practical consequences. The USSR, which indisputably originated from a genuine proletarian revolution, could be regarded as a very special case.

After the Second World War, the creation, by means other than proletarian revolution, of a whole series of states of the same general type exploded the contradiction. The theoretical coherence of Trotskyism—of Trotsky's own Trotskyism—was shattered. In the late 1940s and early 1950s, the Trotskyist movement—more or less united until then—splintered into fragments, largely, though not wholly, under the impact of the enormous upsurge of Stalinism with the emergence of the "socialist camp," and the inability of the Trotskyists to emancipate themselves from Trotsky's error.

But there were other defects in the tradition, too, defects whose seeds were sown in Trotsky's lifetime. They now flourish like rank weeds in the various Trotskyisms.

Propagandism and its price

The opposition is now taking shape on the basis of principled ideological demarcation, and not on the basis of mass actions.... Mass actions tend as a rule to wash away secondary and episodic differences and to aid the fusion of friendly and close tendencies. Conversely, ideological groupings in a period of stagnation or ebb tide disclose a great tendency towards differentiation, splits, and internal struggles. We cannot leap out of the period in which we live. We must pass through it. A clear, precise ideological differentiation is unconditionally necessary. It prepares future successes.
—Trotsky, "The groupings in the Communist Opposition," 1929

The first problem facing Trotsky at the outset of his last exile was how to pull together a coherent oppositional movement within, or at any rate oriented on, the Communist International.

An *independent* movement, a movement seeking to build directly in the working class, was ruled out. "The cry about a second party and a Fourth International is merely ridiculous.... We do not identify the Communist International with the Stalinist bureaucracy."[3]

The perspective was to influence the course of the Communist Parties in the hope that the combined effect of events and the criticism of the Left Opposition could shift them toward realistic revolutionary policies. As in the USSR, Trotsky's aim was *reform* of the existing communist movement, not the creation of a new movement.

The policy failed. The destruction of the German labor movement by the Nazis in 1933, as a result in large part of the criminal lunacy of the Comintern's "Third Period" ultraleftism, which paralyzed the German Communist Party, marked the end of any realistic hope of its success.

Yet it was certainly correct to try. There was no chance at that time of building independent parties. The enormous prestige of the Russian Revolution, still a recent event, had been inherited by Stalin, and some of it had rubbed off onto the Stalinist leaders of the Comintern sections. Moreover, these were the years of the greatest slump in the history of capitalism and, *simultaneously,* of the first five-year plan. The contrast between mass unemployment and industrial decline in the West and the feverish expansion of Russian industry was stark and clear to millions of workers.

And there was Germany—"the key to the international situation," as Trotsky rightly said. Here was a highly industrialized country with the biggest working class in Europe and the biggest Communist Party in the world (for, as Trotsky also said, the CPSU was no longer a party, but a bureaucratic apparatus) plunging into a prolonged social crisis that could be resolved only by the proletarian revolution or the fascist counterrevolution.

To write off the KPD (which claimed 250,000 members in 1932) was to concede victory to Hitler in advance. The KPD however, like all the Comintern sections, maintained that the social democrats—re-christened "social fascists" since 1929—were the main enemy, not the Nazis, and denounced Trotsky's call for a workers' united front against fascism as "the theory of an utterly bankrupt fascist and counterrevolutionary."[4]

The brilliance and cogency of Trotsky's writings on the German crisis have rarely been equaled and have never been excelled by any Marxist, not excluding Marx and Lenin. But ideas become a force only to the extent that they move people; social- ist ideas become significant only to the extent that they become rooted in the working class.

The contrast between Trotsky's writings and the state of the German Trotskyists on the ground was painful. They were a handful. And they were almost all socially marginal people quite outside the workers' movement. The German opposition, Trot- sky noted in 1932, had failed to recruit even "ten native factory workers." It consisted largely of "individualistic, petty-bour- geois, and lumpen elements who cannot tolerate discipline."[5]

The power of the Stalinists had forced the German Trotsky- ists—and not only the Germans, as we shall see—into a political ghetto, which also had a definite *social* location: the fringes of the intellectual section of the petty bourgeoisie. This is the most im- portant simple fact about Trotsky's followers. They originated, for the most part, within a petty-bourgeois milieu, and, with rare exceptions, they could not break out of it. The political conse- quences of this fact profoundly distorted their development.

One of the exceptions, partially at any rate, was the Ameri- can group. They had in their ranks one of Trotsky's most consid- erable non-Russian followers, [James] Cannon, an ex-CP leader of working-class background and considerable experience in the movement, and one or two others—[Vincent] Dunne, [Arne] Swabeck, [Hugo] Oehler—of similar origin. Yet here is Cannon's own description of the membership in the early 1930s:

> We begin to recruit from sources none too healthy.... Freaks al- ways looking for the most extreme expression of radicalism, misfits, windbags, chronic oppositionists who had been thrown out of half a dozen organizations.... Many people came to us who had revolted against the Communist Party not for its bad sides but for its good sides; that is, the discipline of the party, the subordination of the individual to the decisions of the party in current work. A lot of dilettantish, petty-bourgeois minded peo- ple who couldn't stand any kind of discipline, many of the new- comers made a fetish of democracy.... All the people of this type have one common characteristic; they like to discuss things without limit or end.... They can all talk; and not only can but *will*; and everlastingly, on every question.[6]

In more moderate terms—too moderate, for the French sec- tion was one of the worst of the lot—a historian of French Trot- skyism describes the main French group in Paris: "The Paris region included a large proportion of intellectuals, former communist cadres now cut off from their base."[7]

Trotskyism had been *forced* into this milieu and Trotsky was acutely aware of the need to break out of it. Objective conditions made it extremely difficult. Subjective circumstances—the social nature of the Trotskyists—became an additional obstacle. But Trotsky compounded the difficulties. He denounced "closed circles," "literary arrogance," "conceit and grand airs." Yet, at the same time, he insisted: "The cadres can only be educated if all questions are debated by the *whole* Opposition.... Questions of general revolutionary tactics and internal questions should be the property of *every* member of the Opposition organization."[8]

This approach inevitably further strengthened the "intellectualist" tendencies to which the petty-bourgeois nature of the movement gave rise, and made effective involvement in the workers' movement still more difficult. It further strengthened the trend toward "natural selection" of those who wished to "discuss things without limit," the trend to the "one continuous stew of discussion" of which Cannon complained.

Trotsky encouraged the various sections of the Opposition to interest themselves in each others' activities, he wrote interminable circulars and epistles explaining, say, to the Belgians why the French fell out, to the Greeks why the German comrades were in disagreement, to the Poles what were the points at issue between different sets of the Belgian or of the American opposition, and so on and so forth. He did all this in the belief that he was educating and training a new layer of communists, new "cadres of revolution."[9]

Some of this was doubtless unavoidable, a necessary consequence of the propagandist stance that, in turn, was politically correct at the time. Some, but by no means all. Trotsky's method legitimized and encouraged the pretentions of people who, though they could not gain so much as a toe-hold in their own working-class movement, felt able to pronounce on the details of policy and tactics all over the world. It fostered the very "conceit and grand airs" that were such an obstacle to serious work. It helped to give the Trotskyist groups an exotic, hothouse atmosphere remote from the world of working-class militants and thus perpetuated the petty-bourgeois nature of the groups. To all this, Trotsky contributed, in spite of quite opposite intentions. The basic fallacy was that cadres can be trained *outside* the class struggle. And the baleful influence of this tradition was to persist, a poison in the bloodstream of the movement long after propagandism had been officially abandoned as a struggle orientation.

One particular aspect of the evil, factionalism, took a strong hold in the early period and was never subsequently entirely eliminated. Some factional struggles are an inevitable overhead cost in the growth of any serious revolutionary organization. Permanent, persistent factionalism, however, is not an overhead cost, but a disease. As Cannon wrote later: "There is no greater abomination in the workers' political movement than a permanent faction. There is nothing that can demoralize the internal life of a party more efficiently than a permanent faction."[10]

A lightminded toleration of factionalism certainly cannot be attributed to Trotsky. His approach to the development of cadres nonetheless encouraged it precisely because it enabled petty-bourgeois cliques to justify their existence on "theoretical" grounds.

Entrism and its outcome

The period of existence as a Marxist circle ingrafts invariably habits of an abstract approach to the problems of the workers' movement. He who is unable to step in time over the confines of the circumscribed existence becomes transformed into a conservative sectarian.... To a Marxist, discussion is an important but a functional instrument of the class struggle. To the sectarian, discussion is a goal in itself.

—Trotsky, "Sectarianism, Centrism, and the Fourth International," 1935

After Hitler gained power, Trotsky abandoned the reformist orientation toward the Communist Parties. It was necessary, given the utter bankruptcy shown by the failure to even attempt seriously to resist the Nazis, to create new revolutionary parties. Again the political judgment was inescapable. Within two years the Comintern had swung from the ultra-left pseudo-radicalism of the "Third Period" to Popular Frontism—collaboration with the social democrats and "progressive" bourgeois parties on the basis of "defending democracy." The struggle for socialism was thrown out the window.

How could new revolutionary parties (and a new international) be created? It was, and is, an immensely difficult task. Social democracy had been built in the late 19th and early 20th centuries when, so to say, there was a clear space, when rival *workers'* parties were not, in most cases, significant. The Communist Parties came out of the splits in the social democracy on a rising revolutionary tide.

Neither of these conditions existed in the 1930s. At the same time, in these years, the anti-Trotskyist campaign orchestrated from Moscow reached its height. Trotsky was an agent of Hitler and the Japanese emperor—as the line in the period of the Moscow trials goes, "The Trotskyists were fascist agents in the workers' movement."

Any realistic assessment of the failure of Trotskyism to take root, of the failure of successive attempts to break out of isolation, must put overwhelming emphasis on the profoundly unfavorable situation in which the Trotskyists were placed.

In 1939, on the eve of the war, and after many failures, Trotsky frankly surveyed the situation:

> We are not progressing politically. Yes, it is a fact, which is an expression of a general decay of the workers' movements in the last fifteen years. It is the more general cause. When the revolutionary movement in general is declining, when one defeat follows another, when fascism is spreading over the world, when the official "Marxism" is the most powerful organization of deception of the workers, and so on, it is an inevitable situation that the revolutionary elements must work against the general historic current, even if our ideas, our explanations, are as exact and wise as one can demand.
>
> But the masses are not educated by prognostic theoretical conception, but by the general experiences of their lives. It is the most general explanation—the whole situation is against us.[11]

It was true. The blemishes of the Trotskyists in these circumstances are of significance only insofar as they became institutionalized and transmitted to later generations. Three issues of that period are still significant.

To restate the problem as it was, the groups were weak, petty bourgeois, and more or less outside the workers' movement. How to break out of the ghetto, proletarianize Trotskyism, and pull significant numbers of workers into new communist parties?

After initial attempts to "regroup" with various left social-democratic/centrist formations (mainly unsuccessfully), Trotsky proposed entry into the social-democratic parties. Strictly speaking, this was argued for specific cases—France at first—but it came to be generalized in practice. The argument was that the social democrats were moving left, creating a more favorable climate for revolutionary work, that they were attracting new layers of workers, and were an incomparably more proletarian environment than the propaganda groups Trotskyism inhabited.

The operation was conceived as a short-term one: a sharp, hard fight with the reformists and centrists to rally the potentially revolutionary forces, then split and found the party. "Entry into a reformist-centrist party in itself does not include a long-term perspective. It is only a stage which under certain conditions can be limited to an episode."[12]

The first issue was that of the internal democracy of the Trotskyist groups. It was an issue because in many if not most sections the opponents of the "French Turn" (entry) were the majority. Democratic centralism was part of their creed. But what did it mean? An open reciprocal relationship between the revolutionary party and its working-class base, a relationship that requires a correspondingly open party regime? That, of course, was what it was supposed to mean, but very obviously that did not apply to the Trotskyist groups. They were not parties and they were not working class. Or did it mean commitment to accept the majority decision of a petty-bourgeois group?

In practice Trotsky was extremely ruthless. While insisting, rightly, on the maximum feasible internal democracy for *educational* reasons, he insisted on purges and splits with those of his cadres who were deeply wedded to the intellectual milieu. "A revolutionary organization cannot develop without purging itself, especially under conditions of legal work, when not infrequently chance, alien, and degenerate elements gather under the banner of revolution."[13] And again, "The [French] League is passing through a first crisis under the banner of great and clear revolutionary criteria. Under these conditions, a splitting off of a part of the League will be a great step forward. It will reject all that is unhealthy, crippled, and incapacitated; it will give a lesson to the vacillating and irresolute elements; it will harden the better section of the youth."[14]

This approach was denounced by sundry opponents as undemocratic, authoritarian, and so on, all of which was a reflection of the unwillingness of these opponents to break from their background. Because, in the end, entry failed in its strategic aim, because much of the Marxist movement remained petty bourgeois, these attitudes, "making a fetish of democracy" without analysis of the *class* and *political* content, recurred again and again and still recur today.

The second issue was the reemergence of propagandism under a new guise—program fetishism. The arguments with reformists and centrists pushed Trotskyists in the direction of defending the fundamentals of communism rather than applying them in actual working-class struggles. The defense of "the program" inevitably loomed very large, and for some, came to have an almost mystical significance. Some of Trotsky's own formulations (though not his practice) lent some color to this deviation. But Marxism is a synthesis of theory and practice. No program is of any value unless it leads to practical activity necessary to achieve its aims. Again, it has to be stressed that circumstances *forced* a degree of program fetishism on the Trotskyist groups. But this fetishism—the attribution of *independent* power to an inanimate object, a body of writings—did not always disappear when the conditions fostering it had altered. It is still very much alive among some of the Trotskyist grouplets of today.

In particular, one document, *The Death Agony of Capitalism and the Tasks of the Fourth International,* the 1938 transitional program, came to acquire a status close to that of holy writ in the eyes of many Trotskyists. It is a blend of concrete political analysis, which proved to be faulty in a number of important respects; tactical recipes related to the analysis; history; and basic communist ideas. That it was a misleading guide is much less important than the fact that most of Trotsky's followers proved incapable of a critical reappraisal. They did not learn from Trotsky's own unhesitating rejection of positions he had long held when they were clearly inapplicable.

In the end, of course, fetishism too has material roots. Forced back into the specific social environment in which they had begun, powerless to affect the course of events, some succumbed to a quasi-religious faith—for that, after all, is what program fetishism is, no matter how stridently its adherents proclaim their atheism.

The third issue was parasitism. The entrist operates inside an alien body. A certain degree of adaptation to the norms of that body is unavoidable. Adaptation, however, can mean not only care in language, etc., but a shift in political emphasis. Already, in the original short-term entry in France, this occurred. Trotsky wrote of "those [in R. Molinier's circle] who, exhilarated by the initial successes, were anticipating a long perspective of untroubled activity within the reformist party. And it was precisely these elements, leaning on new allies and semi-allies on the right, who began to exercise a very big influence on the political line of our group."[15]

When, in the 1950s and subsequently, long-term entry, the so-called "entry sui-generis" or "deep entry," was adopted by certain Trotskyist groups, the political adaptation of the parasite to the host went very far. It became hard to tell the entrist from his prey. This was accompanied by another sort of mysticism, the belief in "profound historic forces" for socialism, *independent* of actual working-class action.

Here is a specimen, taken from a "World Congress" resolution of the Pablo-Mandel tendency in 1957:

> The fundamental change in the international situation and in the internal situation within the USSR, characterized on the one hand by the world-wide upsurge of the revolutionary forces since 1943 and especially since the victory of the Chinese revolution, and on the other hand by the spectacular successes of planification which made the USSR the second power in the world, destroyed the objective bases for the full sway and power of the Soviet bureaucracy. The evolution of the international correlation of forces in favor of the anti-capitalist social strata was paralleled by an evolution of the correlation of forces inside the USSR in favor of the proletariat and at the cost of the bureaucracy.[16]

And the conclusion?

> The concrete march of the world revolution throughout the world after the Second World War has made of the Chinese and colonial revolutions the principal motor of the world revolution. In reaching the USSR and the countries dominated by the Soviet bureaucracy, the revolutionary wave makes of the political revolution against this bureaucracy the second most powerful motor of the world revolution.[17]

Great historic forces are very comforting things! This deformation, too, is still present in various Trotskyisms.

The heritage

When all is said, the struggle carried on by Trotsky and his followers (with all the weaknesses) did preserve an authentic communist current, if not in the working class then at least on the fringes. The Fourth International, as a serious proposition, was stillborn, but a degree of continuity from the revolutionary period of the

Comintern was maintained in the teeth of near-insurmountable difficulties. We are part of that continuity today; the tradition Trotsky fought for is our tradition.

Traditional Trotskyism, that of Trotsky himself, became partially irrelevant in the same way that Lenin's "democratic dictatorship of the proletariat and peasantry" became irrelevant in 1917. The various Trotskyisms of today are deformed in several ways and unlikely to be capable, in most cases, of further positive development. But the revolutionary essence of Trotsky's politics survives. That is the important thing.

AGAINST THE STREAM:
THE ORIGINS OF
THE FOURTH INTERNATIONAL

THE INTERNATIONAL Socialist Tendency derives ultimately from the Fourth Internationalist movement. It
recognizes the impossibility of purely national "roads to
socialism" and the necessity for the recreation of a revolutionary
international. Immense difficulties stand in the way. A good deal
can be learned about these, and the possibilities of overcoming
them, by an assessment of the first great attempt, Trotsky's
struggle to build a revolutionary alternative to Stalinism and social democracy from 1933 onward. The sequel, the political decline and disintegration of the Fourth Internationalist
movement, will be discussed in a subsequent article.

The August 4 of the Communist International

*An organization which was not roused by the thunder of fascism
and which submits docilely to such outrageous acts of bureaucracy demonstrates thereby that it is dead and cannot be revived.... In all our subsequent work it is necessary to take as our
point of departure the historical collapse of the official Communist International.*

> —Trotsky, *It Is Necessary to Build Communist Parties
> and an International Anew*

First published in *International Socialism,* first series, issue 53,
October–December 1972.

The movement for a Fourth International was born out of a catastrophic defeat for the working class. In January 1933, Hitler came to power and destroyed, in a matter of weeks, the strongest labor movement in the world. He did so without resistance. The collapse of the world's biggest social-democratic party was to be expected. It was a continuation of the collapse of the international social democracy on August 4, 1914. The collapse of the German Communist Party, the largest party in the Communist International outside the USSR, was a different matter altogether.

The point was not simply that the party had been defeated. It was that it had not made any attempt to fight. Its extreme verbal radicalism had gone hand in hand with political passivity. Since 1928–29, the German party, together with all the other Comintern sections, had pursued the ultra-left policies of the so-called Third Period, the period of "ascending revolutionary struggles." In practice, this had meant that, at a time when fascism was a real and growing danger, especially in Germany, the social democrats were regarded as the main enemy. "In this situation of growing imperialist contradictions and sharpening of the class struggle," declared the Tenth Plenum of the Executive Committee of the Communist International (ECCI) in 1929,

> fascism becomes more and more the dominant method of bourgeois rule. In countries where there are strong social-democratic parties, fascism assumes the particular form of social fascism, which to an ever increasing extent serves the bourgeoisie as an instrument for paralyzing the activity of the masses in the struggle against the regime of fascist dictatorship.[1]

It followed that there could be no question of attempting to force the mass social-democratic organizations and the trade unions they controlled into a united front against the fascists. They were themselves social fascists. Indeed, added the Eleventh Plenum of the ECCI (1931), social democracy "is the most active factor and pacemaker in the development of the capitalist state towards fascism."[2]

This completely false estimate of the nature of fascism and the assumption that "strong social-democratic parties" and a "regime of fascist dictatorship" could co-exist led to the view that already, before Hitler became chancellor, Germany was fascist. "In Germany...the Von Papen-Schleicher Government, with the help of the Reichswehr, the Stahlhelm, and the national socialists, has established a form of fascist dictatorship," proclaimed the Twelfth Plenum of the ECCI in 1932.[3]

Against these criminal policies, Trotsky and his handful of supporters had written and argued, with increasing urgency and desperation, over the years. Organized from 1930 as the International Communist League (ICL), they regarded themselves as a faction of the Comintern that had been bureaucratically excluded by the Stalinists and that was fighting to reform the regime in the USSR and in the Comintern. They firmly rejected any idea of forming a rival party. "All eyes to the Communist Party. We must explain to it. We must convince it."[4]

The central theme of all their propaganda is summed up in the title of one of Trotsky's most famous pamphlets, *For a Workers' United Front against Fascism*. But notwithstanding the brilliance and cogency of Trotsky's arguments, the German party, with its quarter of a million members and its six million votes (in 1932), held fast to its fatal course. It followed Stalin's disastrous prescriptions of the Third Period and "social fascism" to the end, notwithstanding some desperate thirteenth-hour maneuvers. It was smashed without resistance along with the "social fascists," the trade unions, and each and every one of the independent political, cultural, and social organizations created by the German working class over 60 years.

In 1931, Trotsky had described Germany as "the key to the international situation":

> On the direction in which the solution of the German crisis develops will depend not only the fate of Germany itself (and that is already a great deal) but the fate of Europe, the destiny of the entire world, for many years to come.[5]

It was an accurate forecast. The defeat of the German working class transformed world politics. The failure of the Communist Party to even attempt resistance was a blow as heavy as the capitulation of the social democracy in 1914. It was the August 4 of the Comintern.

In search of a new Zimmerwald

Up till now these left socialist organizations have held against our refusal to break with the Comintern and to build independent parties. This sharp disagreement has now been removed by the march of development.... The Bolshevik-Leninists must enter

into open discussion with the revolutionary socialist organizations. As the basis for discussion we shall propose the eleven points adopted by our Pre-Conference.
—Trotsky, *It Is Necessary to Build Communist Parties and an International Anew*

In April 1933, the ECCI Presidium met and declared:

> Having heard Comrade Heckert's report on the situation in Germany, the presidium of the ECCI states that the political line and the organizational policy followed by the Central Committee of the Communist Party of Germany, with Comrade Thaelmann at its head, up to the Hitlerite coup, and at the moment when it occurred, was completely correct.[6]

It further resolved:

> Despite fascist terror, the revolutionary surge in Germany will rise; the revolutionary resistance of the masses to fascism is bound to grow. The establishment of the open fascist dictatorship, which is destroying all democratic illusions among the masses and liberating them from social-democratic influence, is accelerating the rate of Germany's advance towards the proletarian revolution.[7]

This lunatic assessment drove Trotsky to conclude that the Comintern was now irrevocably bankrupt, that new parties and a new international must be created.

For some months longer, he resisted the view that reform was no longer possible in the USSR itself. In an article explaining the fundamental change in the line of the Left Opposition, he wrote, "With favorable internal and, above all, international conditions, the edifice of the workers' state can be regenerated on the social foundation of the Soviet Union without a new revolution."[8] Indeed, this view was an essential component of the conception of the USSR as a "degenerated workers' state" as that conception had hitherto been understood by Trotskyists. In the summer of 1933, this was a problem for the future. The immediate questions were what forces were available to form the basis of the new international and what was to be its programmatic basis?

The ICL had finally formulated its 11-point program in February 1933, just after Hitler's victory. It was essentially still the program of a *faction* concerned with the orientation and policies of a much larger organization. It summed up the experience of the Left Opposition's 10-year struggle against Stalinism in the USSR and internationally.

The International Left Opposition stands on the ground of the first four congresses of the Comintern. This does not mean that it bows before every letter of its decisions, of which many had a purely temporary character and in individual practical consequences have been refuted by subsequent practice. But in all the essential principles (relation to imperialism and to the bourgeois state; the dictatorship of the proletariat; the relation to the peasantry and to all oppressed nations; soviets; work in the trade unions; parliamentarism; the policy of the united front) remain even today the highest expression of proletarian strategy in the epoch of the general crisis of capitalism.

The Left Opposition rejects the revisionist decisions of the 5th and 6th World Congresses and considers necessary a radical restatement of the program of the Comintern, in which the gold of Marxism has been rendered completely worthless by the centristic alloy.

In accordance with the spirit and the sense of the decisions of the first four World Congresses, and in continuation of these decisions, the Left Opposition sets up the following principles, develops them theoretically, and carries them through practically:

1. The independence of the proletarian party, always and under all conditions; condemnation of the Kuomintang policy of 1924–28; condemnation of the policy of the Anglo-Russian Committee; condemnation of Stalin's theory of two-class (worker and peasant) parties and the whole practice based on this theory; condemnation of the policy of the Amsterdam Congress, in which the Communist Party was dissolved in the pacifist swamp.

2. Recognition of the international and thereby of the permanent character of the proletarian revolution; rejection of the theory of socialism in one country as well as of the policy of national bolshevism that complements it in Germany (platform of "National Liberation").

3. Recognition of the Soviet state as a workers' state in spite of the growing degeneration of the bureaucratic regime; unconditional command that every worker defend the Soviet state against imperialism as well as against internal counterrevolution.

4. Condemnation of the economic policy of the Stalinist faction both in its stages of *economic opportunism* in 1923 and 1928 (struggle against "overindustrialization" and staking all on the kulaks), as well as its stage of *economic adventurism* in 1928 to 1932 (overstretched tempo of industrialization, thoroughgoing collectivization, administrative liquidation of the kulaks as a class). Condemnation of the criminal bureaucratic legend that "the soviet state has already entered into socialism." Recognition of the necessity of a return to the realistic economic policies of Leninism.

5. Recognition of the necessity of systematic communist work in the proletarian mass organizations, particularly in the re-

formist trade unions, condemnation of the theory and practice of the Red Trade Union organization in Germany and similar constructions in the other countries.

6. Rejection of the formula of the "Democratic dictatorship of the proletariat and peasantry" as a separate regime distinguished from the *dictatorship of the proletariat,* which carries along the peasant and oppressed masses in general behind it; rejection of the anti-Marxist theory of the peaceful "growing over" of the democratic dictatorship into the socialist one.

7. Recognition of the necessity of mobilizing the masses under *transitional slogans* corresponding to the concrete situation in each country, and particularly under *democratic slogans* insofar as it is a question of struggle against feudal relations, national oppression, or different varieties of open imperialistic dictatorship (fascism, Bonapartism, etc.).

8. Recognition of the necessity of a developed *united front policy* with respect to the mass organizations of the working class, both of trade union and political character, including the social democracy as a party. Condemnation of the ultimatist slogan "only from below," which in practice means a refusal of the united front and consequently the refusal to create soviets. Condemnation of the opportunistic application of the united front policy as in the Anglo-Russian Committee (bloc with the leaders without the masses and against the masses); double condemnation of the policy of the present German Central Committee, which combines the ultimatist slogan "only from below" with opportunistic practice on the occasion of parliamentary pacts with the leaders of the social democracy.

9. Rejection of the theory of *social fascism* and of the whole—bound up with it, as serving fascism on the one hand and the social democracy on the other.

10. The struggle for the regrouping of the revolutionary forces of the world's working class under the banner of International Communism. Recognition of the necessity of the creation of a genuine Communist International capable of applying the principles enumerated above.

11. Recognition of *party democracy,* not only in words but also in fact; ruthless condemnation of the Stalinist plebiscitary regime (gagging the will and the thought of the party, the rule of the usurpers, deliberate suppression of information from the party, etc.).

The fundamental principles enumerated above, which are of basic importance for the strategy of the proletariat in the present period, place the Left Opposition in a position of irreconcilable hostility to the Stalinist fraction which currently dominates the USSR and the CI [Communist International]. The recognition of these principles on the basis of the decisions of the first four congresses of the Comintern is an indispensable condition for the acceptance of single organizations, groups and persons into the composition of the International Left Opposition.[9]

The actual strength of the forces at the disposal of the ICL at this stage was tiny. The Spanish group, which had in its ranks the nationally known former Communist Party (CP) leaders Nin and Andrade, was operating in a country where a pre-revolutionary situation was developing. But it was soon to defect to unite with the right-wing communist group led by Maurin to form the Workers' Party of Marxist Unity (POUM), which was to claim 7,000 members by the end of 1935. The price of this amalgamation was the acceptance of the Maurinist position, which was also that of the Comintern, that the coming Spanish revolution was a bourgeois-democratic one, that the proletarian revolution was not on the agenda. This finalized the break between Nin and Trotsky that had occurred in 1934 on the issue of entry into the Socialist Party. Trotsky had no choice. The POUM's perspective was essentially the same as that which had led the Chinese CP to disaster in 1925–27. "A false point of departure during a revolution," he wrote, "is invariably translated in the course of events into the language of defeat." It was yet another accurate forecast.

The fact remained that the ICL had lost the only European section that was in a position to intervene in a real revolutionary movement in the immediate future. Its largest section, the Greek Archio-Marxist organization, which claimed 2,000 members in 1930, was not really Trotskyist and, after a period of denouncing the allegedly "centrist" tendencies of the ICL, broke away to the right.[10]

The most important remaining group, the French, had not more than 200 members, riven by the rival factions of Naville and Molinier and effectively isolated from the working class. There were small groups in Belgium, Britain, Poland, and Czechoslovakia, and for the rest, only émigrés, individuals, or tiny coteries.

In Asia, the Chinese Trotskyists, dispersed and persecuted by the Kuomintang and the Stalinists alike, could not develop a real organization in the face of the repression. In the rest of the continent there were, at best, a few small groups of intellectuals. The Vietnamese, later to form a fairly large group, were at this stage still émigrés in Paris.

Africa was a blank, apart from a group in the Union of South

Africa. The available literature does not reflect much activity in South America at this time.

Only in the U.S. was there a real nucleus. The American Trotskyists were to form, for the next 20 or so years, the strongest and most stable component of the international movement. In 1933, they were still very small. In 1931, they had reported only 154 members, but they were qualitatively superior to most of the Europeans. Potentially they were a force and were soon to make their first breakthrough in the Minneapolis strikes of 1934.

The numerical weakness was not the only problem. A little earlier Trotsky had noted that the German section had failed to recruit even "ten native factory workers."[11] Of the French sections in the early 1930s, Craipeau wrote, "The Paris region [of the Communist League] included a high proportion of responsible communists of long standing, henceforth cut off from their base. This predominance of the intellectuals wasn't surprising. For a rank-and-file worker, the discussions on the Anglo-Soviet Committee or the Kuomintang appeared completely abstract. *Their* preoccupations were elsewhere."[12] Even the Americans, who were better off than most in this respect, suffered from "a lot of dilettantish, petty-bourgeois minded people." Their best-known leader, James P. Cannon, complained:

> All the people of this type have one common characteristic: they like to discuss things without limit or end. The New York branch of the Trotskyist movement in those days was just one continuous stew of discussion.... Walled off from the vanguard represented by the Communist movement and without contact with the living mass movement of the workers, we were thrown in upon ourselves and subject to this invasion.[13]

Trotsky was under no illusions that a new international could be created with such forces. Just as Lenin had participated, though critically, in the attempts of left-wing social democrats to resume international connections in 1915–16 at Zimmerwald and Kienthal, so now Trotsky oriented the ICL toward the various left social-democratic and centrist groupings that were outside the Second and Third Internationals. In the summer of 1933, the British ILP, recently disaffiliated from the Labor Party, called a conference in Paris to discuss the new situation created by Hitler's victory. Fourteen parties and groups, including the ICL, participated.

On the right was the Norwegian Labor Party (NAP), a mass,

left social-democratic organization that was to become, within two years, His Norwegian Majesty's Government. The NAP had affiliated to the Comintern in 1920, and departed from it in 1923. At the other extreme was the German Socialist Workers Party (SAP), a left breakaway from the German social democracy that was now, as an émigré organization, more and more under the influence of ex-members of the right wing of the German Communist Party.

Only four of the organizations—the ICL itself, the SAP and two Dutch groups, the RSP, and the OSP—could be induced to sign the call for a new international. As Pierre Frank noted, the Paris Conference was regarded as the new Zimmerwald.[14] However, the broad left current in which this role could have been played did not develop. The parties and groups represented at Paris were soon, apart from the ICL, drawn rightward as the Comintern began to move out of the Third Period and toward the "United Front." The Paris *Declaration of Four*, itself by no means a Trotskyist platform in the narrow sense, soon became an embarrassment to its non-Trotskyist sponsors.

The sole positive result of Paris was the fusion of the two Dutch groups to form the Revolutionary Socialist Workers Party (RSAP) of the Netherlands. The dominant figure in this party, which had a small but real working-class base, was the veteran communist Heinrich Sneevliet, who had important political differences with Trotsky and who was later to lead his organization out of the Fourth Internationalist movement in support of the Spanish POUM. The SAP leaders, Walcher, Frölich, and Schwab, moved in the same direction even earlier. Nor had Trotsky's efforts to unite with the Zinovievite splinter groups, notably the Maslow-Fischer German émigré group and the Treint group in France, come to anything. A year after the Paris conference, the Trotskyists were as isolated as ever. The attempt to create the nucleus of a new international out of the existing left fragments had *failed*. A new strategy was required.

The French Turn

Only yesterday Doriot was the leader in the fight for the united front, which he, in his own way, made a reality in Saint-Denis. Tomorrow, in case of an agreement between the two bureaucracies, the masses will see in Doriot an obstacle, a splitter, a sabo-

teur of the united front.
    —Trotsky, *The League Faced with a Decisive Turn*

The perspective of remaining as a left opposition in the milieu of the rightward-moving centrist organizations represented at Paris (and soon, for the most part, to be grouped in the "International Labor Community" (IAG) and later in the "International Committee of Revolutionary Socialist Unity," or London Bureau) offered no hope of a revolutionary international in the near future and might well involve the Trotskyists in the decline and disintegration of the centrist parties. Yet, given the total exclusion from the Comintern, the "IAG" parties were the organizations closest to the Trotskyists, and an independent course seemed excluded because of the latter's weakness.

At a deeper level, the problem was that a major long-term effect of the German defeat was to create such a massive groundswell for unity among conscious working-class militants that the call for new parties and a new international, in other words a new split, fell on the stoniest of ground. The Trotskyists had pioneered the call for the workers' united front against fascism. But as this call began to gain ground in the Socialist Parties after 1933, and as the Comintern shifted its position, the pioneers found themselves without influence. They now appeared as the splitters.

In February 1934, the Austrian clerical reactionaries had smashed the Social-Democratic Party and established a military-clerical police dictatorship with fascist trappings under Dollfuss. Unlike their German counterparts, the Austrian Social Democrats did not surrender without a fight. They very reluctantly resorted to armed force in self-defense and were only crushed after a determined resistance. The February fighting had a profound effect on the remaining Social-Democratic parties. Authentic left social democrats began to doubt the possibility of peaceful, parliamentary roads to socialism and to speak about revolution.

That same February, the fascist Croix de Feu staged a riot and attack on the French Chamber of Deputies, in an attempt to exploit popular indignation at the government corruption exposed by the Stavisky affair, to bring down the Daladier government, and to open up the road to a dictatorship. Its near success provoked a general strike in Paris on February 12, in which Communist Party militants demonstrated alongside the "social fascists." This action was soon followed by the abandonment of the Third Period.

For, in the face of the fascist offensive, the French Communist Party (PCF) leadership itself, with Moscow's approval, dropped the theory of "social fascism" and resolved, at the Ivry Conference in June 1934, to press for a pact with the French Socialists (SFIO). The same conference expelled the Communist mayor of Saint-Denis, Doriot, who had dared to advocate this policy "prematurely." The new line was not to be accompanied by any democratization of the now thoroughly Stalinized communist parties. In July, a pact was signed between the PCF and the SFIO for unity of action against fascism. The two parties agreed to refrain from attacking each other as long as the pact lasted. Soon, similar proposals were made to other social-democratic parties. In France, the pact produced an upsurge of working-class activity and enthusiasm that was to be demonstrated on both the political and industrial fronts in the next few years.

The French Trotskyists were now totally without influence. Their main demand appeared to have been met and, although they sharply attacked the dangerous and unprincipled "mutual amnesty" of criticism between the bureaucracies, they could no longer get a hearing among even the most advanced workers. Pierre Frank recalls, "The sympathetic response we had met with [on the united front issue—*DH*], partly in the CP and much more in the SFIO, which had recruited a substantial number of workers, often former CP members—all this sympathetic response was lost to us."[15]

In these circumstances, Trotsky proposed the then radically new tactic of entry into the SFIO, the "French Turn." It was not entirely without precedent. He had already advised the pioneer British Trotskyists, the Balham group, to enter the ILP. But they were a new and very small group—their appeal against expulsion to the 1932 CP Congress had only 13 signatures—and the ILP was then an important section of the "New Zimmerwald" and had broken from the Labor Party to the left. Apparently, he had also advised the handful of Austrian Trotskyists to enter the social-democratic party. But these cases were regarded as exceptional and, in the British case at least, the precedent was not encouraging. The majority of the Communist League of Great Britain rejected the advice of the ICL, and a split occurred—the first of the many that were to plague the Fourth Internationalist movement in Britain.

The "French Turn" proposal provoked opposition in every

ICL section, in many cases, if not most, from the majority of the membership. The critics pointed to the first point of the program, "Independence of the proletarian party, always and under all conditions"; they denounced any "liquidation" into the social democracy, Rosa Luxemburg's "stinking corpse"; they pointed to the propaganda use the Stalinists would make it; and they argued that "the entry into the SFIO means almost automatically the abandonment of the slogan of the Fourth International."[16]

There was substance in some of the criticisms, but the critics could not offer a credible alternative. Given that it was impossible to hope for any reform in the Communist Parties, that the JAG parties were rightward-moving centrists (they included the RSAP, which straddled both camps), that the Trotskyists were tiny, and that the fascist threat was a real and present danger, it was essential to seek *mass* influence in the short term. Independent propaganda groups could not hope to achieve this. Entry into a leftward-moving social democracy might do so. The proposal that the Ligue Communiste enter the SFIO followed the breakaway of the right-wing "neo-socialists" led by Marcel Deat (the Roy Jenkins of the day), which had shifted the center of gravity of the party to the left. This special circumstance played a part in the arguments in the first stage.

There was another consideration. The Trotskyist groups, with partial exceptions, were largely composed of intellectuals and students. "Too many students. Too few workers. The students are occupied too much with themselves, too little with the workers' movement," Trotsky wrote in the summer of 1934.[17] It was to be a recurring theme. The SFIO, which in 1934 had 130,000-odd members compared to the PCF's 30,000-odd, was to some extent a working-class milieu. So, to a much greater degree, were the Belgian and British Labor Parties. And to the extent that "salvation...lies in mobilizing the students for the hard labor of recruiting workers,"[18] so the special circumstances of the French case receded in importance. The entry tactic was generalized. Even in the U.S., where the Socialist Party (SP) did not remotely resemble a mass organization, entry was eventually undertaken.

In view of later developments, it is perhaps necessary to make it clear that the "entry" tactic was essentially a short-term one. The perspective was to rally the best of the leftward-moving workers around the revolutionary program, precipitate a split, and found the revolutionary party. The operation clearly required specific programs, quite different from the ICL program. The best known of these, Trotsky's own "Program of Action for France," appeared in 1934. It was the forerunner of the later "Transitional Program."

Trotsky won over his following at the cost of repeated splits. The ideological uniformity of the movement, upon which he had laid such stress, proved no protection against disruption once disputed practical questions had to be resolved.

The French Turn, though presented as a purely tactical operation, was in fact a change in strategic orientation. It did not involve the abandonment of the call for a new international, as many critics falsely claimed, but it did inevitably transfer the call from the sphere of action to that of propaganda. In this respect, it was no more than a recognition of reality. The *Declaration of Four* had failed to bring in new forces. Such forces were essential. The "entry" at least held out the promise of gaining them.

It failed. The crucial French case is summarized by Pierre Frank as follows:

> For an entire initial period, the activity of the Bolshevik-Leninist Group in the SFIO was conducted with remarkable political clarity. This attracted numerous young people, particularly the whole Jeunesses Socialistes tendency, organized under the name Jeunesses Socialistes Revolutionaire, into the organization's ranks, thus renewing its membership. On the other hand, our exit from the SFIO while the Popular Front was being organized took place under very unfortunate circumstances, and the split among the Bolshevik-Leninists occurring at that time caused us to lose part of the benefits of the entry.[19]

In fact, the Trotskyists were split before the entry, during the entry, and after their expulsion from the SFIO following the Mulhouse Congress in 1935. The Naville group (which had opposed entry, split, and then entered) and the Molinier group (which had supported entry) henceforward led independent existences as the POI and the PCI respectively, an ephemeral unity followed by further splits.

Trotsky was to claim in 1935 that "our section, thanks to the entry, has changed from a propaganda group into a revolutionary factor of the first order."[20] This was undue optimism. Far from becoming a factor of even the second or third order, the movement splintered into quarreling factions. Even Frank concedes "the fragmentation of the French Trotskyists, which reached such a state that at one point the International declared it could no longer accept responsibility for their actions."[21] Of the POI, the "official section," the resolution *On the Tasks of the French Section* adopted at the 1938 "World Congress" paints a sorry picture: "amateurism; the lack of a serious party administration, of a normally functioning national treasury, and a *Lutte Ouvriere* editorship which is stable...; confusion and demoralization of the rank and file...; inability to recruit new members...; the dues are either not paid at all, or, if they are, it is just by luck."[22]

A second entry, which of course produced new splits, was undertaken in 1938, into a new centrist organization, the PSOP, the core of which was the left-wing Seine Federation of the SFIO, which had broken with the Blum leadership. It failed to change the relationship of forces or to improve the composition of the Trotskyist grouplets.

Pierre Frank claims that in other cases, "notably Belgium and the United States, entrism had better results." In the latter case, at least, the claim is dubious. Following the breakaway of the right wing of the Socialist Party (SP) to form the Social-Democratic Federation, the leftish Militant group became dominant in the party. The Trotskyist group, which had already fused with a "native" left organization in 1934 to form the Workers' Party, entered the SP in 1936, after a fierce internal struggle leading to the inevitable split. It was ejected in September 1937, after months of intense factional struggle, having gained "a few hundred people,"[23] mostly from the Socialist Youth. However this gain of largely student youth was to be wiped out in 1940, when the recruits from the SP formed the bulk of the troops of the Abern-Burnham-Schachtman faction, which split away from the main body (SWP) on a confused "anti-leadership" platform and on the Russian question.

The French Turn, then, failed in its object—the creation of serious organizations with some influence in the working-class movement that could form the basis of a new international. Yet the failure was not unqualified. Frank's point about renewal of membership is valid. Nor was the loss of relatively numerous people in the course of the many splits wholly a debit. "Every working-class party, every faction passes during its initial stages through a period of pure propaganda," wrote Trotsky toward the end of 1935.

The period of existence as a Marxist circle ingrafts invariably habits of an abstract approach to the workers' movement. He who is unable to step in time over the confines of this circumscribed existence becomes transformed into a conservative sectarian.[24]

Those who had never known anything but small-group politics were peculiarly susceptible to this disease. Many opponents of the French Turn were infected by it. The sectarians retained the "inner life" of a faction, concentrating on criticizing the "centrism" of the Trotskyists and becoming more remote from reality. A case that happens to be well documented, that of the Oehler group in the U.S., militant opponents of entry, shows them quarreling furiously over "principled" issues and splitting repeatedly, negotiating new fusions with other minuscule sects, setting up their shadowy "International Contact Commission," and finally disintegrating into a welter of microscopic cliques, each known by its leader, Stammites, Marlenites, Meinovites, and the rest, before vanishing into oblivion.[25]

Moreover, the failure of the French Turn was not mainly due to any errors that could have been avoided by the best possible leadership. Profoundly unfavorable developments in the world situation and the working-class movements were the main factors. To understand these, it is necessary to return to events in Russia and to the policies of the Communist International.

The Terror and the People's Front

Every weak, corrupt or ambitious traitor to Socialism within the Soviet Union has been hired to do the foul work of capitalism and fascism. In the forefront of all the wrecking, sabotage, and assassination is the Fascist agent Trotsky. But the defenses of the Soviet people are strong. Under the leadership of our Bolshevik Comrade Yezhov the spies and wreckers have been exposed before the world and brought to judgement.... We express our full confidence in our brother party of the Soviet Union and its great Comrade Stalin, in Comrade Yezhov's determination to root out the last remnants of the anti-Soviet conspiracy.
—Report of the Central Committee to the 15th Congress of the Communist Party of Great Britain, 1938

On December 1, 1934, S.M. Kirov, Stalinist boss of the Leningrad region, was shot and killed by a young man called

Nicolaiev. A fortnight later, Zinoviev, Kamenev, and other former prominent leaders of the CPSU were arrested. The great purges, in which Stalin was to kill most of the prominent members of all wings of the party, had begun. In the course of the next five years, wholesale executions wiped out not only the oppositionists and former oppositionists, but also most of the original Stalinist cadre. It is known from Khrushchev's speech to the Twentieth Congress that the majority of the members of the Central Committee elected at the 1934 Congress (the Seventeenth) were arrested and shot, and the majority of the Congress delegates, who of course were Stalinists, were themselves arrested and charged with "counterrevolutionary activity" in the ensuing years.[26]

In the three great "show trials" (1936–38), prominent former party leaders were induced to confess that, on the orders of Trotsky, they had plotted to wreck the economy and to "restore capitalism" with the help of Hitler and the Japanese emperor. Already, in 1931, Stalin had written,

> Some think that Trotskyism is a school of thought within communism.... It is hardly necessary to point out that such a view of Trotskyism is profoundly mistaken and harmful. Actually, Trotskyism is the spearhead of the counterrevolutionary bourgeoisie, waging the struggle against communism.[27]

Now this was extended to the accusation that Trotsky and his followers were literally agents of the fascists who had to be "exposed" and driven out of the working-class movement. A massive campaign of lies was mounted by the Communist Parties, assisted by the numerous "liberal" and social-democratic fellow travelers that they were now acquiring. It was to be kept up for more than 20 years, and helped to inoculate tens of thousands of CP militants against Marxist criticism of Stalinism and to further isolate the Trotskyists.

As the murderous repression grew inside the USSR and the slander campaign against "Trotsky-fascism" intensified, the Communist Parties moved rapidly to the right. The line of a United Front of workers' parties against fascism changed into the line of a People's Front against war. The Seventh (and last) World Congress of the Comintern (1935) called for

> the united peoples' front in the struggle for peace and against the instigators of war. The struggle for peace opens up the greatest opportunities for creating the broadest united front. All those interested in the preservation of peace should be drawn into this united front.[28]

Among those "interested in peace" were, of course, the imperialist victors of 1918, especially the British and French ruling
classes. They were now the real pivot of Stalin's diplomacy, to
which the Comintern was simply an auxiliary. The USSR had
joined the League of Nations, the instrument of the victorious
powers of the First World War, which Lenin had called "the
League of Imperialist Bandits." For the benefit of the old cadres of
the Communist Parties, who had, after all, been trained in class
politics, revolutionary defeatism, and uncompromising hostility to
"their own" ruling classes, a new theory was developed. It was
the now-familiar one that "progressive" states must be supported
against "reactionary" states. "Today the situation is not what it
was in 1914," declared the ECCI in May 1936.

> Now it is not only the working class, the peasantry and all work-
> ing people who are resolved to maintain peace, but also the op-
> pressed countries and the weak nations whose independence is
> threatened by war.... In the present phase a number of capitalist
> states are also concerned to maintain peace. Hence the possibility
> of creating a broad front of the working class, of all working peo-
> ple, and of entire nations against the danger of imperialist war.[29]

In May 1935, the Franco-Soviet pact was signed. By July, the
CP and the SFIO had come to an agreement with the Radical
Party, the backbone of French bourgeois democracy. In April
1936, the "Front Populaire" of these three parties won a general
election on a platform of "collective security" and reform. The
CP, campaigning on the slogan "For a strong, free, and happy
France," gained 72 seats and became an essential part of the parliamentary majority of Leon Blum, SFIO leader and Front Populaire prime minister. Maurice Thorez, the secretary-general of the
PCF, was able to claim, "We boldly deprived our enemies of the
things they had stolen from us and trampled underfoot. We took
back the Marseilles and the Tricolor."[30]

When the electoral victory of the left was followed by a massive wave of strikes and sit-ins—6 million workers were involved
in June 1936—the erstwhile champions of "ascending revolutionary struggles" exerted themselves to contain the movement
within narrow limits and to end it on the basis of the Matignon
Agreement concessions (notably, the 40-hour week, holidays
with pay). By the end of the year, the Communist Party, now to
the right of its social-democratic allies, was calling for the extension of the Popular Front into a "French Front," by the incorpo-

ration of some right-wing conservatives who were, on nationalist grounds, strongly anti-German.

The French Party pioneered these policies because the French alliance was central to Stalin's foreign policy, but they were rapidly adopted by the whole Comintern. When the Spanish Revolution erupted in July 1936, in response to Franco's attempted seizure of power, the Spanish CP, part of the Spanish Popular Front that had won the February elections and taken power, did its utmost to keep the movement within the framework of "democracy," that is, of capitalism. With the aid of Russian diplomacy and, of course, the social democrats, it was successful. "It is absolutely false," declared Jesus Hernandez, editor of the party's daily paper,

> that the present workers movement has for its object the establishment of the proletarian dictatorship after the war has terminated.... We communists are the first to repudiate this supposition. We are motivated exclusively by a desire to defend the democratic republic.[31]

In pursuit of this line, the Spanish Communist Party and its bourgeois allies pushed the policies of the Republican government more and more to the right, and, in the course of the long drawn-out civil war, drove out of the government first the POUM, then the left-wing leader of the Spanish Socialist Party. The "defense of the Republican order, while respecting property"[32] led to a reign of terror in Republican Spain against the left—symbolized by the murder of Nin and the Barcelona fighting. It was justified by an unprecedented campaign of vilification against all leftist critics as "agents of Hitler and Franco." Trotsky summarized the Spanish events with grim accuracy:

> The republican military commanders were more concerned with crushing social revolution than with scoring victories. The soldiers lost confidence in their commanders, the masses—in the government; the peasants stepped aside, the workers became exhausted, defeat followed defeat, demoralization grew apace.

Notwithstanding the fact that "the Spanish proletariat stood in the first day of the revolution not below but above the Russian proletariat of 1917... [b]y setting itself the task of rescuing the capitalist regime the People's Front doomed itself to military defeat."[33]

Yet the extreme right turn of the Comintern did not seriously benefit the Fourth Internationalists. In the first phase, popular enthusiasm for unity brought enormous gains to the Communist Parties—the French Party grew from 30,000 in 1934 to 150,000 by the end of 1936, plus 100,000 in the Communist Youth; the Spanish party grew from under a thousand at the close of the Third Period (1934) to 35,000 in February 1936, and to 117,000 in July 1937. The recruits were armored against criticism from the left by the belief that the Trotskyists—and indeed the centrists—were literally fascist agents.

In the period of the collapse of the People's Fronts, general demoralization created an extremely unfavorable atmosphere for revolutionaries. The fact was that Stalin had succeeded, through the Comintern, in shifting the whole working-class movement, including the social democracy, far to the right of the 1934 positions. The Trotskyists were swimming against immensely powerful currents. To survive at all, as a revolutionary tendency, was a great achievement in the circumstances. Yet the terrible dilemma, the contrast between ends and means, between the urgency of the need to reverse the defeats and the pathetically weak forces available, was more acute than ever.

The desperate gamble

We are not progressing politically. Yes, it is a fact which is an expression of a general decay of the workers' movements in the last fifteen years.... Our situation now is incomparably more difficult than that of any other organization at any other time, because we have the terrible betrayal of the Communist International which arose from the betrayal of the Second International. The degeneration of the Third International developed so quickly and so unexpectedly that the same generation which heard its formation now hears us and they say "But we have already heard this once."
—Trotsky, *Fighting Against the Stream*

September 1938. The New Zimmerwald is dead. The French Turn has failed in its strategic objective. The Spanish Revolution is strangled. Fascist and semi-fascist regimes control most of Europe. A new world war is clearly imminent. In the remaining bourgeois democracies, social patriotism, in its social-democratic and Stalinist varieties, completely dominates the workers' movement. In these desperately difficult circumstances, the New International is proclaimed, not as an aspiration, but as a fact.

Why? In 1935, Trotsky had denounced as "a stupid piece of gossip" the idea that "the Trotskyists want to proclaim the Fourth International next Thursday."[34] Yet, a year later, he was proposing, precisely, the proclamation of the New International. On that occasion, he was unable to persuade his followers. By 1938, he had won them over.

No significant change in the strength and influence of the revolutionary groups had occurred in the interim. In his foreword to the official record of the founding conference of the Fourth International (later called the "First World Congress"), Max Shachtman wrote, "The delegates represented directly eleven countries—the United States, France, Great Britain, Germany, the Soviet Union, Italy, Latin America, Poland, Belgium, Holland and Greece."[35] Of these delegates, Shachtman himself did indeed represent a very small but real party—the American Socialist Workers Party claimed, with some exaggeration, 2,500 members. He was probably the only one in this position.

The situation in France has already been noted. The British section was a fusion of sectlets, cobbled together for the conference by an SWP representative, which was to decline into insignificance in the next few years—the only British group that was to show some viability (the Workers International League) was unrepresented and indeed was denounced as being "on the path of unprincipled clique politics which can only lead them into the mire."[36] The section in the USSR had been physically exterminated and was "represented" by the Stalinist police spy "Etienne." Germany and Italy were represented by members of minuscule émigré groups. The Dutch were a splinter from the RSAP youth organization. The Poles—who opposed the proclamation of the International—had no independent organization, as the conference resolution on Poland shows, and the Greeks were split between the United Internationalist Communist Organization and the International Communist League, neither of which seem to have amounted to much. The Belgian organization, described by the SWP as "our strongest proletarian section in Europe," may have had some hundreds of members. Even if all the fragments that Shachtman claims ("there were quite a number of others which for a variety of legal and physical reasons were unable to send delegates") are added in, the total does not amount to much, little more in fact than existed in 1933.

Pierre Frank's explanation of the foundation of an "International" without significant sections, without any real base in the working class, amounts to the assertion that this expedient was the only way to preserve the handful of cadres that the movement had acquired. "Why was Trotsky so very insistent on this question?" Frank writes.

> Why did he push it so vigorously, even to the point where the final chapter of his Transitional Program includes an undisguised polemic against those who were opposed to the proclamation of the Fourth International? It was because, for him the most important consideration was not the numerical size of our forces, nor the readiness of a more or less large sector of the workers to understand our decision; but above and beyond all, it was a question of political perspective and political continuity. Trotsky was acutely aware that the workers' movement in general, and our movement in particular, was about to enter an extremely difficult period—the imperialist war—in the course of which we would be subjected to extraordinary pressures by the class enemy and by powerful centrifugal forces. These pressures could very well destroy an organization as weak as our own. Looking back, in examining what happened in our movement during the war, it can be seen that entering the war period without having proclaimed the founding of the Fourth International would have allowed all the centrifugal forces (which appeared during that time) to operate a hundred times, a thousand times more intensively.[37]

The explanation, then, relates to the internal cohesion of the Trotskyist organizations and not at all to the objective possibilities in the working-class movement. Frank has at least the merit of seeing the problem, unlike many latter-day "Trotskyists," but his arguments will not stand critical examination.

First of all, an international Trotskyist organization, the ICL, had existed since 1930. This was a sufficient guarantee of "political continuity," insofar as such a thing can be guaranteed by organizational means, and since the proclamation of the Fourth International merely meant, in practice, renaming the ICL, it is difficult to see what additional resistance to "powerful centrifugal forces" was obtained.

Secondly, the "International" in fact ceased to function with the onset of war. As Frank himself tells us, "Shortly before the war the International Secretariat was transferred to America" and "could keep contact with only a few countries in the 'allied' camp (and even that with great difficulty)."[38] In reality, the SWP acted as international center to the degree that one existed.

Thirdly, and most important, it is merely retrospective justifica-

tion to suggest that Trotsky conceived of "political perspectives
and political continuity" *apart* from developments in the working-
class movement. That kind of revisionism was a later development. On the contrary, he was above all concerned with the mass
movement, and he believed that, in spite of the failure of the two
previous strategies, it was possible to create mass organizations,
given a program and a leadership, out of the crisis that the coming
war would inevitably produce. "Ten years were necessary for the
Third International in order to stamp into the mire their own program and to transform themselves into a stinking cadaver," he declared in an article celebrating the founding conference.

> Ten years! Only ten years! Permit me to finish with a prediction:
> During the next ten years the program of the Fourth Interna-
> tional will become the guide of millions and these revolutionary
> millions will know how to storm earth and heaven.[39]

There is not the slightest shadow of a doubt that, for Trotsky,
the idea of an "International" divorced from the workers' movement was nonsense. There is this much justification for Pierre
Frank's argument. Given that "[i]n the catastrophe of war...the
masses will look for a new orientation, a new direction, and will
find them,"[40] that just as Lenin had been nearly isolated in 1914
but was at the head of a great world movement by 1920, so
would the Fourth International become a great world movement; then it was vital to infuse courage and determination into
the handful of internationalists.

But the proclamation of the new International rested on much
more than this. It rested on a concrete political perspective. This
perspective was, as events were to show, faulty in a number of respects. First, Trotsky believed that capitalism had entered its final
crisis. Not only did "mankind's productive forces stagnate,"[41] but
"the disintegration of capitalism has reached extreme limits, likewise the disintegration of the old ruling class. The further existence of this system is impossible."[42] In consequence, the
reformist workers' parties could not make any gains for their
supporters, "there can be no discussion of systematic social reforms and the raising of the masses living standards; when every
serious demand of the proletariat and even every serious demand
of the petty-bourgeoisie inevitably reaches beyond the limits of
capitalist property relations and of the bourgeois state."[43] Trotsky would, no doubt, have conceded that some economic revival

was possible on a cyclical basis. He excluded the possibility of a prolonged upward movement such as had given birth to reformism in the decades before the First World War. So did everyone else in the revolutionary movement. In fact, an even greater expansion than that of the classic imperialist phase was to follow the Second World War. Reformism got a new lease of life.

Second, Trotsky believed that, with the Popular Front, the Communist Parties had become social democratic. "Nothing now distinguishes the Communists from the Social-Democrats except the traditional phraseology, which is not difficult to unlearn."[44] And, three years later:

> The definite passing over of the Comintern to the side of the bourgeois order, its cynically counter-revolutionary role throughout the world, particularly in Spain, France, the United States, and other "democratic" countries, created exceptional supplementary difficulties for the world proletariat.[45]

And again:

> The Comintern policy in Spain and China today—the policy of cringing before the "democratic" and "national" bourgeoisie—demonstrates that the Comintern is likewise incapable of learning anything further or of changing. The bureaucracy which became a reactionary force in the USSR cannot play a revolutionary role in the world arena.[46]

The reality was to prove more complex, a fact that was to precipitate a fundamental crisis in the Fourth Internationalist movement. Trotsky was pointing to a basic trend, but the timescale was much greater than he thought. In the Cold War after 1948, the Communist Parties did not capitulate to "their own" bourgeoisies. Their loyalty was still to Moscow. Their policies were not revolutionary, but neither were they simply "reformist." They retained a "leftist" position of no loyalty to the bourgeois state, which made the creation of a revolutionary alternative extremely difficult. And, in one great case and some lesser ones, Stalinist parties actually destroyed bourgeois states and replaced them with regimes on the Russian pattern.

The Chinese Revolution of 1949 appeared to put the classic Trotskyist analysis of the Stalinist parties into question, at any rate for the backward countries. For if it was regarded as a proletarian revolution, it destroyed the basis of the Fourth International's existence—the essentially counter-revolutionary nature of Stalinism. If, on the other hand, it was in some sense a bourgeois revolution—a "New Democracy" as Mao Tse-tung claimed at the time—it appeared to destroy the theory of permanent revolution. And, whatever view was taken of it, the fact that it occurred at all refurbished the revolutionary image of Stalinism for a long time.

Third, Trotsky believed that Stalin's regime in Russia was highly unstable. His analysis led him to the view that "either the bureaucracy, becoming ever more the organ of the world bourgeoisie within the workers' state, will overthrow the new forms of property and plunge the country back to capitalism; or the working class will crush the bureaucracy and open the way to socialism."[47] This was not a perspective for decades.

Writing toward the end of 1939, Trotsky had asked critics of his position, "Might we not place ourselves in a ludicrous position if we affixed to the Bonapartist oligarchy [i.e., the bureaucracy—DH] the nomenclature of a new ruling class just a few years or even a few months prior to its inglorious downfall?"[48] In fact, 30-odd years later, the regime still exists. In the interim, the bureaucracy has hardly acted as "the organ of the world bourgeoisie." On the contrary, though fundamentally conservative, it has defended its own interests both against the workers and peasants of Russia and against rival ruling classes. It conquered Eastern Europe and transformed state and society into plausible facsimiles of the Russian original. And, again, these events had a profound effect on working-class consciousness.

Fourth, Trotsky adhered firmly both to the theory of permanent revolution and to Lenin's 1915 analysis of imperialism. Therefore, he believed, the colonial empires that then covered what is now called the "Third World" could be liberated only by struggles led by the working classes. Thus, for example, "The Indian bourgeoisie is incapable of leading a revolutionary struggle," which was undoubtedly true, and at the same time, "The imperialists [in this case, the British rulers of India—DH] can no longer make serious concessions either to their own toiling masses or to the colonies. On the contrary they are compelled to resort to an ever more bestial exploitation." It followed that the "theory that India's position will constantly improve, that her liberties will continually be enlarged and that India will gradually become a Dominion on the road of peaceful reforms...(and) later on perhaps even achieve full independence. This entire perspective is false to the core."[49] And so with the rest of the colonies. Again the reality was more complex. Again, the relatively peaceful liquidation of the colonial empires had a significant effect on working-class consciousness.

The foundation of the new International *in advance* of the recruitment of significant forces rooted in the working classes was a desperate gamble. It was a gamble that could be justified only on the basis of a particular perspective—that outlined in, and indeed summed up in, the title of the program adopted at the founding conference—*The Death Agony of Capitalism*. There was, of course, serious evidence for each and every one of Trotsky's arguments. It is also true that the factors that falsified them were interconnected and that a break in the causal chain could have produced very different results. Thus the survival and expansion of Stalin's regime enormously facilitated the strangling of the European revolutionary movements in 1943–46. This, in turn, permitted the revival of European capitalism and the onset of the Cold War and the permanent arms economy. These, in their turn, made possible the abandonment of the colonial empires without the last-ditch, life-and-death struggle that Trotsky, like Lenin before him, had believed to be inevitable. And so on, and so on.

Nevertheless, the chain was not broken, and when 10 years after 1938 it became possible to hold a "Second World Congress of the Fourth International," the movement remained a collection of small groups. Certainly, the 1948 Congress represented more than that of 1938. Indeed it probably represented more *in the working-class movement* than any of time subsequent "Congresses" of any of the various bodies that now claim the title and/or inheritance of the Fourth International. Yet it represented little enough. A fundamental reappraisal of the situation and of the *perspectives* of the Transitional Program was required. The movement, in its majority, proved incapable of rising to this task. The outcome was tragic. Failing to analyze the mistakes, the movement was doomed not merely to repeat them but to add new and more disastrous ones.

Having failed to advance theoretically, it degenerated, and the various fragments into which it soon splintered came, in most though not all cases, to abandon the fundamental content of Trotskyism, while preserving its forms, and to adapt to Stalinism; to "structural reform" centrism; to pre-Marxian "Third World Socialism"; to Narodnikism; even, in the case of the biggest of the post–Second World War sections—the Ceylonese Lanka Sama Samaj Party—to participation in a counter-revolutionary bourgeois government.

These sorry developments will be examined in "Fourth International in Decline." At this point, it is necessary to remind ourselves of the positive achievements. Without the struggle carried on by Trotsky and his followers, under conditions of incredible difficulty, the revolutionary movement of today would be incomparably weaker, organizationally as well as theoretically, than it in fact is. We stand on the shoulders of those pioneers.

FOURTH INTERNATIONAL IN DECLINE:

FROM TROTSKYISM TO PABLOISM, 1944–1953

Introduction

There was general agreement...that following a postwar period of reactivation and reconstruction, a serious economic crisis would occur. Marxists, basing themselves more particularly on Lenin's concepts of imperialism, believed that the loss of colonies would contribute to the disintegration of the imperialist centers. Yet far from disintegrating, for about 15 years the capitalist world experienced boom, an unprecedented economic prosperity interrupted not by crises but only by "recessions" of varying but always limited size and duration.... A capitalism deprived of its colonies yet flourishing more than ever, with a working class shorn of its political aspirations and almost exclusively preoccupied with its standards of living; in the workers' states an extension of the new relationships of production, with bureaucratic domination maintained and without any workers' mobilizations; in the colonial countries a revolutionary upsurge

This article was first published in *International Socialism*, first series, issue 60, July 1973. (The first part of this article appeared under the title "Against the Stream: The Origins of the Fourth Internationalist Movement," in *International Socialism*, first series, issue 53, October–December 1972.)

based essentially on the peasantry—all this largely explains the proliferation of theories denying, in one way or another, the historical mission of the proletariat as formulated by Marx.
                    —Pierre Frank, *The Fourth International*

IT DOES not, however, explain why the Fourth Internationalist movement itself came to succumb to such theories and so to the most fundamental revision of Marxism. Nor is it an honest formulation of the case. As we shall see, Pierre Frank and the political tendency of which he is part specifically denied, at the relevant time, that there would or could be "a postwar period of reactivation and reconstruction," and insisted on the capitalist nature of all but one of what he now calls "the workers' states."

The fact is that the victory of "substitutionist" ideas in the Trotskyist movement was not due *simply* to the pressure of circumstances. It owed more to the incorrectness of important parts of the Trotskyist heritage of *ideas* and was the outcome a political *struggle* within the movement that led to the victory, initially, of a conservative, "orthodox" group that proved incapable of solving the theoretical or practical problems facing it. When this became obvious even to the "orthodox," they collapsed into a series of unprincipled zigzags that led them ultimately to "critical support" for Stalinism.

The Fourth Internationalist groups went into the Second World War with the perspective that it would end in a revolutionary crisis similar to that of 1917–20, but on a still bigger scale. In 1944, when the German war machine was visibly declining, the newly created European secretariat of the Fourth International (FI) issued theses that proclaimed:

> With an inexorable necessity, the imperialist war is developing towards its *inevitable* transformation into civil war.... [T]he rapid development of revolutionary events and the situation in the USSR will create all *the necessary conditions for a break between the masses and the Stalinist leaders....* The large-scale use of the Red Army as a counterrevolutionary force *is excluded....* The German revolution remains the backbone of the European revolution.... The German proletariat, stronger than ever in numbers, more concentrated than ever, will *from the first* play a decisive role.... *The most favorable conditions* will exist for a victorious revolutionary movement.[1]

And six months *after* the war in Europe had ended, the most authoritative figure in the movement, James P. Cannon, national secretary of the U.S. Socialist Workers Party (SWP), declared

> Trotsky predicted that the fate of the Soviet Union would be decided in the war. *That remains our firm conviction.* Only we disagree with some people who carelessly think the war is over.... The war is not over, and the revolution which we said would issue from the war in Europe is not taken off the agenda.[2]

Thus Trotsky's predictions were elevated to the status of sacred writings, of gospel; and if there was a contradiction between gospel and reality, so much the worse for reality.

The aftermath of the 1940 split

The revisionist opposition attacked the program itself. Their position, at bottom, represented a fundamental break with the programmatic concepts, traditions and methods embodied in the Fourth International.
    —James P. Cannon, *The Convention of the SWP*, 1940

The American SWP was by far the strongest (about 1,500 members)[3] and most stable organization in the FI. The Cannon leadership had been profoundly influenced by the factional struggle and split in 1940, when "the Shachtmanites had not less than 40 percent of the party and a majority of the youth organization. If you count the youth, who were not voting members of the party, it was almost a 50–50 split."[4] The Abern-Burnham-Shachtman group had split from the SWP to form the Workers' Party and thus inflicted a heavy setback in the SWP. They had seceded on a confused and an unprincipled basis.

Though the defectors were in disagreement with Trotsky's analysis of the events following the Hitler-Stalin Pact (1939)— the Russian seizure of the Western Ukraine and Western White Russia from Poland, the Russo-Finnish War, and so on—they had no common position of their own on the "Russian question." As Cannon later conceded, "Shachtman, up to the point of the split, did not openly revise our program on the Soviet Union, which was the central issue in dispute.... As for Abern, he did not yield anything theoretically to revisionism at all."[5] In fact, the Shachtman group had concentrated on the issue of "party regime," which they described as "bureaucratic conservatism." Trotsky's description of them as "a petty-bourgeois opposition" was essentially correct.

The disastrous effect of this split on the international movement was that it confirmed and hardened the view of Cannon and his associates that the "defense of our program was the main, indeed practically the sole, *theoretical* task of the leadership." The SWP leadership became, by default, the effective leadership of the FI. By "program" they meant the letter of *The Death Agony of Capitalism and the Tasks of the Fourth International*. After Trotsky's murder in 1940, they had no competent guide, so they believed, to abate one jot or tittle of that document. The program and the perspective of 1938 were indissolubly connected in the minds of the SWP leadership. After the Shachtman split, any attempt to modify the *perspective* was treated as an attack on the "traditions and methods" of the FI.

The Europeans had much the same outlook, but some of them were capable of learning from experience. Therein lay the difference between the (pre-1948) leadership of the French FI section (PCI) and the British Revolutionary Communist Party (RCP) and of the Americans. These two organizations—small as they were (the PCI claimed 1,000 members in 1947, the RCP 400)—were the only other organizations in the FI of any substance at all, which were in a position to influence its politics.[6]

They came into conflict with the SWP at an early stage, and the erection of a new "international leadership" independent of the only two serious European sections (and therefore dependant on the Americans), together with the fostering of internal opposition to the French and British leaderships, became important SWP policy objectives. The battle was fought, in the first instance, on whether or not there was any possibility of a temporary revival of European capitalism and therefore of a revival of bourgeois democracy after the defeat of fascism. Such a revival was held to be incompatible with the perspective of immediate proletarian revolution. Therefore, it must be excluded.

"Defending our program"

The experience of the countries "liberated" by the Red Army, as in those "liberated" by the Allied armies, already shows that the bourgeoisie, ruined, incapable of making the smallest concessions to the masses...turns from the beginning to "strong" solutions, to

*police and military dictatorships.... A relatively long intermediate
"democratic" period, lasting until the decisive victory either of
the socialist revolution or once again of fascism, will be impossible.... In all the "liberated" countries the bourgeoisie is incapable
of restoring economic life.*
—*The Maturing Situation in Europe and
the Tasks of the Fourth International,*
FI International Executive Committee Resolution, 1945

At The outbreak of the Second World War, the "International
Secretariat" was transferred to New York. In fact, the international leadership elected in 1938 was unable to function. When
certain executive members came out in defense of Shachtman, the
SWP leadership unceremoniously deposed them, with Trotsky's
approval,[7] and appointed a new secretary of the FI, the European
émigré Gerland ("Logan").[8] However, Gerland had a mind of his
own, and, as early as 1943, he, together with the editor of the
SWP's journal, Morrow ("Cassidy") and others, began to draw
attention to the signs of the revival of mass support for the Communist Parties amid social-democratic parties in the European resistance movements. These signs suggested that the tiny FI groups
might confront a real mass revival of reformist parties, rather
than the revolutionary masses looking for leadership.

This, of course, was exactly what happened in 1944–45. Far
from "a break between the masses and the Stalinist leaders," the
Stalinist parties mushroomed into organizations vastly bigger
than before the war. Far from an "inevitable transformation into
civil war" in countries like France and Italy (let alone Germany,
where the working class was atomized by Nazism and then subject to Allied military rule), socialist-communist-liberal bourgeois coalition governments were coming to power in one
country of Western Europe after another and proceeding to
recreate the war-shattered state machines under cover of a cloud
of left-wing rhetoric. Not the proletarian revolution but the
"counterrevolution in its 'democratic' form," as Lenin had
called it, was ascendant.[9]

The Red Army proved only too capable of large-scale use as
a "counter-revolutionary force." All over Eastern Europe (Yugoslavia and Albania excepted), it was used to impose coalition
governments of, apparently, the same political complexion as
those of the West. Where revolutionary enthusiasm threatened

this process, it was firmly repressed. In Bulgaria, for example, the Stalinist-appointed war minister had, in 1944,

> issued a stern order to the troops to return immediately to normal discipline, to abolish soldiers' councils and to hoist no more red flags. Now Sofia reports that the Bulgarian army has been placed under the supreme command of [the Russian] Marshal Tolbukhin. Apparently, the Soviet commander has no patience with Balkan repetitions of 1917.[10]

Gerland, together with Morrow, Goldman, and others in the SWP, saw the way things were going at an early stage and attempted to shift the line of the SWP and the Europeans away from what Morrow, tactlessly but accurately, called "ultra-left braggadocio" and toward immediate demands that took into account the actual consciousness of the radicalized workers supporting the communist and socialist parties, for example, the demand to abolish the monarchy in Italy and Belgium (which was resisted by the CP leaders), for the legalization of the PCI, and so on. They also suggested a short-term "entry" tactic in the Belgian, French, Italian, and other socialist parties and, generally, an end to "revolutionary heroics and chest-beating."

The orthodox reaction to this was to treat it as "an attempt to revise our program," which must, of course, be smashed, and to loudly reaffirm the imminence of the inevitable proletarian revolution. The perspective had clearly been falsified. But it was still defended by the SWP leaders with ferocious vigor. The critics were driven out of the SWP.[11] However, the Europeans began to show disturbing signs of being influenced, in retrospect, by similar ideas. The SWP leadership needed an instrument to combat the heresy in Europe itself. They exerted their influence and financial support[12] to ensure that the new International Secretariat centered in Paris should be impeccably "orthodox," both in its perspectives and, of course, on the sacred "Russian question."

The "unknown men"

Our relations with the leadership in Europe at that time were relations of the closest collaboration and support. There was general agreement between us. These were unknown men in our party. Nobody had ever heard of them. We helped to publicize the individual leaders.... They had yet to gain authority, not only here but throughout the world. And the fact that the SWP supported

them up and down the line greatly reinforced their position.
—James P. Cannon, *Internationalism and the SWP*

The leadership of which Cannon spoke was not, of course, drawn from suspect leaderships of the two major European sections. Cannon's emissary in Europe, Gordon ("Stuart"), had found, and was able to vouch for, a number of "unknown men" who combined the necessary qualifications: no base in a major Trotskyist group, talent, and an unquestioning acceptance of the gospel according to the SWP. The most important of the "unknown men" were Michel Raptis ("Pablo"), a Greek resident in France, and Ernest Mandel ("Germain"), a Belgian. Pablo, an "organization man" of some skill, became the new secretary of the FI; Mandel, a brilliant journalist and master of the arts of polemic, became the "theoretician."

Mandel's most urgent task was to counter the subversive notion, which was gaining ground among the PCI and RCP leaders, that, given the failure of immediate revolutionary prospects in Europe, a major postwar economic boom was in prospect. "There is no reason whatever," he wrote in 1946, "to assume that we are facing a new epoch of capitalist stabilization and development. On the contrary, the war has acted only to aggravate the disproportion between the increased productivity of the capitalist economy and the capacity of the world market to absorb it."[13] Mandel's sleight-of-hand technique was already well developed; his opponents had not predicted "a new epoch of capitalist stabilization"—that was not yet expected by anyone—but merely a major boom.

The RCP reply was blunt and to the point:

> The classic conditions for boom are present in Europe today. A shortage of capital goods; shortage of agricultural produce; shortage of consumer goods.... [T]he specific position of the Secretariat and SWP...that the Western European countries will remain on a level approaching stagnation and slump is entirely false.[14]

But since the SWP was wedded to the idea of "the accelerated ruin of the European economy by the war and the utter impossibility of restoring it to health on a national capitalist basis,"[15] as Cannon had put it two years earlier, Mandel was forced to stick to his thesis.

Meanwhile, Pablo was engaged in the more mundane but es-

sential task of undermining the PCI and RCP leaderships by organizational maneuvers. In France especially, this was an urgent
task. The Craipeau-Demazière leadership had carried the 1946
party congress on a platform calling for an end to sectarian politics and phrase-mongering about "ascending revolutionary
struggles" and for a serious orientation of the organization on
the real mass movement.[16] In short, for a rejection of the politics
of Cannon-Pablo-Mandel.

The PCI was gaining ground. Craipeau had won 14,000
votes in Seine-et-Oise in the 1946 election. *La Verité* was growing in circulation and influence. The Renault strike (influenced
by members of what is now Lutte Ouvriere) had shattered the
"no-strike" campaign of the Communist trade union federation
and the government. The Socialist Youth organization, nominally 5,000 strong, had broken with its parent party and was negotiating with the PCI for unity on a revolutionary basis, as was
a smaller group from the adult party headed by the former joint
national secretary of the socialists, Yves Dechezelles. The fusion
of these forces had to be stopped at all costs. If successful, or
even partially successful, it would give the Craipeau-Demazière
leadership an unassailable majority and, even worse, would alter
the whole balance of forces in the FI and end the hegemony of
the SWP and its European acolytes.

Accordingly Pablo, assisted by Pierre Frank (also a member of
the secretariat), set to work to cobble together a coalition of tendencies to oust the leadership before the fusion could take place.
The coalition consisted of elements that had nothing in common
except their opposition to the "dilution" of the PCI by fresh
forces, i.e., to its serious growth. There were the former Molinierists, headed by Pierre Lambert, then, as now, sectarian phrase-
mongers. There was the personal following of Frank, still officially
part of the Lambert tendency but soon to be its most violent opponent. There was the ultra-left Peret group (which, incidentally, regarded the USSR as state capitalist); the Shachtmanite-influenced
group of Chaulieu, which regarded the USSR as a new kind of exploitative society, and the French Communist Party as the embryo
of the new "bureaucratic collectivist" ruling class in France; and
the future Stalinist apologist Mestre and his friends.

The coalition could not possibly lead the PCI, but, aided by
the full weight of the SWP-Secretariat support, it did manage to
scrape together enough votes to depose the leadership at the end

of 1947, and so kill the fusion and the hopes of breaking out of the sectarian ghetto.[17] This achieved, the coalition fell apart, its constituent parts seceding or being expelled, until a few years later all that was left of the PCI was a small rump presided over by Pierre Frank.

In Britain, Pablo was less successful. Building on the earlier work of "Stuart," he and Mandel did their best to develop the Healy-Lawrence minority, which was slavishly devoted to the SWP line, into a credible alternative to the Haston-Grant leadership. When this proved to be impossible—Healy could gain the support of only about one-fifth of the membership—the Secretariat intervened to split the RCP into two sections, both officially recognized (1947). The Healy group entered the Labor Party, the RCP continuing the open-party tactic. Pablo had failed to destroy the RCP leadership. In the event, that leadership solved his problem for him. It destroyed itself. The rock on which it foundered was the "Russian question," the question which was to disorient and demoralize the whole Trotskyist movement.

"A complete petty-bourgeois revision"

The bureaucracy which became a reactionary force in the USSR cannot play a revolutionary role on the world arena.
—Trotsky, The Death Agony of Capitalism
and the Tasks of the Fourth International

In 1944–45, the Russian Army gained control of most of Eastern Europe. Russia's political masters proceeded to erect new bureaucratic state machines to replace the shattered German puppet regimes that had been destroyed. The personnel were drawn from the servants of the previous semi-fascist regimes, reinforced by émigré and underground members of the Communist Parties. These "people's democracies" were headed by the same type of CP-socialist-liberal bourgeois (or peasant) party governments as in the West. The difference lay in the fact that military and police machines were under effective Stalinist control, backed by the Russian Army.

The line of the FI, affirmed in April and June 1946, was to call for "the withdrawal of all occupation troops including the Red Army."[18] There was, however, a complication. As Mandel wrote:

The bureaucracy in general began by curbing and breaking the revolutionary upsurge of the masses. A year and a half later, however, the situation in these countries is marked by a more or less widespread introduction of agrarian reforms and nationalization of heavy industry.[19]

In fact, virtually all modern industry was nationalized.

What sort of regimes were these? The term "buffer" regimes was coined to describe them, implying that the Russian interest in them was purely military. Mandel declared, "In the 'buffer' countries the state remains bourgeois."[20] "The bourgeois character of the state," he explained,

> flows from the capitalist relations of production and is expressed in a special kind of state structure. This structure (hierarchical and centralized administration, apparatus of repression, etc.) is present everywhere, with the old officials still functioning.

But in these new Russian-controlled states, the decisive sections of industry were nationalized. Surely this changed their nature? "Nationalizations," replied Mandel,

> in no way change the capitalist character of the "buffer" nations; they merely express, in a new and concentrated form, the total incapacity of the native private capital of these countries to develop and even to run industry.[21]

There was, however, a difficulty. For the first 10 years of the Left Opposition—until the end of 1933—Trotsky had maintained, as an essential component of his conception of Russia as a "degenerated workers' state," that "the edifice of the workers' state can be regenerated on the social foundations of the Soviet Union, without a new revolution."[22] That is to say, Stalin's despotism can be ended by reformist means. Trotsky abandoned this position and maintained, for the last seven years of his life, first, that only a revolution could "regenerate" the USSR; second, that it nevertheless remained a degenerated workers' state, but only because the means of production were state owned; third, that such state ownership of the decisive means of production could arise only from a proletarian revolution.

In the postwar period, 100 million people in a third of Europe were subjected to regimes that were counter-revolutionary in origin but satisfied the "state ownership" criterion for "workers' states." Inevitably, the argument was advanced that Poland, Hungary, Bulgaria, and so on were in fact "degenerated workers' states" of the Russian type that had been created by "revolution

from above." To these arguments, the "orthodox" Trotskyists re-
acted with violent hostility, partly because the suggestion undermined the whole argument for the necessity of a new
international by implying that the Bonapartist bureaucracy of the
USSR was not necessarily counter-revolutionary, partly because
their class and revolutionary instincts were outraged at the idea
that the repressive despotisms erected in Eastern Europe without
or against the working class could be put on a par with the off-
spring, however degenerated, of the great October Revolution.

The "revolution from above" thesis, later associated with
Deutscher and Pablo, was first advanced by the French renegade
from Trotskyism, Leblanc. Mandel, as usual, replied for the orthodox:

> The facts thus prove the complete falsity of Leblanc's theory that
> the Stalinist bureaucracy would be compelled "objectively to
> carry through the socialist revolution in other countries."
>
> This theory is a complete petty-bourgeois revision of the
> Marxist-Leninist concept both of the state and of the proletarian
> revolution.... Finally Leblanc's thesis completely revises the Trot-
> skyist conception of the objectively counterrevolutionary role of
> the Stalinist bureaucracy both in Russia and in other coun-
> tries.... [I]t is clear that what we have here is a capitulation
> under the pressure of Stalinism...a very powerful pressure
> amongst the French intelligentsia.[23]

All of which was incontestable. But what then of the USSR? It,
too, had long had "hierarchical and centralized administration,
apparatus of repression, etc." Its sole essential distinguishing fea-
ture was that nationalization of the means of production, which
Mandel, following Engels, now proclaimed "in no way
change[s] the capitalist character."

The truth was that it was no longer possible to maintain both
the Marxist-Leninist theory of the state and the proletarian revolution and Trotsky's theory that the USSR was still, in some sense,
a workers' state, even though the only way the workers could ob-
tain power was by smashing it in the course of a proletarian revolution. No longer possible, that is, unless the relevant facts were
ignored. But the essence of "orthodox Trotskyism" (the term was
coined by Cannon) was adherence to the letter of the sacred texts
of 1938–40. And so, it was maintained, those who grasped either
horn of the dilemma were damned. All who understood the essential identity of the class character of the USSR and the East Euro-

pean states were beyond the pale; those who maintained that both were in some sense workers' states were damned equally with those who maintained that both were in some sense state capitalist. "The parallelism of these two revisionist tendencies strikes the eye," declared the Second World Congress (1948). "There is no room for them in the revolutionary movement."[24]

From Trotsky to Tito

Were the path they have taken to be followed, that is, bringing liberation on the bayonets of the Red Army, which would really be but enslavement of peoples in another form, the science of Marxism-Leninism would perish.
—Joseph Tito, in *Yugoslav Fortnightly,* November 2, 1949

The survival and expansion of Stalinism precipitated a crisis that ultimately destroyed "orthodox Trotskyism" as Cannon and his supporters understood it. There were two related problems: the survival of Stalinism in the USSR itself and the existence, now, of other Stalinist states of essentially the same type.

The first problem could be met by dogmatic assertion. The end of Stalinism, the destruction of the bureaucracy, is at hand. The war, the Secretariat reiterated in 1946,

> marks the beginning of the period in which the fate of the regime established by the October revolution will be definitely and finally decided.... [O]nly the intervention of the proletarian revolution can save the Soviet Union from an early and fatal end.[25]

The second problem could be approached in a number of ways. The facts about the "people's democracies" were denied or minimized—actually there is still a lot of private industry, agriculture hasn't been collectivized, and so on (all of which was equally true of the Russia of the mid-1920s). Then, ignoring altogether the qualitative differences between the events of 1939–40 and those of 1944–45, there was much pseudo-learned argument about the degree of "structural assimilation" of the "people's democracies" with the USSR.

The point here was that Trotsky himself had noted that when the Western Ukraine was forcibly incorporated into the USSR, its economy had been transformed to conform to the Russian model. The various arguments were juggled with great sophistical skill, but always to lead to the required conclusion—the East

European states are capitalist, the USSR is a degenerated workers' state; the apparent identity of their social structures is a
snare and a delusion.

The "orthodox" position was formulated yet again at the
1948 World Congress.

> The capitalist nature of the economy of the "buffer zone" is ap-
> parent.... In the "buffer" countries the state remains bourgeois....
> [T]he state of the "buffer" countries represents at the same time
> an extreme form of Bonapartism.[26]

And then came the conflict between Stalin and Tito. Within
weeks of the congress, the Pablo-Mandel Secretariat issued a declaration of support for the "capitalist" regime of Tito in its struggle against Stalin's "workers' state"! Their position was the more
awkward because Tito soon began to receive substantial U.S. aid!

How to justify this complete reversal of position? By swallow-
ing all the words that had been written against "revisionism" and
proclaiming that what had occurred in Yugoslavia four years earlier was "the Yugoslav socialist revolution."[27] Stalin's Comintern
never made a more abrupt abandonment of a previous line. It
took some time longer for the SWP to eat its words (it did so in a
formal statement, *The Tito-Stalin Conflict*, in 1949). This was
the first time that Pablo-Mandel had acted independently.

Frankenstein was no longer fully in control of his creation.
The monster had developed a mind and a will of its own. And
having taken the first step, it soon went all the way to that "complete petty-bourgeois revision of the Marxist-Leninist concept
both of the state and of the proletarian revolution" it had so vehe-
mently denounced. It had been preceded by the RCP leadership.

Haston and Grant of the British RCP had recognized much
earlier that the "orthodox" position was untenable. In 1947,
they had flirted with the idea that the USSR was state capitalist
but had failed to carry it through and then, before Pablo and
Mandel, had collapsed into the Pabloite position. There had indeed been a "revolution from above" in most of Eastern Europe,
and in Yugoslavia and Albania there had been a revolution from
below, led by Stalinist parties and not based on the working
class, which had nevertheless led to the creation of "workers'
states," in which, from the beginning, the workers were excluded from all trace of power.

Pablo himself took a little longer to swallow the poison,

Mandel and Cannon longer still. But swallow it they did and, having done so, found that they could not stop. The drug was addictive. By 1951, it was accepted that the new Stalinist states were "deformed workers' states," deformed rather than degenerated because, so to say, they had never been undegenerated, the workers had never held power.

Thus "orthodoxy" had led to the most profound revisionism. The FI had itself abandoned "the historical mission of the proletariat as formulated by Marx." But what, then, remained of the historical justification for the FI?

Centuries of deformed workers' states?

An epoch of transition between capitalism and socialism, an epoch that has already begun and is quite advanced.... This transformation will probably take an entire period of several centuries, and will, in the meantime, be filled with forms and regimes transitional between capitalism and socialism, and necessarily deviating from "pure" forms and norms.
— Pablo, *Where Are We Going?* 1951

When Arne Swabeck came to the plenum a few days later he said, "What is this—centuries of degenerated workers' states?" And he told us that a girl comrade got up in the Chicago branch and asked..., "If there are going to be centuries of Stalinism, what's the sense of my going out and selling 10 papers on the street corner?" A very good question.
— Cannon, *Internationalism and the SWP*

The FI'S flirtation with Tito was short-lived. For this was the era of the Cold War, which erupted into a limited hot war in Korea in 1950. Kim Il Sung of North Korea, although he was probably not aware of the fact, was transformed along with his East European analogues from the Bonapartist dictator of a capitalist police state into the leader of a "workers' state," albeit a deformed one. The "award" was made retrospective, so to say, to the time he was installed by the Russian army in 1945. But Kim Il Sung, at that time, was a Russian puppet pure and simple. Tito was not; and well aware that his survival depended in the last resort on U.S. support, he flatly refused to support the Russian bloc against the U.S. and its satellites in the Korean War. The FI, on the other hand, swung behind Stalin.

For now, the "very powerful pressure of Stalinism" was being felt not merely by the "French intelligentsia," but by Trotskyists themselves. The Cold War sharply polarized the European working-class movement, with the Left (even in Britain) strongly under Stalinist influence. The Communist Parties were everywhere eliminated from government and adopted a "leftish" line—promoting strikes and demonstrations, etc. The right wing, including the leadership of the British Labor Party (and the Tribune ex-lefts), became violently pro-American. There wasn't much breathing space between the right and the Stalinists. There was immense pressure to "choose sides"—for Stalin or for Truman. The Secretariat chose Stalin and, in doing so, precipitated the first and biggest of the international splits in the FI.

This capitulation was not simply a question of lack of moral fiber. The leaders of the FI had resisted infinitely greater pressure to "choose sides" in the Second World War. But then they had a clear, if false, perspective. Now, having swallowed the "bureaucratic revolution from above" thesis and Tito's "proletarian revolution" from below carried out by a peasant army under Stalinist control, there was no firm ground under their feet. The effect of Mao Tse-tung's conquest of China with another peasant army (1947–49), a "Yugoslav socialist revolution" on a vastly greater scale, completed their disorientation.

Under the impact of events, Pablo had rediscovered a previously little-noted passage in the 1938 program that stated:

> One cannot categorically deny in advance the theoretical possibility that, under the influence of completely exceptional circumstances (war, defeat, financial crash, mass revolutionary pressure, etc.) the petty-bourgeois parties, including the Stalinists, may go further than they themselves wish along the road to a break with the bourgeoisie.

But this "highly improbable variant," as Trotsky had called it, now became the real perspective. At the same time, the "transitional period," which for Marx and Lenin had been the period after the conquest of power by the working class until the final withering away of the state (i.e., the period of the proletarian dictatorship), was redefined by Pablo as the present ("an epoch that...is quite advanced"). In plain words, Stalinist dictatorships are the dictatorship of the proletariat! This, the notorious "centuries of deformed workers' states" thesis, went hand in hand with the proposal for "entry sui generis" by the FI group into the Stalinist (and other "petty bourgeois") parties.

In the autumn of 1950, an extended plenum of the FI executive adopted the perspectives that were to be endorsed by the Third World Congress (1951). These theses predicted "a new world war in the relatively near future." They added that, by its nature, this war would be a "war-revolution."[28] The two power blocs were now described as "imperialism and the anti-imperialist camp"—the same labels as those used by the Stalinists—and, in the "war-revolution," the Stalinist states, the "colonial revolution," and the working class, led by Stalinist parties, would be the anti-imperialist side.

From this and the imminence of "war-revolution" flowed "entry sui generis," an entry intended not to split but to influence the Stalinist parties. As Pablo explained it:

> These organizations cannot be smashed and replaced by others in the relatively short time between now and the decisive conflict. All the more so since these organizations will be obliged, whether they wish it or not, to give a leftward turn to the whole or at least a part of the leadership.[29]

This was a return to the "reformist" Trotskyism (reformist with respect to Stalinism) of pre-1933. Though the need for the FI was still proclaimed, the political basis for it was completely abandoned.

The 1953 split

But the revisionism of 1940 was by no means as deep and definitive as the revisionism that we have split with today. There is not a single member of this plenum who contemplates any later relations in the same party with the strike-breakers of the Pablo-Cochran gang.... [T]he split of 1940 was by no means as definitive and final as is the split today. We are finished and done with Pablo and Pabloism forever, not only here but on the international field.
—Cannon, *Factional Struggle and Party Leadership*

By 1951, practically all the critical tendencies had been eliminated from the FI, or, like the RCP leadership, had eliminated themselves. The split was a split among the erstwhile "orthodox," and it was a split between those who retained some attachment to the traditions of revolutionary Marxism, in however distorted a form, on the one hand, and those who followed Pablo, Mandel, and Frank, on the other. At the beginning of 1952, the Secretariat "reconstructed" the PCI, deposing the then-majority leadership (the followers of Pierre Lambert) and replacing them by a minority coalition of Frank and Mestre. The Lambertists, for all their defects, could not swallow pro-Stalinism. "If these ideas are correct," they wrote of Pablo's theses, "stop chattering about the tactic of entrism, even entrism sui generis, and pose clearly our new tasks: that of a more consistent tendency, not even a left opposition...whose role is to aid Stalinism to overcome its hesitation."[30] After they had been deposed, Lambert and his followers, a considerable majority of the organization, seceded.

In the following year, there were fierce faction fights in the SWP and the reconstructed British section (now led by Healy and Lawrence). The pro-Pablo forces led by Cochran (U.S.) and Lawrence (Great Britain) took Pablo's ideas to their logical conclusion, as did Mestre and his followers in France; three pro-Stalinist splits resulted, the splitters going right over, in the cases of Lawrence and Mestre, to the Stalinists. Another split divided the Bolivian Partido Obrero Revolucionario (POR), by this time a relatively big organization, which the Pablo-Mandel Secretariat was pressing to "enter" the bourgeois nationalist party, the Movimiento Nacionalista Revolucionario (MNR). The majority (Lora group) refused to accept this and was thrown out, recognition being transferred to the Pabloite splinter group of Moscosco.

Cannon, Healy, Lambert, and others set up a rival "International Committee of the FI." The International Secretariat was left, as Pablo complacently put it, "at the same time ideologically more homogenous and organizationally weaker." In fact, it dwindled into insignificance for many years, its remaining sections vanishing into the CP or Socialist Party organizations, where they were to lose as many people as they gained. As to the International Committee, it was politically paralyzed from birth because its leaders, while rejecting Pablo's conclusions, accepted his basic political premises. Its major component (the SWP) was to return, after 10 years, to the original fold.

To return to the starting point. Unfavorable circumstances played a part in the decline of the Fourth Internationalist movement. More important were the fundamental weaknesses of the 1938 program, especially its quite wrong analysis of Stalinism.

In addition, the very pretensions of an "International" without any real working-class base were themselves an added handicap. The ludicrous notion that an "international leadership" could be constructed from people who had no serious practical experience of leadership in national organizations was another of Trotsky's errors, which had a most harmful effect on the movement. As long as Trotsky lived, he could substitute for such a leadership. Without him, the "World Party of the Socialist Revolution" was even weaker in the head than it was in the arm.

TROTSKY'S HERITAGE:

ON THE 50TH ANNIVERSARY OF
THE FOUNDING OF
THE FOURTH INTERNATIONAL

IN MARCH 1935, Trotsky, then an exile in France, made this entry in his diary:

> Rakovsky was virtually my last contact with the old revolutionary generation. After his capitulation there is nobody left....
> Now nobody remains. For a long time now I have not been able to satisfy my need to exchange ideas and discuss problems.... And still I think that the work in which I am engaged now, despite its insufficient and fragmentary nature, is the most important work of my life—more important than 1917, more important than the period of the civil war or any other....
> There is now no one except me to carry out the mission of arming a new generation with the revolutionary method over the heads of the leaders of the Second and Third Internationals.... I need at least about five more years of uninterrupted work to ensure the succession.[1]

Rakovsky, a veteran revolutionary internationalist who had been head of the Ukranian Soviet government after the revolution and a prominent leader of the Left and United Oppositions, had been in exile in Central Asia since late 1927. Old, chronically ill, and totally isolated, he was induced in March 1934 to declare that he "will give up his struggle and submit to discipline."[2]

First published in *International Socialism*, new series, issue 40, Autumn 1988.

He was the last of the leading members of the left in the USSR to submit to Stalin and his fate evidently affected Trotsky deeply. His sense of isolation, of inability to "exchange ideas," that is to discuss informally and to explore possibilities with comrades of experience and independent mind, in no way weakened Trotsky's indomitable will or his superb self-confidence ("too far-reaching self confidence" Lenin had written in his Testament). Yet it was a serious handicap, one for which Trotsky was in no way responsible and about which he could do nothing, but a serious handicap all the same. His associates now were chiefly young revolutionaries who inevitably stood toward him as pupil toward master. The few exceptions (the Dutch revolutionary Sneevliet for example) were not very close to the Left Opposition tradition and were soon to diverge widely.

"There is now no one except me" was thus not arrogance but a simple, rueful recognition of reality. Trotsky was to have his five years (plus a few months), but they were far from uninterrupted, as we shall see.

First, however, look at the magnitude of the claim. His outstanding role in 1917 (he might have added 1905, too), his leading role in the civil war and in the early years of the Comintern, his leadership of the Left Opposition in 1923, of the United Opposition—along with Zinoviev and his associates in 1926–27, his pioneer role in analyzing the roots of the degeneration of the regime that emerged from the Russian Revolution, all this, he thought, was less important than "the work in which I am engaged now," the work, that is to say, of his third exile (1929–40).

Nor is that all. Trotsky, an internationalist to the marrow of his bones, had already, before his final exile, written a devastating critique of the failures of both the Communist International and the leadership of the German Communist Party (KPD) in the revolutionary crisis of 1923, *The Lessons of October*.[3] He had also energetically opposed the reliance of the British Communist Party (encouraged by the leadership of the Communist International) on "left" union officials, and predicted the disastrous outcome of the General Strike of 1926 and the debacle of the Anglo-Soviet Trades Union Committee,[4] had written (and spoken) at length against the subordination of the Chinese Communist Party to the Kuomintang and the whole disastrous course of the Comintern in China,[5] and he had produced the classic critique of the Bukharin-Stalin "socialism in one country" thesis in *The Draft Program of the Communist International, A Criticism of Fundamentals.*[6] All this and many other lesser but valuable contributions before 1929. Yet Trotsky's assessment was essentially correct. His last eleven years were indeed the years of his most important contributions. Of course, the distinction is in some ways artificial. But for what had gone before he could not have done what he did, would not have been the man that he was. A great part of his work after 1929 was repetition and development of what had gone before.

However, if one accepts his view that Stalinism internationally was the greatest single disaster that ever affected the workers' movement—worse than reformist accommodation precisely because it affected the best, most revolutionary and self-sacrificing workers—and that it was, in Trotsky's words "the syphilis of the workers' movement," then his judgment is amply justified. Moreover, how many of Trotsky's writings would be available to us today but for his post-1929 struggle and his creation of a living, *organized* tradition?

At the beginning of 1929, when he was deported to Turkey, Trotsky's mood was not so somber. He accepted that the Opposition had been defeated in the USSR (temporarily, he believed) but he looked to the communist parties outside the USSR, above all to the KPD, the biggest and most influential, but also to the French (PCF) and, indeed, to any he could influence. He had always rejected (as had Lenin) the notion that these parties could be regarded as mere imitations or satellites of the Russian party—now Stalin's apparatus. They had, he believed (rightly), native roots, native strengths, and native weaknesses. All his work for the next four and a half years was directed to influencing them. "All eyes to the Communist Party. We must explain to it. We must convince it."[7]

How to do this? By writing, by polemics of course. He had learned though, through his pre-1917 struggle against Lenin and through his experience in the revolution and in the early years of the Communist International, the importance of cadres, of organization, and he sought simultaneously to influence the cadres (especially the leading cadres) of the Comintern parties and to build up his own cadre. "Faction, not party" was the guiding thread of his activity in these years.

The Comintern, he believed (rightly), then incorporated the cream of the politically conscious working class internationally. Therefore, the handful of people he was able to gather together in 1929–34 were oriented on the Comintern parties. If we look back objectively, emancipating ourselves from the knowledge of what was to follow, then it must be said that he was unquestionably right. Even with the great wisdom of hindsight, no better road appears. There were, at the time, those who thought otherwise, especially and most importantly in Germany.

A digression will be useful here. After the debacle of the German October of 1923, the left (a left with ultraleftist tendencies) had won the leadership of the KPD (April 1924) in spite of the unsuccessful attempts of the Comintern to "moderate" their victory by including some of their opponents in the leadership. This left, however, was both fairly heterogeneous and, most important, not very impressed by the Moscow leadership of the Comintern or unduly subservient to it. Therefore for Stalin, Zinoviev, and then Bukharin it had to be destroyed. The Germans, however, proved to be stiff-necked. It required three years of maneuvering (in which Bukharin played a leading role) to split the lefts into various factions, to expel the most intransigent, and to promote the obedient Thaelmann (who had impeccable left credentials, was an impressive speaker, and was also incapable of initiative) to the central leading role.[8] By 1928, all this had been achieved and there were five or six "leftist" groups of various sizes and persuasions outside the KPD. Most important was the Leninbund, led by Hugo Urbahns, a veteran of the 1923 rising in Hamburg and a leading leftist ever since.

Trotsky naturally tried to win the Leninbund (which had several thousand adherents in 1929–30) but was quickly repulsed. Urbahns and his cadre believed that the KPD had to be written off. A new communist party had to be built. They also believed that a counter-revolution had occurred in the USSR (a belief common amongst German left communists too) and that the Russian regime now represented a species of state capitalism. Trotsky would not entertain or compromise with either of these positions or with the generally ultraleftist yet erratic orientation of Urbahns. He was firmly convinced that the break-up of the "right-center bloc" in the USSR in the summer and autumn of 1929 (when Stalin and his supporters broke with Bukharin, Rykov, Tomsky, etc., and launched the mass collectivization of agriculture by coercion and industrialization at breakneck speed) represented a left zigzag by the (he thought) basically "centrist" Stalin faction. Indeed, as he wrote in April 1930:

The course of 1928–31—if we again leave aside the inevitable waverings and backslidings—represents an attempt of the bureaucracy to adapt itself to the proletariat....

> The zigzags of Stalinism show that the bureaucracy is not a class, not an independent historical factor, but an instrument, an executive organ of the classes. The left zigzag is proof that no matter how far the preceding right course had gone, it nevertheless developed on the basis of the dictatorship of the proletariat.[9]

At the same time:

> The elements of dual power contained in the apparatus have not disappeared.... They have undoubtedly become even stronger as the plebiscitary degeneration of the apparatus has progressed.... Not only ideological but organizational tentacles of the counter-revolution [i.e., of the bourgeoisie, DH] have penetrated deeply into the organs of the proletarian dictatorship.[10]

Thus a new shift "rightwards," a "Thermidor," remained a real danger. Against that danger Stalin had to be supported. Thus Trotsky profoundly underestimated the fundamental transformation that was occurring in the USSR in these years and, although he was to modify his views in 1934, the long-term effects of this error were to prove enormous.

On the question of attempting to create new communist parties, Trotsky was eminently realistic. Only the impact of great events could create such a possibility and those events might be by no means favorable. Indeed, within a short time the impact of the world depression and the extraordinarily rapid growth of fascism in Germany highlighted the matter starkly.

In 1931, Trotsky wrote:

> Hugo Urbahns, who considers himself a "left communist," declares the German party bankrupt, politically done for, and proposes to create a new party. If Urbahns were right, it would mean that the victory of the fascists is certain. For, in order to create a new party, years are required.[11]

In fact the project was, in those years, utterly utopian. The myth of the "workers' fatherland," the USSR, however rapidly the reality was departing from it, and the gravitational pull of the Comintern parties, especially the bigger ones, were far, far too powerful. Moreover, those parties were still, in spite of all the Comintern's blunders, made up of revolutionaries. Even their apparatuses, allowing for an inevitable quota of cynics and bureaucrats, were subjectively revolutionary. To write them off, without the most strenuous and persistent efforts at reform, was, as Trotsky said, truly capitulation under the cover of radical phrases.

A new factor was emerging. To a considerable extent, from the Sixth Congress of the Comintern (August–September 1928) and, most violently, since the Tenth Plenum of its Executive (July 1929), the communist parties had been pulled sharply to the left, in fact to ultraleft positions (most crucially the rejection of the United Front tactic—just as it was becoming centrally important), although these were to be periodically punctuated by opportunist maneuvers. Moreover, to "explain" the new term, it was discovered that the Social Democrats had now become social-fascists! This was, in Comintern parlance, the so-called "Third Period," that of "ascending revolutionary struggles."

Trotsky's criticism of Comintern policy from 1925 onwards had been from the left (Britain, China, and so on). Now he appeared as a critic from the right. His splendid polemics *The Third Period of the Comintern's Errors*[12] (January 1930) and *The Turn in the Communist International and the Situation in Germany*[13] (September 1930) are still indispensable reading as models of analysis and tactical prescription.

Naturally, they did not endear him to the "lefts," superficially his most obvious constituency. They also brought to the fore the relationship of the International Left Opposition (the first conference of which took place in Paris in April 1930) to the considerably bigger right oppositional forces, expelled from or seceding from some of the Comintern parties in this period. The right, most important of which was the German KPO led by Heinrich Brandler, Thalheimer, Frolich, and Walscher (all prominent KPD leaders up to and including 1923), had retained a following of thousands, especially union militants, agreed entirely with Trotsky about the absurdities of the Third Period and the centrality of the United Front tactic in and after 1929. Were these not natural allies?

Trotsky decisively rejected this notion. As early as March 1929, he had written:

> Communist opportunism expresses itself in the urge to re-establish under present day conditions the pre-war Social Democracy. This is to be seen with especial clarity in Germany. Today's Social Democracy is infinitely removed from Bebel's party. But history testifies that Bebel's party became converted into present day So-

cial Democracy.... Yet so far as I can see the efforts of Brandler, Thalheimer, and their friends are aimed in this direction.[14]

He specified three basic criteria for the cadre he was striving to create. First, the British question and opposition to the line of subordination of the Communist Party of Great Britain to the Anglo-Soviet Trades Union Committee:

> a classic example of the policy of centrism sliding to the right...a basic question of European politics. The Stalinist course on this question constitutes the most flagrant, cynical, and ruinous violation of the principles of Bolshevism and the theoretical ABC of Marxism.... Whoever has still failed to understand this is not a Marxist, not a revolutionary politician of the proletariat.[15]

Second, the Chinese question.

> The study of the problems of the Chinese Revolutions [of 1925—27, DH] is a necessary condition for the education of the opposition and the ideological demarcation within its ranks. Those elements who have failed to take a clear and precise position on this question reveal thereby a national narrowness which is itself an unmistakable symptom of opportunism.[16]

Finally, the Russian Question.

> Because of the conditions created by the October revolution the three classic tendencies in socialism, i) the Marxist tendency; ii) the centrist tendency; and iii) the opportunist tendency, are most clearly and precisely expressed.... So far as I know, Brandler and Thalheimer have all these years considered as absolutely correct the policy of the CPSU [the Communist Pary of the Soviet Union] on economic questions.[17]

Was this, perhaps, a sectarian attitude? Were some thousands (perhaps some tens of thousands or so internationally) rejected, alienated because of an insistence on a "narrow" Trotskyist platform? Not so. The Right Oppositional groupings were, or rapidly became, rightward moving centrists. Wrong as I believe Trotsky was on the Russian question, he had touched a raw nerve. Brandler, Lovestone (his American counterpart), and the rest professed to believe that Stalin was right about everything in the USSR (up to and including the first great show trial—that of Zinoviev, Kamenev, etc., in 1936) and was merely misinformed about the rest of the world. As Trotsky wrote of the KPO at the beginning of 1932:

> Their practical goal is self evident.... "If you place me at the head of the party in Germany," says Brandler to Stalin, "I on my

part shall bind myself to recognizing your infallibility in Russian matters, provided you permit me to put through my own policies on German matters."

Needless to say, the rightists would have no truck with the Left Opposition's criticisms of the Bukharin-Stalin policies in Britain and China. Occasional tactical agreements apart, there was no common basis for unity. This issue is of more than historical significance.

In the next years Trotsky wrote some of his most important contributions to revolutionary theory. If we think of Trotsky's *heritage*, then a major element, by any reckoning, must be his devastating criticisms of the policies of the Comintern and the KPD in the years of Hitler's rise to power. For not only are these writings a brilliant exposition of revolutionary tactics, they also represent a genuine deepening of our understanding of living Marxism in theory and practical application alike. To select only one, *Germany: What Next?*[18] (January 1932) has rarely been equaled and never (in my view) excelled in the whole body of Marxist writing from 1848 onwards. Add to these works that profound analysis of the dynamics of the revolutionary process, *The History of the Russian Revolution* (1932), and our debt to the Trotsky of this period is enormous.

Yet the immediate effect of all this was small. Although various communist parties, notably the KPD, did experience various internal crises during the Third Period,[19] the Moscow line held. There was no struggle for a United Front against the fascists. Hitler came to power without civil war in January 1933.

In 1931, Trotsky had written:

Yes, should the fascists really come to power that would mean not only the physical destruction of the Communist Party, but veritable political bankruptcy for it.... The seizure of power by the fascists would therefore most probably signify the necessity of creating a new revolutionary party, and in all likelihood also a new International. *That would be a frightful historical catastrophe.*[20]

That catastrophe now had to be faced. Hitler's victory was not merely a German phenomenon. By August 1940, the time of Trotsky's murder by a Stalinist killer, Hitler controlled all Europe west of the USSR (and was in alliance with Stalin) and east of Britain. Europe was then a much more important part of the world than it is now. Trotsky's worst case predictions had been more than fulfilled.

Trotsky did not despair in 1933—or ever. He sought to reorient his forces to face the catastrophe, calling now precisely for a new International. What did they amount to? Less than a month after Hitler became chancellor of Germany, a conference of the Left Opposition was held in Paris. According to the report, "representatives of oppositionist organizations from...the USSR, Germany, France, Britain, Belgium, the United States, Greece, Italy, Spain, Bulgaria, and Switzerland" attended.[21] The conference did not seriously discuss the new situation (it had been convened and prepared prior to Hitler's victory). What concerns us here is what was really represented. The opposition in the USSR had ceased to exist as an organized body. Trotsky had no contact with it after 1932. Repression, the capitulation of most of the leading oppositionists to Stalin's "left course," the defection of most of the young intransigents to the position that the Thermidor had already occurred, had fragmented it. The German section was soon reduced to coteries of émigrés. Of the rest, the French section had about 200 members (and was riven by the struggle between two factions), the Americans had nearly as many (154 were claimed in 1931), the Belgian and British group were smaller but real, the Italians were émigrés in Paris, the Greeks and the Spaniards were soon to defect, and little was to be heard subsequently of the Bulgarians or the Swiss.

In short, there was very little, but a "window of opportunity" seemed to be opening. In the immediate aftermath of Hitler's victory, a temporarily strong leftist current flowed through various centrist and left reformist organizations and fourteen of them (all European) attended a conference in Paris in the summer of 1933 called by the British Independent Labor Party (ILP) to discuss the new situation. The International Left Opposition naturally seized the opportunity to attend. I have written elsewhere at some length about this and the subsequent vicissitudes of Trotsky's movement to 1940.[22] Here a very brief summary will have to suffice.

Trotsky had reluctantly concluded (in April 1933) that the Comintern was finished as a revolutionary force. Therefore it was necessary to take preliminary steps toward the creation of a new international. The Paris conference was seen, on the analogy of 1915, as a new Zimmerwald, whose left should be rallied around the platform of the Opposition (now called the International Communist League). The results fell far short of Trotsky's hopes, but some gains were made out of this orientation (notably in the Netherlands and the U.S.), but it soon became clear that the centrist currents were being pulled rightwards again. The year 1933 was the high point of their development, further gains were unlikely in this milieu.

A most important factor in this development was the partial abandonment of the Third Period, social-fascist line of the Comintern. This was marked, most strikingly, by the conclusion of an agreement between the French party (PCF) and the socialists for joint anti-fascist action (July 1934). Trotsky was not deceived for one moment that this thirteenth hour conversion represented a return to revolutionary politics. On the contrary, he saw it as a bloc between two apparatuses to stifle a real United Front of struggle. Nevertheless, it called for a new orientation. For the main emphasis of the groups had been on the United Front. This now appeared to be a reality in France. It was necessary to get inside. Given the relationship of forces, that could only mean entering one of its components. Hence, given the Stalinist control of the PCF, entry into the much looser socialist party was proposed.

The argument was that the danger of French fascism was imminent (so Trotsky believed) and that the Socialist Party had a considerable and potentially revolutionary left wing. It was here that the nucleus of the new party in France could be forged. The operation was conceived as a fairly short term one. It was attempted in France and then generalized to those other countries where there were real groups. It failed to produce major results. The Trotskyist organizations remained small and not influential. Again, for more detail the reader is referred elsewhere.

What must be stressed here is that the whole situation was becoming rapidly more and more unfavorable. The short-lived United Front line of the Comintern quickly gave way to the Popular Front—for "the defense of democracy" in alliance with whatever bourgeois forces could be induced to join. Class politics was out, and "national defense," military alliances with the USSR against Hitler (the sole point of the Popular Front from Stalin's point of view) were the order of the day. The mass working class organizations, Stalinist and social-democratic alike, were pulled sharply to the right, the centrist groups tagging along, protesting but moving the same way a certain distance behind. Most of the allies or half allies of 1933 became hostile to the Trotskyists. They were now more isolated than ever.

There was another factor. More or less simultaneously with the Popular Front line came the terror in the USSR, the wiping out by mass executions and wholesale imprisonment of most of the prominent members of all the former tendencies of the Russian Communist Party, including many of Stalin's own former supporters—and a vast host of others. The three great show trials of former old Bolshevik leaders (1936–38) were the tip of the iceberg in this slaughter, but they served a very important purpose. For the accused were convicted of acting in concert with Trotsky and in the interests of Hitler, to "restore capitalism" in the USSR, dismember the country, and serve the interests of fascism, and the accused were induced to confess to these crimes.

A torrent of lies and fabrications flowed from the communist parties around the world to sustain the absurd charges and to prove (as Stalin put it) that "Trotskyism is the spearhead of the counter-revolutionary bourgeoisie."[23] The leaders of the Popular Front socialists (the French and Spanish parties, the British Labor left, etc.), with very rare exceptions, would not denounce the monstrous slanders. After all, they were for class collaboration and very much against the class struggle politics for which "Trotskyism" had become a synonym. Trotsky himself was driven from France, found a temporary refuge in Norway and finally in Mexico. None of the major "democracies" would admit him, not Britain, not the U.S.

This was the nightmare background to the last great working class upsurge in Europe of the thirties—the Spanish Revolution and civil war of 1936–39. That revolution was strangled by the Spanish Popular Front, which paved the way for Franco's victory. The Trotskyist forces in Spain were negligible and quite unable to affect the course of events. From the point of view of the political heritage, however, these years produced Trotsky's last writings on a major revolutionary process and are of great value.[24]

Towards the end of the 1930s, then, the situation for revolutionary Marxists was grave. The fascists were gaining victory after victory, the Comintern, founded as the instrument of international proletarian revolution, had become a counter-revolutionary force. In 1938, Trotsky had written of "the definite passing over of the Comintern to the side of the bourgeois order, its cynically counterrevolutionary role throughout the world."[25] And yet the Comintern was bigger and more influential than ever. The various attempts to remedy the strategy of seeking to influence the communist parties until 1933, the attempted regroupment with (temporarily) leftward moving centrists in 1933–34, the entry tactic, and the attempts to establish independent parties from 1934 onwards all had failed in a strategic sense—gains (and losses) had been made but nowhere had the relationship of forces been altered.

Trotsky summed up the experience in April 1939:

> We are not progressing politically.... We are in a small boat in a tremendous current. There are five or ten boats and one goes down and we say it was bad helmsmanship. But this was not the reason—it was because the current was too strong. It is the most general explanation.[26]

This is surely true. Whatever errors had been made by the Fourth Internationalist groups, and inevitably there were errors, had only a trivial effect compared to the overwhelming difficulties of a profoundly adverse situation.

What then had been achieved? A good deal, in spite of everything. The *living* continuity of the tradition of Marx and Lenin had been maintained, although by very slender forces, and it had been *enriched* by application to new problems. Trotsky's heritage, embodied in his writings, is a major and very important part of our political armory. Now these writings would not, for the most part, have been produced at all but for Trotsky's extreme tenacity in seeking to create a revolutionary cadre in the struggle to change the course of events. Our own international tendency was born out of that cadre, which, with all its manifold defects, was the only living continuation of the tradition of Lenin.

Of course, the heritage also had negative features, weaknesses, which were to prove of great importance. Three, in ascending order of importance, must be noted.

First, the proclamation of the Fourth International in 1938 (proclamation rather than foundation since nothing was changed). No new forces were brought in nor could any reasonably be hoped for in that time of extreme ebb. It simply gave a new and excessively grandiose title to the existing and very weak international Trotskyist current. In itself, this might not seem to be of great importance, yet it helped to generate delusions of grandeur in the "International leadership" that managed to establish itself in the mid-1940s and hindered their ability to make realistic assessments of the new post-war situation.

Second, and more important, Trotsky held a very catastrophic view of the immediate prospects for capitalism toward the end of his life, "even in the absence of proletarian revolution." He even committed himself (in 1939) to the proposition that:

> The disintegration of capitalism has reached extreme limits, likewise the disintegration of the old ruling class. The further existence of this system is impossible.[27]

This assessment was not grounded in any serious economic analysis and represents a specimen of the "automatic breakdown of capitalism" school of thought, which had always been rejected by Lenin and runs counter to the main thrust of Trotsky's own thinking. His entire record entitles us to believe that he would have abandoned it had he lived longer. Unfortunately, he was murdered in 1940 and nearly all his followers took the catastrophic view very seriously. Hence they adopted an entirely false economic (and so political) perspective after the war and, in many cases, persisted in it long after its falsity should have been obvious.

Third, and most important, Trotsky's analysis of the USSR after 1928–29 was quite wrong. The argument is familiar enough to readers of this journal and will not be repeated here. What is important is that the belief that the Stalinist regime was near to collapse ("a few years or even a few months"[28] was his estimate in 1939) colored the views of his followers so that they were totally unprepared for the expansion of Stalinist states after 1944, both by Russian arms and by indigenous Stalinist parties in backward countries, becoming disorientated and pulled, in many cases, toward a "critical" support for Stalinist regimes[29] and hence into various other forms of substitutionism. Here they tended to preserve the forms of Trotsky's views on the USSR whilst departing more and more from the spirit of his revolutionary Marxism, from the working class as the subject of history.

These were serious faults on Trotsky's part, but it is unreasonable to blame him for all the errors of his disciples. He himself had changed his mind repeatedly in the past in the light of new situations and new circumstances. The fact that, as he wrote in 1935, "There is now no one except me," nobody, that is, of the older generation that had been through Lenin's school, is a measure of the extreme devastation wrought by Stalinism. Such devastation could not fail to have its effect in imposing a near impossible burden on Trotsky.

He bore that burden to the end. We owe him an immense debt and we can best discharge it by a serious, critical study of his great works on strategy and tactics and the dynamics of revolution.

NOTES

INTRODUCTION TO THE 2003 EDITION

1. Isaac Deutscher, *The Prophet Armed*, *The Prophet Unarmed*, and *The Prophet Outcast*, first published by Oxford University Press (1954–1963), are scheduled to be reissued in 2003 and 2004 by Verso.
2. Trotsky, *The Stalin School of Falsification* (London: New Park, 1974). Trotsky, *My Life* (Harmondsworth: Penguin, 1975).
3. Slavoj Zizek, *Revolution at the Gates: Selected Writing of Lenin from 1917* (London and New York: Verso, 2002). Zizek explains why Trotsky is a "special" case:

> Quite logically, "de-Stalinization" was indicated by the opposite process of "rehabilitation," of admitting "errors" in the past politics of the Party. The gradual "rehabilitation" of the demonized Bolsheviks' ex-leaders can thus serve as perhaps the most sensitive index of how far (and in what direction) the "de-Stalinization" of the Soviet Union was going. The first to be rehabilitated were the senior military leaders shot in 1937 (Tukhachevsky and others); the last to be rehabilitated, in the Gorbachev era, just before the collapse of the Communist regime, was Bukharin—this last rehabilitation, of course, was a clear sign of the turn towards capitalism: the Bukharin who was rehabilitated was the one who, in the 1920s, advocated a pact between workers and peasants (owners of their land), launching the famous slogan "enrich yourselves!," and opposed forced collectivization. Significantly, however, one figure that was *never* rehabilitated, excluded by the Communists as well as the by the anti-Communist Russian nationalists: Trotsky, the "wandering Jew" of the Revolution, the true anti-Stalin, the arch-

enemy, opposing the idea of "permanent revolution" to the idea of "building socialism in one country."

I am tempted here to risk a parallel with Freud's distinction between primordial (founding) and secondary repression in the Unconscious: Trotsky's exclusion amounted to something which can never be readmitted through "rehabilitation," since the entire Order relied on this negative gesture of exclusion. Trotsky is the one for whom there is no room either in pre-1990 Really Existing Socialism or in the post-1990 Really Existing Capitalism, in which even those who are nostalgic for Communism do not know what to do with Trotsky's permanent revolution—perhaps the signifier "Trotsky" is the most appropriate designation of that which is worth redeeming in the Leninist legacy."

4. Duncan Hallas, Introduction to Leon Trotsky, *The Lessons of October* [1924] (Chicago and London: Bookmarks, 1987), pp. 6–7.

5. Zizek, *Revolution at the Gates,* p. 192.

6. Leon Trotsky, diary entry of March 25, 1935, in Trotsky, *Trotsky's Diary in Exile: 1935,* trans Elena Zarudnaaya (Cambridge: Harvard University Press, 1958), pp. 46–47.

7. Hallas, "Trotsky's Heritage," *Trotsky's Marxism and Other Essays,* p. 184.

8. Introduction to *The Fourth International* (Chicago and London: International Socialism Reprints, 1988), p. 1.

9. Hallas, "The Meaning of Marxism (London: Pluto, 1971).

10. Hallas, "The Legacy of Karl Marx," *Socialist Worker,* March 1983, reprinted in *Socialist Worker,* September 27, 2002, p. 9.

TROTSKY'S MARXISM

INTRODUCTION TO THE 1984 EDITION

1. Perry Anderson, *Considerations on Western Marxism* (London: New Left Books, 1976), p. 29.

CHAPTER I. PERMANENT REVOLUTION

1. Engels to Kautsky, *Marx and Engels: Selected Correspondence 1846–1895* (London: Lawrence & Wishart, 1936), p. 399.

2. "Manifesto of the Russian Social Democratic Workers' Party (1898)," in R.V. Daniels, ed., *A Documentary History of Communism*, vol. 1 (New York: Vintage, 1962), p. 7.
3. V.I. Lenin, *Collected Works*, vol. 9 (Moscow: Foreign Languages Publishing House, 1960), pp. 55–57. Emphasis in original.
4. Lenin, *Collected Works*, vol. 21, p. 33.
5. Leon Trotsky, "Our Differences," *1905* (New York: Vintage, 1972), p. 312.
6. Trotsky, "Our Differences," p. 312.
7. Trotsky, "Our Differences," pp. 313–14.
8. Trotsky, "Results and Prospects," *The Permanent Revolution and Results and Prospects* (London: New Park, 1962), pp. 194–95. Emphasis added.
9. Lenin, *Collected Works*, vol. 9, p. 28.
10. Trotsky, "Our Differences," p. 317.
11. It would take us too far afield from the limited purpose of this book to attempt to justify these statements. Trotsky's own *History of the Russian Revolution*, vols. 1 and 2 (London: Sphere, 1977, and Pluto Press, 1978) and Tony Cliff's *Lenin*, vol. 2 (London: Pluto Press, 1976) provide, from slightly different angles, the decisive evidence.
12. Cliff, *Lenin*, vol. 2, p. 138.
13. Isaac Deutscher, *The Prophet Unarmed* (London: Oxford University Press, 1959), p. 323.
14. Trotsky, "The Chinese Communist Party and the Kuomintang," *Leon Trotsky on China* (New York: Monad, 1976), pp. 113–15.
15. Trotsky, "First Speech on the Chinese Question," *Leon Trotsky on China*, p. 227.
16. Trotsky, "Summary and Perspectives of the Chinese Revolution," *Leon Trotsky on China*, p. 297.
17. Trotsky, "The Chinese Revolution and the Theses of Comrade Stalin," *Leon Trotsky on China*, pp. 162–63.

CHAPTER 2. STALINISM

1. Lenin, *Collected Works*, vol. 33, pp. 65–66.
2. E.H. Carr, *The Bolshevik Revolution*, vol. 2 (Harmondsworth: Penguin, 1963), pp. 194–200.

3. Victor Serge, *From Lenin to Stalin* (New York: Monad, 1973), p. 39.
4. Trotsky, in Isaac Deutscher, *The Prophet Armed* (London: Oxford University Press, 1954), p. 509.
5. Lenin, *Collected Works,* vol. 32, p. 24.
6. Lenin, *Collected Works,* vol. 32, p. 48.
7. A detailed account is given in Deutscher, *The Prophet Unarmed*, especially chapters 2 and 5.
8. *Platform of the Opposition* (London: New Park, 1973), pp. 35–36.
9. Stalin, in Trotsky, *The Revolution Betrayed* (London: New Park, 1967), p. 291.
10. Trotsky, "Where is the Soviet Republic Going?" *Writings of Leon Trotsky, 1929* (New York: Pathfinder Press, 1975), pp. 47–48.
11. Trotsky, "Where is the Soviet Republic Going?" p. 50.
12. Trotsky, "Where is the Soviet Republic Going?" p. 51.
13. Trotsky, "Problems of the Development of the USSR," *Writings of Leon Trotsky, 1930–31* (New York: Pathfinder Press, 1973), p. 215.
14. Trotsky, "Problems of the Development of the USSR," p. 225. Emphasis in original.
15. Alec Nove, *An Economic History of the USSR* (Harmondsworth: Penguin, 1965), p. 206.
16. Trotsky, "The Class Nature of the Soviet State," *Writings of Leon Trotsky, 1933–34* (New York: Pathfinder Press, 1972), pp. 117–18. Emphasis in original.
17. Trotsky, "The Workers' State, Thermidor, and Bonapartism," *Writings of Leon Trotsky, 1934–35* (New York: Pathfinder Press, 1971), pp. 166–67.
18. Trotsky, "The Workers' State, Thermidor, and Bonapartism," p. 182.
19. Trotsky, "The Workers' State, Thermidor and Bonapartism," pp. 182.
20. Trotsky, quoted in Deutscher, *The Prophet Unarmed*, p. 139.
21. Trotsky, "The Workers' State, Thermidor and Bonapartism," pp. 172–73. Emphasis in original.
22. Trotsky, "The Death Agony of Capitalism and the Tasks of the Fourth International," *Documents of the Fourth International* (New York: Pathfinder Press, 1973), p. 210. Em-

phasis in original.
23. Trotsky, "The Death Agony of Capitalism," p. 211.
24. Trotsky, "The Death Agony of Capitalism," pp. 211–12.
25. Trotsky, *The Revolution Betrayed* (London: New Park, 1967), p. 278.
26. Trotsky, "The Death Agony of Capitalism," p. 213. Emphasis in original.
27. Trotsky, *The Revolution Betrayed*, p. 254.
28. Trotsky, *The Revolution Betrayed*, p. 255.

CHAPTER 3. STRATEGY AND TACTICS

1. Trotsky, "Manifesto of the Communist International to the Workers of the World," *The First Five Years of the Communist International*, vol. 1 (New York: Pioneer, 1945), pp. 29–30.
2. Jane Degras, *The Communist International, 1919–43*, vol. 1 (London: Cass, 1971), p. 16.
3. Degras, *Communist International, 1919–43*, p. 6.
4. Lenin, *Collected Works*, vol. 28, p. 455.
5. S. Haffner, *Failure of a Revolution: Germany 1918–19* (London: Andre Deutsch, 1973), p. 152.
6. Lenin, *Collected Works*, vol. 21, p. 40.
7. Degras, *Communist International, 1919–43*, pp. 12–13.
8. Degras, *Communist International, 1919–43*, p. 19.
9. Lenin, *Collected Works*, vol. 25, p. 393.
10. Lenin, *Collected Works*, vol. 29, p. 311.
11. Degras, *Communist International, 1919–43*, p. 13
12. Lenin, *Collected Works*, vol. 31, pp. 206–07.
13. Lenin, *Collected Works*, vol. 31, p. 206.
14. Degras, *Communist International, 1919–43*, p. 109.
15. Trotsky, "Speech on Comrade Zinoviev's Report on the Role of the Party," *The First Five Years*, vol. 1, pp. 97–99.
16. Trotsky, *First Five Years*, vol. 1, p. 101.
17. Trotsky, *First Five Years*, vol. 1, p. 141.
18. Trotsky, *First Five Years*, vol. 1, pp. 303–05.
19. Trotsky, *First Five Years*, vol. 1, pp. 294–95.
20. Degras, *Communist International, 1919–43*, p. 230.
21. Trotsky, *First Five Years*, vol. 2, pp. 91–95.
22. Trotsky, *Writings of Leon Trotsky, 1932–33* (New York: Pathfinder Press, 1972), pp. 51–55.

23. E.H. Carr, *The Interregnum, 1923–1924* (Harmondsworth: Penguin, 1965), p. 221.
24. Trotsky, "Lessons of the General Strike," *Trotsky's Writings on Britain*, vol. 2 (London: New Park, 1974), pp. 241, 245.
25. Trotsky, "Lessons of the General Strike," p. 244. Emphasis in original.
26. Trotsky, "Lessons of the General Strike," pp. 252–53.
27. Degras, *The Communist International: Documents,* 3 vol. (London: Cass, 1971), p. 44.
28. Degras, *Communist International: Documents,* p. 159.
29. Degras, *Communist International: Documents,* p. 224.
30. Trotsky, "The Turn in the Communist International," *The Struggle against Fascism in Germany* (New York: Pathfinder Press, 1971), pp. 57–60. Emphasis in original.
31. Trotsky, "What Next?" *The Struggle against Fascism in Germany,* p. 248.
32. Trotsky, "What Next?" p. 254.
33. Degras, *Communist International: Documents,* p. 375.
34. Degras, *Communist International: Documents,* p. 390.
35. Degras, *Communist International: Documents,* p. 384.
36. See Felix Morrow, *Revolution and Counter-Revolution in Spain* (New York: Pioneer, 1938), p. 34.
37. Morrow, *Revolution and Counter-Revolution in Spain,* p. 35.
38. Trotsky, "The Lessons of Spain: The Last Warning," *The Spanish Revolution (1931–39)* (New York: Pathfinder Press, 1973), pp. 322–23.

CHAPTER 4. PARTY AND CLASS

1. Deutscher, *The Prophet Armed,* p. 45.
2. *1903: Second Congress of the Russian Social Democratic Labor Party* (London: New Park, 1973), p. 204.
3. Trotsky, "Our Political Tasks," in Daniels, ed., *A Documentary History of Communism,* vol. 1, p. 31.
4. See Schurer, "The Permanent Revolution," in Leopold Labedz, ed., *Revisionism* (London: Allen & Unwin, 1962), p. 73. Emphasis added.
5. Schurer, *Permanent Revolution,* p. 74.
6. See Cliff, *Lenin,* vol. 1 (London: Pluto Press, 1976), pp.

168–179; vol. 2, pp. 97–139.

7. Trotsky, "What Next?" p. 163. Emphasis in original.
8. Trotsky, "What Next?" pp. 163–64.
9. Trotsky, "What Next?" p. 159.
10. Trotsky, "Manifesto of the Communist International," p. 29.
11. Trotsky, "What Next?" p. 254.
12. Trotsky, "The Spanish Revolution and the Danger Threatening it," p. 133.
13. Trotsky, "The Groupings in the Communist Opposition," *Writings of Leon Trotsky, 1929*, p. 81.
14. Trotsky, "The International Left Opposition: Its Tasks and Methods," *Writings of Leon Trotsky, 1932–33*, p. 56.
15. Trotsky, *History of the Russian Revolution*, vol. 1, p. 306.
16. Trotsky, "The Evolution of the Comintern," *Documents of the Fourth International*, vol. 1, p. 128.
17. Trotsky, "Thermidor and Bonapartism," *Writings of Leon Trotsky, 1930–31*, p. 75.
18. Trotsky, "For a Workers' United Front against Fascism," *The Struggle against Fascism in Germany*, p. 134. Emphasis in original.
19. Trotsky, "Germany: Key to the International Situation," *The Struggle against Fascism in Germany*, pp. 121–22.
20. Trotsky, "The Stalin Bureaucracy in Straits," *Writings of Leon Trotsky, 1932* (New York: Pathfinder Press, 1973), p. 125.
21. Trotsky, "To the Editorial Board of *Prometeo*," *Writings of Leon Trotsky, 1930* (New York: Pathfinder Press, 1975), pp. 285–86.
22. Cliff, *Lenin*, vol. 2, p. 12.
23. J. van Heijenoort, *With Trotsky in Exile* (Cambridge: Harvard University Press, 1978), p. 38.
24. Trotsky, "Lessons of the SFIO Entry," *Writings of Leon Trotsky, 1935–36* (New York: Pathfinder Press, 1970), p. 31.
25. Trotsky, "It Is Time to Stop," *Writings of Leon Trotsky, 1933–34*, pp. 90–91.
26. Trotsky, "Centrist Alchemy or Marxism," *Writings of Leon Trotsky, 1934–35*, p. 274.
27. Trotsky, "A Great Achievement," *Writings of Leon Trotsky, 1937–38* (New York: Pathfinder Press, 1976), p. 439.

CHAPTER 5. THE HERITAGE

1. See *The Moscow Trials: An Anthology* (London: New Park, 1967), p. 12.
2. See Deutscher, *The Prophet Outcast* (New York: Vintage, 1964), p. 171.
3. Trotsky, "Fighting against the Stream," *Writings of Leon Trotsky, 1938–39* (New York: Pathfinder Press, 1974), pp. 251–52.
4. Trotsky, "The Death Agony of Capitalism," p. 180; Trotsky, "The USSR in War," *In Defense of Marxism* (London: New Park, 1971), p. 9.
6. Trotsky, "The Death Agony of Capitalism," p. 183.
7. Trotsky, "The Death Agony of Capitalism," p. 182.
8. Trotsky, "The Comintern's Liquidation Congress," *Writings of Leon Trotsky, 1935–36*, p. 11.
9. Trotsky, "The USSR in War," p. 10.
10. Michael Kidron, *Western Capitalism Since the War* (Harmondsworth: Penguin, 1967), p. 11.
11. Trotsky, "The Founding of the Fourth International," *Writings of Leon Trotsky, 1938–39*, p. 87.
12. Trotsky, "The Death Agony of Capitalism," p. 183.
13. Trotsky, "The USSR in War," pp. 4–5.
14. Trotsky, "The USSR in War," p. 21.
15. Trotsky, "The USSR in War," p. 18.
16. Trotsky, *The Revolution Betrayed*, pp. 245–46.
17. Trotsky, "Ten Years," *Writings of Leon Trotsky, 1938–39*, p. 341.
18. Karl Marx, *Poverty of Philosophy* (London: Lawrence & Wishart, 1937), pp. 129–30.
19. Marx, "Wage Labor and Capital," *Selected Works of Marx and Engels* (London: Lawrence & Wishart, 1934), pp. 265–66.
20. Cliff, *State Capitalism in Russia* (London: Pluto Press, 1974), p. 276.
21. Trotsky, "The USSR in War," pp. 16–17.
22. Harold Isaacs, *The Tragedy of the Chinese Revolution* (London: Secker & Warburg, 1938), p. 394.
23. See Cliff, "Permanent Revolution," *International Socialism*, first series, number 12, 1962, p. 17.
24. Cliff, "Permanent Revolution," p. 18.
25. Cliff, "Permanent Revolution," p. 18.

26. Cliff, "Permanent Revolution," p. 18.

OTHER ESSAYS

TROTSKYISM REASSESSED

1. Trotsky, *Writings of Leon Trotsky, 1932–33,* pp. 51–52.
2. Trotsky, *Writings of Leon Trotsky, 1930–31,* p. 225. Trotsky's emphasis.
3. Deutscher, *The Prophet Outcast,* p. 143.
4. Deutscher, *The Prophet Outcast,* p. 206.
5. Trotsky, *Writings of Leon Trotsky, 1930,* p. 293.
6. James P. Cannon, *History of American Trotskyism* (New York: Pathfinder Press, 1972), pp. 92–93.
7. YvonCraipeau, *Le Mouvement Trotskiste en France,* p. 39.
8. Trotsky. *Writings of Leon Trotsky, 1930,* p. 297. Trotsky's emphasis.
9. Deutscher, *The Prophet Outcast,* p. 60.
10. Cannon, *Speeches to the Party* (New York: Pathfinder Press, 1973), p. 185
11. Trotsky, *Writings of Leon Trotsky, 1938–39,* pp. 251–52.
12. Trotsky, *Writings of Leon Trotsky, 1935–36,* p. 31.
13. Trotsky, *Writings of Leon Trotsky, 1933–34,* p. 90.
14. Trotsky, *Writings of Leon Trotsky, 1933–34,* p. 91.
15. Trotsky, *Writings of Leon Trotsky, 1935–36,* p. 31.
16. *The Development and Disintegration of World Stalinism,* Socialist Workers' Party (U.S.), p. 28.
17. SWP, *Development and Disintegration,* p. 47.

AGAINST THE STREAM

1. Degras, *Communist International: Documents,* p. 44.
2. Degras, *Communist International: Documents,* p. 159.
3. Degras, *Communist International: Documents,* p. 224.
4. Trotsky, "What Next?" p. 254.
5. Trotsky, "Germany: Key to the International Situation," pp. 121–22.
6. Degras, *Communist International: Documents,* p. 257.
7. Degras, *Communist International: Documents,* p. 262.

8. Trotsky, "It Is Impossible to Remain in the Same International with Stalin," *The Struggle against Fascism in Germany*, p. 430.

9. CLGB, *The Fundamental Principles of the International Left Opposition*, 1934.

10. Craipeau, *Le Mouvement Trotskiste en France*, p. 83.

11. Deutscher, *The Prophet Outcast*, p. 206.

12. Craipeau, *Le Mouvement Trotskiste en France*, p. 39.

13. Cannon, *History of American Trotskyism*, p. 93.

14. Pierre Frank, *Histoire de la IV Internationale*. This work has recently been serialized in English by Intercontinental Press. As I have used the serialized version, page references are not given. The author tells us that he "has participated in this 'long march' of the Trotskyists for more than forty years, first becoming part of the international leadership of the Trotskyist movement in 1931." While this is not entirely candid—Frank took part in the breakaway movement led by Raymond Molinier in the thirties—it is true that there are few, if any, better placed to attempt a serious assessment of the struggle to build a revolutionary alternative to Stalinism and social democracy since 1933. Unfortunately the book fails to attempt this. It is an uncritical exposition of the views of the Mandel tendency.

15. Frank, *Histoire de la IV Internationale*.

16. From a statement of the Belgian Communist League, quoted by Trotsky in *Writings of Leon Trotsky, 1934–35*, p. 95.

17. Trotsky, "On the Theses 'Unity and Youth,'" *Writings of Leon Trotsky, 1934–35*, p. 92.

18. Trotsky, "On the Theses 'Unity and Youth,'" *Writings of Leon Trotsky, 1934–35*, p. 95.

19. Frank, *Histoire de la IV Internationale*. At that time, the Trotskyists referred to themselves as "Bolshevik-Leninists."

20. Trotsky, "A New Turn is Necessary," in *Writings of Leon Trotsky, 1934–35*, p. 315.

21. Frank, *Histoire de la IV Internationale*.

22. "On the Tasks of the French Section," in *The Founding Conference of the Fourth International* (New York: Socialist Workers' Party, 1939), pp. 96ff.

23. Cannon, *The Struggle for a Proletarian Party* (New York: Pathfinder Press, 1972), p. 154.

24. Trotsky, "Sectarianism, Centrism, and the Fourth International," in *Writings of Leon Trotsky, 1935–36*, p. 16.
25. Max Shachtman, "Footnote for Historians," *New International*, December 1938.
26. N.S. Khrushchev, "Special Report to the 20th Congress of the CPSU," in *The Moscow Trials: An Anthology* (London: New Park, 1967), pp. 4ff.
27. Stalin, quoted in Deutscher, *The Prophet Outcast*, p. 171.
28. Degras, *Communist International: Documents* p. 375.
29. Degras, *Communist International: Documents*, p. 390.
30. Degras, *Communist International: Documents*, p. 384.
31. Quoted in F. Morrow, *Revolution and Counter-Revolution in Spain*, p. 34.
32. "Statement of the CC of the Spanish CP," quoted in Morrow, *Revolution and Counter-Revolution in Spain*, p. 35.
33. Trotsky, *The Lesson of Spain* (London: Merit, 1969), p. 21.
34. Trotsky, "Centrist Alchemy or Marxism," in *Writings of Leon Trotsky, 1934–35*, p. 274.
35. The Founding Conference of the Fourth International, p. 7.
36. The Founding Conference of the Fourth International, p. 114. The congress also "finally" excluded the Molinier-Frank group. "It is clearer than ever that the whole question of the PCI and the journal *La Commune* has no political significance, but is purely and simply the personal question of R. Molinier and his financial affairs" (p. 108).
37. Frank, *Histoire de la IV Internationale*.
38. Frank, *Histoire de la IV Internationale*.
39. Trotsky, "The Founding of the Fourth International," p. 59.
40. Trotsky in a letter to Emrys Hughes in *Writings of Leon Trotsky, 1938–39*, p. 147.
41. Trotsky, "The Death Agony of Capitalism," p. 11.
42. Trotsky, "The USSR in War," p. 9.
43. Trotsky, "The Death Agony of Capitalism," p. 15.
44. Trotsky, "The Comintern's Liquidation Congress," *Writings, 1935–36*, p. 11.
45. Trotsky, "The Death Agony of Capitalism," p. 13.
46. Trotsky, "The Death Agony of Capitalism," p. 52.
47. Trotsky, "The Death Agony of Capitalism," pp. 47–48.
48. Trotsky, "The USSR in War," p. 17.

49. Trotsky, "India Faced with Imperialist War," in *Writings of Leon Trotsky, 1938–39*, p. 37.

FOURTH INTERNATIONAL IN DECLINE

1. Quoted by Morrow in *New International*, January 1946, p. 13. All emphases added.
2. Cannon, *The Militant*, November 17, 1945. Emphasis added.
3. The membership was variously reported in the internal literature of the period as 1,200 to 1,600.
4. Cannon, "Fractional Struggle and Party Leadership," *Defending the Revolutionary Party*, p. 25.
5. Cannon, "Fractional Struggle and Party Leadership," p. 25. Burnham, of course, was a renegade who later became an active supporter of U.S. imperialism during the Cold War.
6. The Vietnamese Trotskyists were fairly numerous until Ho Chi Minh's Stalinists liquidated them by physical violence in and after 1946. The Bolivian POR had a real base among the tin miners—demonstrated by the return of four POR deputies in the general election, following the overthrow of the pro-Nazi dictator Villaroel (1945). The Ceylonese Lanka Sama Samaja Party, an established organization that adhered to the FI in 1940, after expelling its Stalinist minority, emerged from illegality as the major opposition party in the immediate postwar period. None of these organizations, which clearly did enjoy serious support, had any real contact with, or influence on, the "international leadership" until the "Second World Congress" (1948).
7. Trotsky, *In Defense of Marxism*, p. 205.
8. Formally speaking, it was an "emergency conference" of the FI held in New York in May 1940 that did these things. In fact, this quite unrepresentative gathering was no more than a rubber stamp for the SWP.
9. An important exception was Greece, where British military intervention, with Stalin's tacit approval, smashed the left and imposed a right-wing regime.
10. Ygael Gluckstein, *Stalin's Satellites in Europe* (London : Allen & Unwin, 1952), p. 133. The quotation is from *The Economist*, October 7, 1944.
11. Goldman joined Shachtman. Morrow left revolutionary

politics in despair and, like many others in the same position, ended up supporting a reactionary cause—in his case, Zionism.

12. The European sections were desperately poor, and the secretariat depended on SWP financial aid.

13. "The New Imperialist Peace and the Building of the Parties of the FI," *Workers' International News,* November–December 1946.

14. *Workers' International News,* November–December 1946.

15. Cannon, *Letters from Prison* (New York: Merit, 1968) p. 208.

16. Craipeau, *Le Movement Trotskiste en France,* p. 201.

17. Craipeau, *Le Movement Trotskiste en France,* p. 203. Craipeau and his associates left the party in the ensuing period, and many of them drifted into centrist politics. Craipeau now leads a tendency in the PSU. As usual, this defection, in disgust, was used to "prove" that they had "always been centrists"! In fairness to Pierre Frank, it should be said that he does not make this charge in his *History.* He simply fails to mention this decisive turning point in postwar French Trotskyism or his own role at the time.

18. SWP, *International Information Bulletin,* March 1947, p. 1.

19. Ernest Mandel, "The Soviet Union After the War," *International Information Bulletin,* March 1947, p. 10.

20. "The USSR and Stalinism," *Fourth International,* June 1948.

21. Mandel, "The Soviet Union After the War," p. 12.

22. Trotsky, *Writings of Leon Trotsky, 1933–34,* p. 20.

23. Mandel, "The Soviet Union After the War," p. 13.

24. "The USSR and Stalinism."

25. "The New Imperialist Peace."

26. "The USSR and Stalinism."

27. "Open Letter to CPY," quoted in *New International,* September 1948.

28. Frank, "The Fourth International," *Intercontinental Press,* April 14, 1972.

29. Quoted in ISFI, *A Recall to Order,* 1959.

30. Quoted in *Spartacist* (New York), number 21, p. 10.

TROTSKY'S HERITAGE

1. Trotsky, *Trotsky's Diary in Exile: 1935* (New York: Atheneum, 1963), pp. 45–47.
2. Trotsky, *Writings os Leon Trotsky, 1933–34*, p. 245. In 1938, Rakovsky was put on trial, along with Bukharin and his supporters and others, and sentenced to 20 years imprisonment for "counter-revolutionary activities." He was then a 65 year-old invalid and has not been heard of since. The Supreme Court of the USSR has ruled that all the accused except one (Yagoda) were entirely innocent of the crimes charged against them. Bukharin has even had his party card (posthumously) restored. Not so Rakovsky, an oppositionist of the left.
3. Trotsky, *The Lessons of October* (London: Bookmarks, 1987).
4. Trotsky, *Leon Trotsky on Britain* (New York: Monad, 1975). Part III gives a convenient selection. A fuller collection is Trotsky's *Writings on Britain*, 3 vol. (London: New Park, 1974).
5. Trotsky, *Leon Trotsky on China.*
6. Trotsky, *The Third International After Lenin* (New York: Pioneer,1936). This volume also contains Trotsky's important "Strategy and Tactics in the Imperialist Epoch."
7. Trotsky, "What Next?" p. 254.
8. E.H. Carr, *Foundations of a Planned Economy,* vol. 3 (London: MacMillan,1976), pp. 401–18.
9. Trotsky, "Problems of the Development of the USSR," *Writings of Leon Trotsky, 1930–31.*
10. Trotsky, "Problems of the Development of the USSR," pp. 219–29.
11. Trotsky, "For a Worker's United Front against Fascism," p. 134.
12. Trotsky, *Writings of Leon Trotsky, 1930,* pp. 27–68.
13. Trotsky, *The Struggle against Fascism in Germany,* pp. 55–74.
14. Trotsky, "The Groupings in the Communist Opposition," *Writings of Leon Trotsky, 1929,* p. 81.
15. Trotsky, "The Groupings in the Communist Opposition," pp. 81–82. Emphasis in the original.
16. Trotsky, "The Groupings in the Communist Opposition,"

p. 82.

17. Trotsky, "The Groupings in the Communist Opposition," pp. 82–83.

18. Trotsky, *The Struggle against Fascism in Germany*, pp. 142–154.

19. See, for example, Carr, *The Twilight of the Comintern 1930–35* (London: MacMillan, 1982), pp. 3–82.

20. Trotsky, "For a Workers United Front against Facism," p. 134. Author's emphasis.

21. Trotsky, *Writings of Leon Trotsky, 1932–33*, p. 129.

22. Duncan Hallas, "Against the Stream," *International Socialism,* first series, number 53. This article, together with a later one "The Fourth International in Decline," *International Socialism,* first series, number 60 have been reproduced by Bookmarks in 1988 under the title *The Fourth International.* [Both essays appear in this volume.]

23. Deutscher, *The Prophet Outcast*, p. 171.

24. Trotsky, *The Spanish Revolution.*

25. Trotsky, "The Death Agony of Capitalism and the Tasks of the Fourth International," p. 182.

26. Trotsky, "Fighting against the Stream," pp. 251–53.

27. Trotsky, "The USSR in War," p. 9.

28. Trotsky, "The USSR in War," p. 17.

29. Hallas, "The Fourth International in Decline."

INDEX

A

Abern-Burnham-Schachtman faction, 140, 155
Aesop's Fables, 73
Africa, 133
Albania, 97, 106, 108, 157, 165
Algeria, 22
America, 147; Americans, 81, 134, 156, 167, 179
Amsterdam Congress, 131
Andrade, 133
Anglo-Russian Committee, 68, 131–132, 134
Anglo-Soviet Joint Trade Union Advisory Committee, 68
Anglo-Soviet Trade Union Committee, 67, 75, 82, 172, 177
Angola, 36
Anti-Dühring, *16*
April Theses, 30
Asia, 133; Central, 171
Austria, 31, 87; Austria-Hungary, 39, 59, 79; Austro-Hungarian Empire, 57; Austrian Social Democrats, 136; Austrian Heinfeld Program, 16

B

Babeuf, 81, 84
Bakunin, 77
Balham Group, 137
Barcelona, 144
Bebel, 176
Belgium, 21, 133, 146, 158, 179; Belgian Labor Party, 138
Berne, 58
Belorussia (Western), 100

Bessarabia, 100
Blanqui, 35, 77
Blum, Leon, 74, 140, 143
Bolshevik-Leninists, 129, 139
Bolshevik Party, 6–8, 48, 78, 88
Bolshevik Revolution, 6
Bolshevik Revolution, The, 39
Bolsheviks, 25, 30, 35, 51, 81, 94; Bolshevism, 85
Bonaparte, Napoleon, 45; Bonapartism, 132
Borchard, Julian, 89
Bordiga, 88
Brandler, Heinrich, 176–177
Brest Litovsk, 38–39
Britain, 21, 39, 41, 73, 100, 109, 133, 137, 146, 161, 167, 176, 178–179
British Independent Labor Party, 61
British Labor Party, 67, 137–138, 161, 167
British Revolutionary Communist Party (RCP), 156, 159–161, 165, 168
Bronstein, 15
Bruno, 101
Brussels, 88
Bukharin, 34, 44, 56, 172, 178
Bukovina, 100
Bulgaria, 106, 158, 162, 179
Bulgarians, 81, 179
Bureaucratization of the World, The, 102
Bund, 17

C

Cannon, James, 118–120, 134, 155–156, 159–160, 166, 168–169
Canton, 31–32, 34–35

Canton Commune, 35, 106
Carr, E.H., 39
Ceylonese Lanka Sama Samaj Party, 152
Chang Tso-lin, 31
Chaulieu group, 160
Chiang Kai-shek, 34, 166
Chicerin, 56
China, 21, 97, 106–108, 114, 149, 167, 172, 176, 178
Chinese Revolution, 31, 33, 35, 67, 82, 97, 124, 149, 177
Chu Teh, 106–107
Ciliga, 101
Civil War in France, 38
Cliff, Tony, 30, 105, 109, 114–115
Cochran, 168–169
Cold War, 149, 151, 166–167
Communist International, 18, 34, 55–56, 60–64, 67, 69–70, 79, 81, 86–87, 90, 93–94, 96–97, 114–117, 120, 125, 127–129, 131–132, 135, 140–141, 143–145, 149, 165, 172– 176, 178, 180–181; Executive of (ECCI), 32, 63, 65, 73, 143; Eleventh Plenum of, 70; Presidium of, 130; Tenth Plenum, 69, 128; Fifth World Congress 66; First, 55–56, 88; World Congress of, 14; Fourth, 9, 66, 91–92, 99, 101, 117, 124, 127, 138, 146–148, 156–157, 166, 168, 171, 181; Second World Congress, 62; Second World Congress of the Fourth International 151, 164; Second, 9, 15, 23, 29, 60,80, 88, 92, 134, 145, 171; Seventh World Congress of, 142; Sixth World Congress, 66, 69, 176; Third World Congress, 62, 168; Third, 9, 55–56, 60–61, 88, 92, 134, 145, 148, 171
Communist League, 88; of Great Britain, 137
Communist Manifesto, 55, 62, 88
Communist Party, 64–65, 80, 96, 99, 117–118, 120, 129, 138, 142–143, 145, 149, 157–158, 161, 167, 173, 178; Bulgarian, 60, 66; Central Committee of, 94; Chinese (CCP), 31, 33–35, 84, 106–107, 133, 172; French

(PCF), 74, 136–138, 143–145, 160, 173, 180; French Communist Youth, 73, 145; GB Congress of, 94; German (KPD), 56, 67, 71–73, 85–86, 117, 128, 130, 135, 172–174, 178; Great Britain (CPGB), 67–69, 172, 177; Report of the Central Committee to the 15th Congress, 141; Russian (RCP), 41, 48, 56, 58, 181; Soviet Union (CPSU), 35, 84–85, 142, 177; Spanish, 74–75, 81, 133, 144–145; Yugoslavian, 60
Constituent Assembly, 58
Council of People's Commissars, 38
Craipeau, 134, 160
Croix de Feu, 136
Cuba, 36
Czechoslovakia, 58, 106, 133

D

Daladier, 136
Deat, Marcel, 138
Death Agony of Capitalism and the Tasks of the Fourth International, The, 123, 151, 156, 161
Declaration of Four, 135, 139
Dechezelles, Yves, 160
Demaziére, 160
Deutscher, Isaac, 5–7, 15, 19, 32, 77, 163
Dmitroff, Georgi, 7
Dollfuss, 136
Doriot, 135, 137
Draft Program of the Communist International, A Critique of Fundamentals, 172–173
Dunne, Vincent, 118
Dutch Revolutionary Socialist Workers Party (RSAP), 87, 135, 138, 146

E

East Germany, 106
Eastern Europe, 150, 157, 161–163, 165
Eberlein, 56

Egypt, 23
Emancipation of Labor Group, 23
Engels, Frederick, 12, 16–17,
    22–23, 29, 59, 77, 88, 163
Ethiopia, 21
Eurocommunism, 75
Europe, 16, 22–23, 25–26, 37,57,
    61, 66, 82, 86, 94, 99, 109, 117,
    146, 155, 162, 178, 181; West-
    ern, 28, 60, 157–158

F

Factional Struggle and Party Lead-
    ership, 168
February Revolution, 83
Fighting Against the Stream, 145
Finland Station, 79
First Congress of Russian Social
    Democrats, 25
First World War, 98, 143, 149
"For a Workers' United Front
    Against Fascism," 70, 129
Fourth Internationalists, 95, 97,
    144, 154, 169, 182; Executive
    Committee Resolution of, 157;
    French (PCI), 156, 158–160, 169
France, 5, 21, 24, 27, 39, 45, 60,
    73–74, 89, 94, 96–97, 100, 121,
    123, 137, 143, 146, 149, 157,
    159–160, 171, 179–181; Franco,
    74–75, 144, 181; Franco-Soviet
    Pact, 74, 143
Frank, Pierre, 135, 137, 139–140,
    146–147, 154, 160–161, 169
Frankenstein, 165
French Chamber of Deputies, 136
French Revolution, 25, 45
French Social-Democratic Party, 136
French Socialist Party (SFIO), 60, 74,
    139–140, 143
French Socialists, 137
French Turn, 122, 135, 137,
    139–140
Frölich, 135, 176
Front Populaire, 74, 143

G

Gerland, 157–158
German KPO, 176

German Independent Social Democ-
    rats (USPD), 61
German International Socialists, 89
German Social Democratic Party
    (SPD), 58, 61, 67
German Socialist Workers' Party
    (SAP), 135
Germany, 16, 21 25, 31, 39, 57, 61,
    64, 67, 69–71, 86–87, 90, 96,
    117, 128–132, 146, 157, 174,
    179; Empire, 59
Germany: What Next? 178
Goldman, 158
Gordon, 159
Grant, 161, 165
Gorter, 63
Greece, 58, 179; Greeks, 146, 179
Greek Archio-Marxist organization,
    87, 133
"Groupings in the Communist
    Opposition, The," 116

H

Hamburg, 67, 174
Han Dynasty, 108
Haston, 161, 165
Healy, 161, 169
Heckert, 130
Hernandez, Jesus, 74, 144
Hicks, 69
History of the Russian Revolution,
    83, 178
Hitler, Adolph, 70, 72–73, 86, 94,
    96, 100, 120–121, 128, 130,
    142, 144, 178–179, 181
Hitler-Stalin Pact, 97, 100, 155
Holland, 146
Hong Kong, 32
Hungary, 31, 87, 106, 162

I

India, 21, 150
International Committee of Revolu-
    tionary Socialist Unity, 136, 169
International Communist League,
    129–131, 134–135, 138–139,
    146–147, 179–180
International Contacts Commis-
    sion, 141

International Labor Community (IAG), 136
International Labor Party (ILP), 137, 179
International Left Opposition, 66, 115, 130, 133, 176
International Secretariat, 147, 157,–158, 169
International Socialism, 113, 127, 153, 171
International Socialist Organization, 10–11
International Socialist Review, 113
International Socialist Tendency, 127
Internationalism and the SWP, 159
Iran, 21, 79
Iskra, 17, 23, 77–78
Islam, 37
"It Is Necessary to Build Communist Parties and an International Anew," 127, 130
Italy, 21, 31, 64, 97, 146, 157–158, 179; Italians, 81; Italian Socialist Party, 61, 63
Ivry Conference, 137

J

Jacobins, 27
Jacson-Mercader, 95
Japan, 21, 96; Japanese Emperor, 94, 121
Jenkins, Roy, 138
Jeunesses Socialistes, 139
Jeunesses Socialistes Revolutionaire, 139

K

Kamenev, 7–8, 66, 142, 177
Kapp Putsch, 61
Kautsky, Karl, 16, 21, 62
Kerensky, 99
Khruschev, Nikita, 5, 142
Kiangso Soviet Republic, 106
Kidron, Michael, 98
Kienthal, 134
Kim Il Sung, 166
Kirov, S.M., 141
Korea, 166; Korean War, 166
Kremlin, 56

Kronstadt, 40
Krupskaya, 17
Kuomingtang (KMT), 31–35, 107, 131, 133–134, 172; Executive, 32

L

Lambert, Pierre, 160, 169
La Verité, 160
Lawrence, 161, 169
Latin America, 146
League of Nations, 143
League Faced with a Decisive Turn, The, 136
Leblanc, 163
Left Opposition, 43, 46–47, 49, 66, 83, 86, 117, 119, 130, 132, 134, 162, 171–173, 178–179
Lenin, Ilyich, 7–10, 16–17, 19, 23, 25–28, 30, 35, 38, 41, 44, 51, 55–61, 66, 77–79, 83, 91–92, 99, 115, 118, 125, 143, 148, 151, 153, 157, 167, 172–173, 182–184; Leninism, 131
Leninbund, 174
Leningrad, 141
Lessons of October, 6, 172
Liebknecht, Karl 81, 84
Ligue Communiste 138
Lin Piao, 107
London Bureau, 136
London Central, 10; East, 10; King's Cross Station, 17
Lora Group, 169
Lovestone, 177
Lutte Ouvriere, 140, 160
Luxemburg, Rosa, 16, 56, 78, 81, 138

M

Manchuria, 107
Mandel, Ernest, 114, 159–163, 166, 169
Mao Tse-tung, 97, 106–107, 150, 167
March Action, 63
Marseilles 143
Marlenites, 141
Martov, 17
Maslow-Fischer Group, 135

Marx, Karl, 8–12, 19, 28–29, 37–38, 77, 88, 103–104, 108, 118, 154, 166–167, 182
Matignon Agreement, 74, 143
Maturing Situation in Europe and the Tasks of the Fourth International, The, 157
Maurin, 133
Meinovites 141
Menshevik Party, 8, 17
Mensheviks, 24–25, 27, 30, 78
Mestre, 160, 169
Mexico, 181
Minneapolis, 134
Militant group, 140
Minority Movement, 68–69
Molinier, R., 123, 133, 139
Molinierists, 160
Morrow, 157–158
Moscosco, 169
Moscow, 39, 57, 59–60, 69, 97, 121, 137, 149, 174, 178
Moviemto Nacionalista Revolucionario (MNR), 169
Mulhouse Congress, 139

N

Narodniks, 23
National Socialism, 63
Naville, 133, 139
Nazis, 70, 117, 120
Nazism, 157
Nepmen, 41, 43–44, 46, 48
Netherlands, 180
Neumann, Heinz, 35
"New Communist Parties and the New International," 83
New Economic Policy (NEP), 38, 40–41,44–47, 51
New International, 91, 146
New York, 134, 157
New Zimmerwald, 137, 145, 179
Nicolaiev, 142
Nin, 133, 144
1905 Revolution, 18, 24–25, 78
1938 Transitional Program, 51, 93–94, 139, 147, 151
Nkrumah, 114
North Korea, 106, 166
Norway, 181
Norwegian Labor Party (NAP), 56, 60, 134–135
Nove, Alex, 47

O

October Revolution, 19, 30, 37–38, 49, 51, 58, 61,79, 92, 96, 103
Oehler, Hugo, 118
Oehler Group, 141
On the Tasks of the French Section, 140
Oppositionists, 45
Orwell, George, 102
OSP, 135

P

Pablo-Mandel Tendency, 124
Paris, 25, 35, 88,118, 134–135
Paris Commune, 59
Paris Conference, 135
Partido Obrero Revolucionario (POR), 169
Parvus, 27
Peasant Party, 67
Peking, 107
People's Commissar for War, 38, 56
People's Front, 141–142, 144–145
People's Liberation Army, 107
Petrograd (Leningrad), 39
Petrograd Soviet, 17
Plekhanov, G.V., 16–17, 23–24
Poland, 11, 16, 58, 100, 106, 133, 146; Poles, 146
Popular Front, 52, 67, 73–76, 84, 90, 95, 100, 139, 144, 149
POUM (Worker's Party of Marxist Unity), 75, 87, 133, 135, 144
Pravda, 64
Preparing for Power! 109
Program of Action for France, 94, 139
Proudhon, 77, 103
Purcell, 69

R

Radek, Karl, 89
Radical Party (French), 74, 143
Rakovsky, 171

Raptis, Michel (also "Pablo"),
   159–161, 163
Red Army, 6, 18, 61, 64, 106, 154,
   156–157, 164
Red Trade Union, 132
Reichswehr, 70, 128
Revolution Betrayed, The, 51, 53,
   102
"Revolutionary Traditions," 114
Rhineland, 88
Right Oppositional groupings, 177
Rizzi, Bruno, 102
Romania, 106
Rosmer, 62
RSP, 135
Ruhr, 67
Russia, 6, 8–9, 11, 16–18, 21–23,
   25, 28–29, 34, 38–41, 44, 55, 57,
   59, 77–79, 81, 85, 101, 141, 150,
   162–164; Western White, 155;
   Russian Army, 161; Empire, 23;
   Revolution, 5–6, 8, 18–19, 24,
   27–28, 30, 37–38, 49, 99, 117,
   172; Social Democratic Labor
   Party, 17; Social Democratic
   Labor Party Congress of 1903,
   77–78
Russo-Finnish War, 155
Rykov, 174

S

Saint-Denis, 135, 137
Sapronov, 49
Saxony, 67
Scandinavians, 81
Schapper, 77
Schactman, Max, 146, 155–157;
   Schactmanites, 155
Scheidemann, 62
Schwab, 135
Second World War, 95, 98, 100, 109,
   116, 124, 149, 154, 157, 167
"Sectarianism, Centrism, and the
   Fourth International," 120
Seine-et-Oise, 160
Seine Federation, 140
Serbs, 81
Shanghai, 32, 35, 107
Shensi, 106
Siberia, 15–16, 39, 77
Smirnov, V.M., 49

Sneevliet, Heinrich, 135, 172
Social Democrats, 97, 149, 176
Socialist Party U.S., 138, 169;
   French, 180; Socialist Parties, 136
Socialist Worker, 11
Socialist Workers Party (U.S.), 91,
   100, 108, 146, 155–158, 165;
   Convention of, 155
Socialist Youth, 140, 160
Sofia, 158
Soviet Republic, 56, 62
Soviet Trade Union Federation, 68
Soviet Union, 53, 68, 94, 130, 141,
   146, 155, 162
Spain, 91, 96, 144, 149, 179, 181;
   Spanish Revolution, 73–74, 91,
   144–145, 181; Spanish Socialist
   Party, 75
Spaniards, 179
Spartakus rising, 57
Stahlhelm, 70, 128
Stalin, Joseph, 5–8, 18, 33–34, 38,
   41, 44, 46–48, 52, 53, 66–67,
   74–75, 81, 94, 100, 105,
   116–117, 129, 131, 141,
   144–145, 150–151, 162, 165,
   167, 172–175, 177–178,
   180–181; Stalinism, 164, 166 ;
   Stalinists, 86, 89, 138, 154
Stalin School of Falsification, The, 5
Stammites, 141
Stange, 56
State and Revolution, 38
State Capitalism in Russia, 105
Stavisky affair, 136
Stuttgart Congress, 55
Sun Yat-sen, 31
Swabeck, Arne 118, 166
Swedish Social Democrats, 61
Switzerland, 179; Swiss, 179

T

Tambov, 40
Thaelmann, 85, 130, 176
Thalheimer, 176–177
Thailand, 21
The League (French Trotskyists),
   90, 122, 134
Theses on the World Situation, 64
Third Period, 117, 120, 128–129,
   135. 137, 145, 176, 178, 180

Third Period of the Comintern's Errors, 176
Third Republic (French), 55
Third World, 19, 21, 150
Thorez, Maurice, 74, 143
Tito, Joseph, 164–167
Tito-Stalin Conflict, 165
Tolbukhin, Marshal, 158
Tomsky, 174
Trade Unions in the Epoch of Imperialist Decay, 94
Trades Union Council (TUC), 68
Treint group, 135
Tribune, 167
Tricolor, 74, 143
Truman, 167
Turkey, 21, 173; Turkish Empire, 21
Turn in the Communist International and the Situation in Germany, 176
Twelfth Party Congress, 48, 129
Twentieth Congress, 142
Two Tactics of Social Democracy in the Democratic Revolution, 25, 28

U

Ukraine (Western), 100, 155, 164; Ukrainian Soviet, 171
United Front, 90, 135, 142, 176, 178, 180
United Internationalist Communist Organization, 146
United Opposition, 43, 171_172
United States, 10, 21, 31, 39, 96, 104, 107, 109, 134, 138, 141, 146, 149, 179–180
Union of South Africa, 133–134
Urbahns, Hugo, 85, 174–175
USSR, 5–6, 18, 32–33, 35, 38, 41, 45–53, 55, 67, 69, 73, 81, 83–85, 89, 94, 96, 100–101, 103–105, 115–117, 124, 128, 130, 132, 142–143, 146, 149, 160, 163–164, 172–173, 175, 177, 181, 183

V

Verkholensk, 17
Vietnam, 36; North, 97, 106, 108
Vladivostok, 39
Von Papen-Schleicher, 70, 128

W

Walscher, 135, 176
Wang Ching-wei, 34
Warsaw, 61, 64
Weimar Republic, 59
Where Are We Going? 166
White Terror, 67
World Congress, 131, 140
Workers' International League, 146
Workers' Opposition, 41
Workers' Party, 140, 155
Wu P'ei-fu, 31
Wuhan (Hankow), 34, 107

Y

Yagoda, 95
Yangtze River, 31, 107
Yezhov, 94, 141
Yugoslav Fortnightly, 164
Yugoslavia, 58, 97, 106, 108, 157, 165

Z

Zanzibar (also Tanzania), 36
Zasulich, Vera, 17
Zimmerwald, 129, 134–135; Zimmerwald Left, 88
Zinoviev, 7–8, 56–57, 62, 66, 68, 142, 172, 174, 177

ABOUT HAYMARKET BOOKS

We believe that activists need to take ideas, history and politics into the many struggles for social justice today. Learning the lessons of past victories as well as defeats can arm a new generation of fighters for a better world.

As Karl Marx said, "The philosophers have merely interpreted the world; the point however is to change it."

We take inspiration and courage from our namesakes, the Haymarket Martyrs, who gave their lives fighting for a better world. Their struggle for the eight hour day in 1886, which gave us May Day, the international workers' holiday, reminds workers around the world that ordinary people can organize and struggle for their own liberation. These struggles continue today in every corner of the globe—struggles against oppression, exploitation, hunger and poverty.

It was August Spies, one of the Martyrs who was targeted for being an immigrant and an anarchist, who predicted the battles being fought to this day. "If you think that by hanging us you can stamp out the labor movement," Spies told the judge, "then hang us. Here you will tread upon a spark, but here, and there, and behind you, and in front of you, and everywhere, the flames will blaze up. It is a subterranean fire. You cannot put it out. The ground is on fire upon which you stand."

Visit our online bookstore at www.haymarketbooks.org.

Also by Haymarket Books

THE STRUGGLE FOR PALESTINE
Edited by Lance Selfa   ISBN 1931859000   2002   256 pages

In this important new collection of essays, leading international solidarity activists offer insight into the ongoing struggle for Palestinian freedom and for justice in the Middle East.

THE FORGING OF THE AMERICAN EMPIRE
By Sidney Lens   ISBN 0745321003   2003   468 pages

In this comprehensive history of American imperialism, Sidney Lens shows how the U.S., from the time it gained its own independence, has used every available means—political, economic, and military—to dominate other peoples. With a new introduction by Howard Zinn.

Haymarket Books is a non-profit, progressive book distributor and publisher, a project of the Center for Economic Research and Social Change.